The Craft of Teaching Adults

Revised Edition

THE CRAFT OF Teaching Adults

Thelma Barer-Stein
& James A. Draper,
Editors

KRIEGER PUBLISHING COMPANY
MALABAR, FLORIDA
1994

Original Edition 1988
Revised and Enlarged Second Edition 1993
First U.S. Printing 1994

Printed and Published by
KRIEGER PUBLISHING COMPANY
KRIEGER DRIVE
MALABAR, FLORIDA 32950

Library of Congress Cataloging-in-Publication Data

The craft of teaching adults / Thelma Barer-Stein & James A. Draper, eds. -- Enlarged ed.
p. cm.
Includes bibliographical references.
ISBN 0-89464-867-5 (U.S.) ISBN 0-921472-16-1 (Canada)
1. Adult education--Canada. I. Barer-Stein, Thelma. II. Draper, James A., 1930-
LC5254.C73 1994
374'.971--dc20 93-33837
CIP

10 9 8 7 6 5 4 3 2

DEDICATED TO THE CONTINUING PRESENCE OF J. ROBY KIDD

Dr. Kidd was the first chairman of the department of adult education at The Ontario Institute for Studies in Education (OISE) University of Toronto, and the founder of the International Council for Adult Education.

Nationally and internationally, even before his death in 1982, Dr. Kidd's devotion to adult education impressed and continues to impress those who knew him, heard him, or read his works. It is in this way that J. Roby Kidd is a continuing presence in adult education.

Contents

INTRODUCTION

Introducing a book is very much like introducing a person. It is important to state the name correctly and it is also helpful to explain just a tantalizing bit about it. At least that is what we usually do to provide an introduction that will slip effortlessly into dialogue, and perhaps a new friendship.

This is a book for students of adult education, for part-time teachers of adults, and for professionals in many fields who may not yet recognize that one of the most important daily tasks is that of teaching an adult. This is also a book for the adult educator whose years of practice may have encrusted and buried the pithy discussions of philosophies, of differing modes and methodologies of teaching, of techniques of handling groups of adults, and of principles into a well-worn daily pattern of taken-for-granted teaching. Novice or well-practiced, here is a book that will entice, stimulate, provoke, enlighten. And yes, excite.

Culture Concepts is very proud that this was the book that two academic presses said would never sell. Now, to celebrate this well-travelled, well-used textbook, we are presenting this enlarged and updated second edition of what has now become a classic for many students and teachers alike. We consider classics to be ... "books that won't stay on the shelf."

In the first printings of this book, I was so excited about the results of my own doctoral research, that I patterned this whole introduction following the five steps of the Learning Process that emerged from that research: Being Aware, Observing, Participating, Rote Internalizing, Confronting and Reflective Internalizing. This time, I am content to have shared that excitement with you in joining Carmen Connolly to put it all in a chapter!

The Beginnings of This Book

Years ago when James Draper delivered the keynote address to the Colleges '79 conference in Saskatchewan, the title of his address was, "The Craft of Adult Education."[1] At that time he noted that this craft was based on certain assumptions:

- that adults can and do learn
- that adults can and do take responsibility for all aspects of learning (planning, participating, and evaluating)
- that we are all teachers and learners.

He noted too, that 'craft' can be thought of along two basic dimensions: the *production craftsperson* concerned with replication and a uniform end-product, and the *artisan craftsperson* who is continually refining and perfecting his or her process through ,confronting difficulties,experimenting and innovating.

1. Draper, J.A. "The Craft of Adult Education" in Proceedings of Saskatchewan Community Colleges, *The Practice of the Craft of Adult Education*, Saskatchewan, April 19-21, 1979.

Returning to his department of adult education at the Ontario Institute for Studies in Education (OISE), James pursued this notion of the artisan craft of teaching adults and recognized its presence in the contagious enthusiasm and expenditure of time and effort by students and colleagues alike. That was when he nudged the faculty members and some graduate students to share the reflections on many years of experience and to produce this book.

Immediately, several questions beg attention:

1. How does teaching as a craft differ from just teaching?
2. How does teaching become a craft?
3. What characteristics distinguish the practitioner of a craft?

In that Saskatchewan address, James had also noted that what determines craft is not the acquisition of highly specialized skills and/or knowledge, but the genuine faith in its worth.

And if we question the source of that faith, we may find it in Alan Thomas' words:

> *...the impact that a single teacher in a single course or class can have on any individual learner ....*

For any teacher, the first tangible response from a student indicating clearly how much and to what degree you have influenced their thinking, their behaviour or their life direction is unforgettable. I am sure that is what Thomas is speaking about. In a very real sense, it is the recognition that you as a teacher, have made a difference to someone. Just one single someone is all it takes. That is impact.

How Does Teaching As a Craft Differ from Just Teaching?

In many ways, it is difficult to be just an average teacher when teaching adults. Unless courses are taken for credit or specific updating programs, adults vote their opinion of teachers with their feet and their voice. Adult students are usually here because they want or need to be and usually the intensity and eagerness they bring to the class, the life experiences and the searching questions, their often heroic efforts to overcome responsibilities, tiredness and countless other commitments to be in a course; the family and financial difficulties they often have to hurdle, cannot help but incite a level of intensity and commitment from the teacher that may not be provoked in teachers of children. There is rarely a passive complacency in teaching adults.

Teaching as a craft begins with this kind of intensive tug from the adult students. Their eagerness, their experiences, cannot be ignored. In fact, they are infectious. Teaching classes after a full day of other work, I often felt that "This evening will be a drag ..." but inevitably I became infected with their excitement to learn and found renewed energy from my adult students. I believe we enthusiastically infected each other, for classes often carried on past the final hour.

On the other hand, teachers of Basic Skills, English as a Second Language (ESL) and sometimes parenting groups, find that some adults bring to the course together with their eagerness to learn, a self-defeating anxiety about "making it." Not every adult enters studies with confidence and with the support of family and co-workers or friends. And sometimes too, the overwhelming weight of personal problems closes the adult to learning. These are the times and the situations when time must be taken either to share concerns and experiences, or to permit that adult to be quiet, to observe, rather than participate.

Teaching as a craft encompasses and embodies a holistic view (philosophy) and a holistic mode of teaching. Emotions, feelings, knowledge, skills, physical and mental states of being all combine in each adult, and all must be accounted for in the planning, the teaching/learning and in a collaborative attitude that permeates teacher and student from day one to the final assessment of how things went.

How Does Teaching Become Craft?

Teaching becomes a craft only with a continuous conscious awareness of the method and the content and the process of teaching and learning. It becomes a craft only when the teacher retains a vigilance for his or her own learning as a teacher, as a facilitator, as a counsellor, as a guide, and as a nurturer of the learning of self and of others.

This implies that the craft of teaching – teaching adults or children – is never fully perfected, never fully completed. Like the individuals in the class, it is always diverse, complex, and forever shifting and changing in attitudes, needs and emotions. What works one time may bomb the next. Especially when teaching adults, the teacher needs to be flexible, open to differing ways and differing ideas, and teach with an attitude and a firm belief in the meaning of partnership and collaboration in learning. Some of my own most exciting classes and workshops developed unexpectedly when students added insights and experiences and discussions flared far from any original outline. These were the times we will all remember. Unplanned, disorganized, unpredictable but thoroughly exciting.

What Characteristics Distinguish the Practitioner of a Craft?

James Draper hoped that as these pages became a reality, dreams turning into a book, the written reflections of these experienced practitioners of the craft of teaching adults would clearly display the devotion, the scholarly expertise, and their own special personal pleasures in teaching adults. They do. In the ensuing pages you will be continually fascinated by the interplay of theory and practice, of reflection and research. A genuine interest and respect for their adult learners, have marked each contributor as a craftsperson.

But as you read and share their insights, you will be aware of something else. Underlying all their experience and their knowledge and skills exists an unquenchable curiosity, their inner driving need and desire to learn more. This is a delicious heady feeling, it drives you, it keeps you up nights, it writes notes in the middle of the night, and it ignites your energy when you think there isn't any left. Curiosity to learn.

About this Enlarged Edition

We asked the previous authors of chapters to update and enhance if they wished to do so. Surprisingly – or maybe not a surprise at all – many felt that they had exposed the core of their topic and wanted to leave it that way. More current research could always be seen and compared with the essence they had rendered. Other authors made minor changes.

Perhaps this alone attests to the classic quality of this book.

To enhance our previous publication, we invited several new scholars and adult education practitioners to contribute the nuggets of their own expertise, and we asked them to write in their own way, but to be aware of the wide audience this book has enjoyed. We know that when you browse and study the new chapters you will be as pleased as we have been in reading and learning from them.

In arranging the order of the chapters, we have interspersed some of the old with some of the new to provide a range of topics. These flow from the foundational understandings offered to us with definitions, history and philosophy, differing theories and aspects of adult learning to considerations of what is involved in distance education, in comparison studies and even a look into the future.

And a Final Word

You may recall that I began this introduction to our Craft of Teaching Adults by equating an introduction to a book with an introduction to a person. My intent was to indicate that being introduced to a person or to a book was in so many ways similar, especially in being able to dialogue together, in always 'being there' as a resource.But, you might be thinking, dialogue with a book?

Think of those times that you have been in the presence of someone so fascinating, so erudite and so challenging, that your total being was held immobile in absorbed listening. Taking leave of such a presence is done always with a mix of exhilaration and reluctance. Exhilaration because now your mind is racing in many new and exciting directions forming inferences, images and possibilities all stimulated by that single contact. You know the reflections will bounce excitedly for a long time. Reluctance because of course it would be pleasant to listen and to share much longer. The person, like a book, has stirred an ongoing dialogue of ideas and notions that won't rest until you have taken hold of them and settled them firmly into your own world, your own personally meaningful world of relevance. And after all, that is the only real goal of any learning, isn't it? Enjoy this book like an old dear friend.

Thelma Barer-Stein
Toronto, 1993

Introducing the Contributors

James originally envisioned this book as a collaboration of all the faculty members of the department of adult education at the Ontario Institute for Studies in Education which is the graduate Faculty of Education of the University of Toronto. Not all were able to commit themselves. Together with some recent OISE graduates, we have invited distinguished adult educators to share their expertise with us in this enlarged and updated second edition of *The Craft of Teaching Adults*, and take pleasure in introducing them to you.

Thelma Barer-Stein

Born in Vancouver, B.C. and presently living in Ontario, Thelma holds an undergraduate degree (University of British Columbia.) and internship as a dietitian, an M.Ed. (University of Western Ontario) in educational administration and a Ph.D in adult education (OISE) but these do not really speak of Thelma's lifelong interest in understanding cultural differences. It is the thread that links her seemingly disparate research, writing and teaching in cultural food differences (her book, *You Eat What You Are: A Study of Ethnic Food Traditions* is widely used as a classic text), in the human experience of learning ("Learning as a Process of Experiencing the Unfamiliar") and in phenomenology as a serious approach to research in human experience.

As an independent scholar and consultant, her work has taken her to many universities in Canada, as well as to Australia, Thailand, India and most recently (1987) on a tour of universities in England, Scotland and Wales sponsored by The British Council. She helped to develop and co-taught the OISE adult education department's course, Adult Education in Cross-Cultural Contexts and she is also the founder and president of Culture Concepts Inc.

Donald H. Brundage

Don was born and raised in Alberta. After receiving his BA from the University of Alberta he began a career with the Calgary YMCA and continued his academic studies at George Williams College receiving his Masters in Social Work in 1952. Eleven years of work with the YMCA in Calgary and Toronto was followed by six years in New York City where he received his Ed.D. at Teacher's College, Columbia University while working at International House. He has been associated for the past 20 years with the department of adult education, OISE in Toronto, before his recent retirement.. His collaborative work with Dr. Dorothy MacKeracher, *Adult Learning Principles and Their Application to Programme Planning* is well known in Canada and abroad.

Dr. Ross Keane and Dr. Ruth MacKnenson, his co-authors, are graduates of the department of adult education, OISE.

Elizabeth J. Burge

Elizabeth is the Distance Learning Coordinator of the Ontario Institute for Studies inEducation (OISE), the Graduate School of Education of the University of Toronto. The Distance Learning Office of OISE has been established to integrate distance education field development and research, relating especially to audio and computer mediated communication.

She is a learning designer with experience in audio conferenced classrooms, has published and taught in the areas of adult and distance learning design, and has run workshops in various countries. She has been active in the Canadian Association for Distance Education and the International Council for Distance Education, and has served on the editorial boards of the *Journal of Distance Education* and *The American Journal of Distance Education.*

She graduated B.A. (University of Adelaide) and (post graduate) Diploma in Educational Technology (University of South Australia) before coming to Canada in 1980 for the (intended) short stay to complete an M.Ed. at OISE. She completed her Ph.D. at OISE with a thesis focusing on students' descriptions of the learning in a computer-conferenced environment.

Carmen R. Connolly

Carmen is Acting Chief of the Nutrition Programs Unit in the Health Promotion Directorate, Health and Welfare Canada. She has been with the Directorate since July, 1989. Carmen's responsibilities include program management for the implementation of *Canada's Guidelines for Healthy Eating* and the new *Canada's Food Guide to Healthy Eating.*

She obtained a Post Graduate Diploma in Public Health Nutrition from the University of Toronto and an M.A. in Adult Education from the Ontario Institute for Studies in Education (OISE). Throughout her career she has been actively involved in professional activities and has chaired several committees for The Canadian Dietetic Association. Carmen is currently co-chair of the Nutrition Expert Advisory Group of the Canadian Cancer Society.

Lynn E. Davie

Lynn, an adult educator for more than twenty-five years, is currently a professor in the department of adult education at The Ontario Institute for Studies in Education. His writing and research has focused on distance education by computer mediated communication, participation rates in adult education, and program evaluation.

His current research interests include tracking the changing demographic patterns of adults who participate in adult education or training. He is a member of the research team that conducts the *OISE Survey of Public Attitudes Toward Education in Ontario* every two years, including a series of questions on adult education for the past ten years.

Also, he continues his research interests in the design of distance education programs which utilize computer networks for their distribution. Research interests include the development of cooperative learning strategies, the cognitive processing of information received through text based computer networks, and the effectiveness of different program structures.

James A. Draper

James has been a faculty member of the department of adult education, OISE, since 1967. Graduate courses which he has taught include: Introduction to the Field of Adult Education, Community Education and Development, Adult Basic Education, Adult Education in Cross-Cultural Contexts, Comparative Studies in Adult Education, and the Social History of Adult Education.

Much of his field work and writing has been on adult education in India. During the past few years, his research has focused on the part-time instructors of adults who are employed by school boards and colleges in Ontario. Currently, he is doing a study of graduates from faculties of education to see how many of these graduates eventually teach adults. He is on the review board of *The McGill Journal of Education* and has contributed four articles to the *New Canadian Encyclopedia.* Since 1987 he has served on the governing Council of the Commonwealth Association for the Education and Training of Adults (CAETA).

Virginia R. Griffin

Ginny has been a member of the adult education faculty at OISE since 1968. During that time she has taught program planning and courses on processes of learning, facilitating adult learning and holistic worldview in adult learning and education.

Her research interests focus on the processes of learning, especially those that enable us to be most fully human. A special enjoyment in her work is supervising thesis students, and learning with them the complexities and beauty of adults' learning especially when they find more possibilities within themselves than they knew were present.

A recent book, edited with David Boud, *Appreciating Adults Learning: From the Learners' Perspective* exhibits her learning with thesis students and the perspective she takes in her teaching and her research.

Reg Herman

Reg entered adult education in 1967 as a Project Director for research and development at OISE. From 1968 to 1972, he was Managing and Features Editor of *Convergence,* the international journal edited by J. Roby Kidd. Aside from the projects listed in the References (the film, *Innovations for Learning: Case Studies of Training in Industry; The Design of Self-Directed Learning*), Reg feels that the research that most influenced the creative decision-making model were: a study for UNESCO of the national disaster of community access to cable TV in Canada, *The Heritage of Adult Education*, two video programs with Roby Kidd produced by the University of Guelph; *A Social Services Model of Adult Basic Education*; and *LOGS: a Language of Group Skills*.

Reg has left OISE to devote full time to consulting, research and writing on group problem-solving and decision-making skills.

J. Roby Kidd

Probably best known for his widely-translated book, *How Adults Learn*, Roby was the first chairman of the department of adult education (1966) at OISE; chaired or directed many international organizations such as the Second World Conference on Adult Education (Montreal 1960), UNESCO International Committee for the Advancement of Adult Education (1961-66), International Cooperation Year, Canada (1964-65), the adult education division of World Confederation Organization of the Teaching Profession, and the Canadian Association for Adult Education (1951-61).

Internationally, he is probably best remembered as founder and first secretary-general of the International Council for Adult Education. Roby wrote his chapter for this book out of a depth of practical experience, for it is he who established the first Comparative Studies Program in Canada which attracted international fellows and students for graduate study. His death in the spring of 1982 characteristically found him in the midst of many national and international writings, travels and activities in his beloved field of adult education.

Alan M. Thomas

Alan was born in Toronto, studied for his B.A. (English and philosophy) at the University of Toronto, his M.A. (History of Education) and Ph.D. (Social Psychology), both at Teacher's College, Columbia University. His teaching includes experience at the University of British Columbia (1955-60) in the Faculty of Education, and at The Ontario Institute for Studies in Education, University of Toronto since 1971.

From 1960-1969 he was the executive director, Canadian Association for Adult Education, and served as executive assistant for the Minister of Communications, Government of Canada from 1970-71. His major research interests centre around large scale programs in adult education; Learning in Organizations; Labour Canada's Labour Education Program and a Review of the Educational Programs in the Canadian Corrections System; as well as writings in policy formation for adult education and learning and the law.

Currently he is working on a project concerning the use of "prior learning" for determining admission or advanced standing in Canadian education as well as a study of the impact of older-full-time students in Ontario secondary schools.

Allen Tough

For many years, Allen studied the adult's intentional efforts to learn and change. *The Adult's Learning Project* and *Intentional Changes* discussed his ideas and the implications for teachers. More recently he has been writing about our responsibilities to future generations. His most recent book is *Crucial Questions About the Future* (University Press of America). He is a professor in the department of adult education at the Ontario Institute for Studies in Education at the University of Toronto. He teaches graduate courses on future studies, global issues, and intentional changes.

Dorothy MacKeracher

Dorothy professes, teaches, advises, inquires and writes about adult education at the University of New Brunswick (Fredericton), with some degrees of proficiency in the areas of women's (and men's) learning, development and aging, instructional methods and design, and research. Her expertise is attested to partly by her doctoral degree from the Ontario Institute for Studies in Education, but mostly by her lifelong experiences as a learner.

Michael R. Welton

Michael R. Welton is an associate professor of adult and continuing education at Dalhousie University, Halifax, Nova Scotia. He loves trying to retrieve pearls from the past, and has been working for a few years with the thoughts of Jurgen Habermas. He likes the mix and interplay of story-telling and social theory. He is very interested, too, in dialogue. How can we listen to one another? He also thinks that history is really just a conversation with the past.

USING THIS BOOK

This is not another basic how-to-book. In offering a distillation of long-practiced skills and deeply reflected wisdom in teaching adults, the contributors have displayed a smorgasbord of possibilities. It is for the reader to browse, select, and hopefully make use of these in distinct and personally relevant ways.

You may be just contemplating a shift into full-time or part-time teaching of adults or perhaps you have been engaged in teaching or planning adult learning for some time. This book is intended for all who feel a need and a desire to learn more and to become even more effective in what they already do.

But we don't always have the time we would like to have, to do the things we would like to do. Settling down with this book and reading it from cover to cover would be like listening attentively in a good conversation. Failing that, one could skip through and read only the *Practitioner's Summary* at the start of each chapter; this is rather like eating a meal of appetizers. Intrigued with a particular author or topic, we invite you to flip the pages quickly and read the *Marked Sections*; this would be like eating the whole meal, but only little bites.

Focusing in on a particular aspect of adult teaching, you will find the author's own *References and Suggested Reading*, as well as the *Bibliography* helpful in extending your own learning.

You will see that not all the author's agree, either in theories or in practice methodologies, in terminologies or in definitions. Some even refer to the same sources but arrive at differing conclusions. Just like in the everyday world! These differing styles, preferences and views form valuable entries for discussions and for further research and refinement of practice.

Just more reasons why we believe this book engages and provokes reflection, discussion and action and just "... won't stay on the shelf."

Thelma Barer-Stein

Chapter 1

The New World of Continuing Education

Alan M. Thomas

Practitioner's Summary

This chapter is an attempt to help the part-time instructor of adults feel more at home in the wider context of the field of adult education. The author attempts a difficult task: to clarify commonly-used terms within the field despite the differing contexts in which they might be used and the diverse lives and interests to whom they may be directed. Such a young field presents few agreements or traditions, but Thomas offers several definitions as a foundation for understanding and discussion of: *Education Permanente, Lifelong Learning, Continuing Education* and *The Learning Society*.

Other current confusions centre around concepts of the learner as student or pupil and the teacher of adults as leader, resource person, facilitator or expert.

Canadian history, past and recent confirms the importance and diversity of adult learning: to learn or teach a language, to propagate religious faith, to proliferate secular organizations and volunteer groups, citizenship education, martial training and later to educate employees in industry workplaces. When one considers all of these as forms of adult education and multiplies them by the countless industries, hospitals, government departments, etc. then we can agree with Thomas that "it is not surprising that no one knows...the exact amount of adult education in Canada."

But this same diversity and its unbridled growth has also exacerbated relationships among all forms of adult education and the varying levels of government. This presupposes an alertness on the part of all adult educators to be able to deal separately and in conjunction with educational policies as they change through varying influences, and the needs of the learners change as well.

Canada's present period indicates "steady and explosive growth of adult education" – by whatever definition – even though such growth often defies detection or definition. Nearly half the upper-income adults in Ontario are or have been involved in part-time learning. What is of concern here and in other societies, is the lack of participation in educational opportunities by the "lower half of the population".

An impressive growth area lies in "labour education" and it is here that monies are increasingly directed by the Federal Government. But what is most important to note is that such education is voluntary from both sides.

Presentations of such educational opportunities and the increasing diversity of the burgeoning needs of adults leads us to concerns of process and content, and how best to achieve the evaluation of these for all concerned.

Adults have become a focus of interest for research and studies dealing with the adult life stages and how these may relate to adult learning. Two major writings include Kidd's *How Adults Learn* and the UNESCO *Learning To Be, Report of the Faure Commission* which stresses (among other points) that it has been wrong to invest exclusively in education for the young and that further research into learning itself as a distinct discipline called *Mathetics* may be of benefit for all societies.

Many studies indicate the decreasing importance of chronological age and the increasing importance of experience, circumstance and context as far as the giving and receiving of learning. This is important, because all such understandings call for differing educational planning that is sensitive to and inclusive of the changing needs of the adults who are participating.

Thomas's conclusions include not only issues related to the broad national or community scope of adult education, but also to the impact that a single teacher in a single course or class can have on individual adult learners and therefore on the results of large-scale provision of learning opportunities. Adult learners expose themselves. They reveal their ambitions as citizens and workers, their hopes as parents, their anxieties as individuals. Instructors of adults must tread warily, for they tread on adult dreams.

Chapter 1
The New World of Continuing Education

Alan M. Thomas

What Is Adult Education?

This article attempts to provide some perspective and some context for the current practice of adult education in Canada. While there are agreed traditions for the education of the young, there are none for the education of adults.

I will try to provide some glimmering of the complexities, the scope, the vitality that characterizes the adult end of the spectrum of continuing education, acknowledging that no single presentation could possibly do justice to the variety that is to be found both from region to region and student to student.

Any reply to the first legitimate question by the uninitiated: "What is adult education?" produces the first confusion. Depending on who is asked, the response is likely to include a torrent of terms, mostly familiar words in unaccustomed combinations: adult education, continuing education, recurrent education, education permanente, life-long education, vocational/technical training. And most likely a few others. Each of these terms comes with its particular definition. Each frequently claims to be the best term, but the astute listener will see that each one is based on slighly different grounds, and often reflects the interests of a specific organization or group of organizations in the society. Adult lives are so diverse, and the interests of modern societies so complex and demanding, that it is not surprising that there should be competition for the most precious possession of all adult citizens: their attention, and their will to learn.

While there is obvious competition for the imaginations and will of the young in our society at least, that competition takes place in a deliberately publicly responsive forum, the elected school board. It takes place also within some generally agreed upon traditions about the auspices of the education of the young, and the general methods of carrying out such education. No such agreements or traditions are associated with the education of adults.

To approach the adult sector of continuing education from a preoccupation with the education of the young, that is, the children and youth sector of continuing education, is almost to ensure confusion and misunderstanding. In general it is easier to explain adult education to people in business, the military, even in government, than it is to those whose professional lives have been devoted to the practices and language of the formal system of education. It is no one's fault that this is the case, only that for a variety of reasons, for the past ninety-years or so, the two sectors of educational practice have been sharply separated from each other.

These have been separated by professional language, by methods of practice, by sponsoring agencies, and by methods of finance. The only common link has been the learners themselves who, as adults pursuing some form of self development, are the same people who as children, enjoyed or endured the attentions of the educational system designed for them.

> *What has been given little serious attention, in this context at least, is that success as a child or young person in the school system nearly guarantees the likelihood of that person participating successfully in some form of adult education.*

Whether this can be explained by the fact that those who do succeed in formal schooling usually take up roles and places in the society that demand their further learning, or by the fact that success as a child in formal schooling creates habits of learning that demand participation in formal educational settings as adults, or by a combination of both factors (which is most likely the case) is a matter of some debate.

However, the apparent functional relationship between the two sectors is of increasing importance, as the demands of the present and future society make their professional isolation from each other both impossible and increasingly destructive.

Adult Education

The most common term is of course *adult education*, as defined by UNESCO, a definition that is now very wide-spread in acceptance throughout the world:

> *The entire body of organized educational practices, whatever the content level and method, whether formal or otherwise, whether they prolong or replace initial education in schools, colleges, or universities, as well as in apprenticeships, whereby persons regarded as adult by the society to which they belong, develop their abilities, enrich their knowledge, improve their technical or professional qualifications or turn them in a new direction and bring about changes in their attitudes or behaviour in the twofold perspective of full personal development and participation in balanced and independent social, economic and cultural development. Canadian Commission for UNESCO, 1980.*

But who is an adult?

A close examination indicates that this definition equates *adult education* with the education of adults, since it says that adult education is "any form of education participated in by persons regarded as adults in the society to which they belong." As simple as that sounds, a moment's reflection reveals that for one group in our society (those between 15 and 19 years of age) the question of just who is an adult is a hazy and often painful one. On the one hand, at sixteen we have entrusted individuals with the privilege of driving a car, with all of the potential for manslaughter or suicide or both, that that implies. On the other hand, we reserve other such adult privileges as drinking and voting to later ages, and there remains considerable confusion in the eyes of the system of criminal justice with respect to just who is an adult and when. Even after that, while the law may be all of a piece in this respect, there are a range of informal sanctions, regarding whether an individual has indeed acted like a grown-up, that can be, and often are, applied to any age.

For many years, the British defined adult education not by the age of the participants, but by the nature of the subjects studied. It was in essence liberal education, the type of education designed to develop and maintain adult behaviour. The point is important simply because the term adult education frequently conceals an ideology related to who ought to be the participants, or what the objectives ought to be. These various ideologies have to be identified as they occur. For all round practical purposes, the UNESCO definition seems to serve us best providing we realize that it is a technical definition only.

Education Permanente

Education Permanente is a definition one is likely to encounter in Quebec or among French-speaking Canadians. It is not well translated as permanent education, but probably more accurately as continuing education.

Recurrent Education

Recurrent Education is a phrase introduced since World War II by the Organization for Economic Cooperation and Development. This organization is made up of industrially advanced countries for the most part, and its purpose is to provide information and research regarding their development, development primarily of an economic nature. Recurrent education means an educational policy or policies which supports alternate periods of work and school, sometimes consecutive, sometimes concurrent, which will lead to the development and maintenance of a work force adequate to a modern technical state. It can be considered a sub-system of the broader definition of adult education, and it is to be found operationally among economists, and those who do perceive a relationship between learning and economic surival. This is also the arena in which the more familiar term, vocational/technical training, applied to adults, is commonplace.

Lifelong Learning

Lifelong Learning, while often casually introduced into these responses is, of course, an entirely different term because it is based on the capacity and likelihood of individuals engaging in learning throughout their entire lives. It is quite independent of the existence of formal or even informal educational agencies and programs, or of publicly identified goals of the kind represented by various degrees, certificates, diplomas, and the like. This is the realm of the work of Allen Tough and his associates, who argue that up to 80% of the learning activities of adults is carried out quite independently of educational systems. These discoveries are important for anyone concerned with what is being learned in any society, as distinct from what is being taught, but they are of equal importance to those working in the educational system, since the learning taking place outside that system or systems bears directly on the success or failure of their efforts.

Continuing Education

Continuing Education has been left to the last, mostly because it is now a matter of public discussion in most provinces, and because the predominant definition seems unsatisfactory. In the document entitled *Continuing Education: The Third System* issued by the Ministry of Education, Ontario, 1981, continuing education is defined as:

> *the provision of opportunities for lifelong learning in English and in French to adult learners who are not involved in traditional fulltime credit programs. Adult learners are those people at least sixteen years of age or older who are engaged in purposeful learning activities.*

There is some tradition in Ontario as in other provinces for this kind of definition, that defines continuing education as only that education undertaken after the participation in formal programs. It is largely a definition based on what various educational institutions have done in the past, and for that reason is recognizable to almost all educators. However, it does not seem particularly suitable for the present or future in which traditional student bodies are changing with great rapidity, and it does not seem to fit the experience of these new students, or even some of the conventional ones. Recently an alternative definition that may be better on both counts was advanced by the Department of Adult Education, The Ontario Institute for Studies in Education (1981). Continuing Education is defined in this case as:

> *a system(s) of education which includes formal and non-formal education; is defined with respect to its various parts and agencies (elementary schools, secondary schools, colleges and universities) in terms of specific educational objectives to be fostered, rather than in terms of the age or circumstances of learners. The system is available to persons of any age, part-time or full-time, voluntary or*

compulsory, and is financed by a mixture of public and private resources. It is distinguished from other educational activities in the society by the possession of the exclusive right to provide public recognition or certification for those completing its programs, though not all of its programs need lead to such certification.

The authors felt that such a definition provided a more coherent framework from which to judge and evaluate the contributions of various agencies in the system and that it reflected more accurately the view of the child moving from grade five to grade six, the youth moving from high school to college, and everyone else moving in and out of the system for various purposes and at various times. Each can claim with authority that he or she is continuing his or her education.

> *The conflict and confusion that abounds with respect to definitions is likely to remain for some time. It is, after all, the result of a field of activity experiencing rapid growth both in practice and in thinking about practice. The important thing is to try to use consistently whichever definition most appeals to you. That alone will be an important improvement in future discourse.*

Using Familiar Terms in Unfamiliar Ways

The second immediate confusion presents itself in the use of familiar terms in unfamiliar ways. For example, the word student (adult education in Canada would not dare to use the word pupil, though some other countries do) can mean a very much wider range of experience and conditions than attending a school every day and being present in classes.

The other source of confusion is the use of unfamiliar terms to describe what would seem to be familiar events or circumstances. For example, the word curriculum was rarely used, at least until recently, as more formal agencies became active in adult education. Most noticeable perhaps are the words used in place of the word teacher. Leader, resource person, facilitator, expert, are all likely to be found in the literature. Some of them to be sure, grate on the sensibilities, but they are products of the experience that has accumulated as adult educators have worked with adults as learners in settings and circumstances quite unlike the formal ones usually associated with all education.

> *What the proliferation of words associated with teaching represents is the fact that the teacher in a formal classroom plays a combination of roles, often simultaneously, that differentiate themselves when working with adults. For example, in working with adults, the person who is the source of expert knowledge (resource person) need not be the same person who arranges for exchange among students and with the expert (facilitator).*

A process of disassociating from formal schooling

To a certain extent, the different language found is the result of the history of adult education in Canada. As a matter of principle, adult educators disassociated themselves and their practice from formal schooling because they believed, often correctly, that adults did not want to be approached as though they were children. The image of grown men and women crammed into desks created for children however apocryphal it may have been, had an enormous influence on adult educators in the first part of this century.

Recent History

Citizenship education takes the lead

> *As an immigrant country, Canada has had to maintain a tradition of adult learning and of adult education for its entire history. It is relatively safe to assert that there has not been a minute in Canadian history when someone was not trying to learn or teach a language.*

A new geography, a new agriculture, a new society, the fundamental experience of the adult immigrant, had to be learned as an adult, usually informally, and by trial and error. There was and is always the need for citizenship education of some kind.

The most important agencies in this enterprise during the nineteenth century were the churches, which were engaged not only in the propagation of the faith in competitive religious environments but in a variety of other services as well. However, as the century moved on, secular agencies appeared such as the Mechanics' Institutes, and various other lodges, associations, and voluntary movements. Before the century ended, the Boards of Education, among others, were offering evening classes to young men and women in a rising middle class. There is no doubt that during that period adults were learning proportionately as much as adults are learning today. The major difference today is the number who are learning publicly and under public auspices, that is, participating in formal adult education.

However, the long tradition of concern for adult education was interrupted at the turn of the century by a succession of events. The first was the increasing introduction of compulsory education for children and young people. While the almost universal application of that policy was not completed until nearly half way through this century, the ideology of a movement that promised to "fill the churches and empty the prisons" also created the belief that the education of adults was no longer necessary.

> *The belief, imbedded more deeply and profoundly in those in charge of public education than in any other group, that any lapse or failure*

> *in educational achievement noticed among adults could be eliminated by rearranging the school program of the children, captured the popular imagination and remained an official doctrine for fifty years or more.*

Citizenship education, martial skills and invisible workplace education

At the same time a second conviction took root. This was that adult education was necessary only as citizenship education for adult immigrants who had never been to school, and the provision of limited opportunities for those who for one reason or another, had missed their chance at school as children. Adult education was perceived to be a safety net for those who had fallen through a crevice in the society.

Despite the lengthy popularity of this view, from the turn of the century to the end of World War II, other currents were developing. Two world wars, for example, involved enormous programs of adult education, as young men and women were obliged to learn martial skills never taught in school. Research applied to industry, and accelerating technical growth and changes, persuaded large technically based enterprises such as oil companies, to provide training and education for many of their employees as early as the mid-thirties.

By the mid-fifties, an American professor, Harold Clark (1953) argued that in the United States a third system of education had been created, rivalling in resources and numbers the public school system and the universities. This system was entirely preoccupied with the education of adults. It was to be found not in spacious buildings clearly announcing their educational purposes, but spread almost invisibly throughout the workplaces of the United States.

Education in Canada

In Canada, the same development occurred. It took place more slowly than in the United States partly because of the predominant "branch-plant economy", with the result that most of the research and consequent training that would have taken place in Canada remained at head office, usually in the United States. However by the seventies, one high technology company in Canada maintained nineteen permanent teaching centres in the province of Ontario alone, through which passed some eight to ten thousand students a year.

> *When the volume of education is multiplied by all of the other middle and large-sized industries, and by the hundreds of government departments, hospitals, and other large organizations, it is not surprising that no one knows precisely the exact amount of adult education in Canada, nor the extent of resources it consumes, either in time or money. The same growth and development has led to new complications in the relationships between varying levels of government.*

Education in Canada is generally assumed to be an exclusive right of provincial governments, though the interpretation that the founding fathers meant to include the education of adults in their decision-making remains open to judicial challenge. In addition to the overall responsibility of the Federal Government for the state of the economy, and the relentlessly increasing dependence of that economy on the availability of constantly proliferating skills that must be learned by both young and old, the Federal Government cannot ignore the educational provisions (or lack of them) made available by the provinces.

While there have been few if any, skirmishes between the two levels of government over the education of the young, there has been almost constant dispute and acrimony since the early years of the century over the technical and vocational education of adults. As Canadians have become increasingly dependent for survival upon adult learning, these disputes are likely to continue.

> *The consequence is that anyone engaged in the practice of adult education has to keep an eye on several levels of government simultaneously, and must be able and willing to deal with them both separately and in conjunction as their policies change, and as the needs of the relevant groups of adult learners express themselves.*

Adult Learning: Differentiating Andragogy from Pedagogy and a New Discipline: Mathetics

With the publication of J. Roby Kidd's, *How Adults Learn,* (1959) self-consciousness with regard to the distinct nature of the learning of adults was established. Earlier references to the special terms associated with adult education suggested the contrast in experience with learning of the young in school, and learning of other ages under other and diverse circumstances. Kidd's book drew on an enormous range of research and experience that had not been previously organized into a single presentation.

Since that time attempts have been made to assert a distinct theoretical field under the term of andragogy, teaching of adults as distinct from pedagogy, teaching of children. Information has accumulated with respect to processes of maturation and how those processes affect the learning potential of adults. At a more popular level, much attention has been given to varying life stages and the range of attitudes, expectations, aspirations, and capabilities that are associated with each of these stages.

Since 1958, when the first full time graduate program of studies in adult education appeared at the University of British Columbia, approximately ten more programs offering various graduate degrees have been created at Canadian universities. Though they have led a somewhat uneasy existence in association with much larger faculties wholly preoccupied with the learning and schooling of the young, they have for the most part survived and, in recent years, numbers of applications for admission by students have surpassed those experienced by the school centred programs.

Next to Kidd's work, the major landmark was the publication of the UNESCO report on education throughout the world, *Learning To Be, Report of the Faure Commission*, (1973). UNESCO had witnessed, during the twenty years following the conclusion of World War II, the largest expenditure on formal education in the history of the world. These expenditures were not confined to the advanced industrial world, but undertaken by nearly every country, rich or poor, in the belief that investment in formal education was the secret formula to economic growth. The UNESCO study at the end of that period was an attempt to assess the validity of that formula. Results were mixed. More children had experienced increased schooling, and there was some progress in the battle against poverty, disease, and malnutrition. However, no one had anticipated the millions of rebellious students, the hundreds of thousands of discontented teachers, and the alarmed and uneasy public that developed during the same time. The Report drew two important conclusions:

> *First, it argued that despite the turmoil and the imbalances, it had not been wrong to invest heavily in education. What was wrong was to invest so heavily and exclusively in the education of the young.*

That conclusion laid to rest one of the oldest North American beliefs that you could fundamentally alter a society by concentrating on the education of the children.

> *Second, the Report argued that learning as a human, individual activity was and is more fundamental than education, which is only a response to the existence of the potential, and that it might be more profitable to enlarge the psychological, sociological, political, etc. study of learning if we are to understand the true nature and function of education.*

It also pointed out that a good deal of the most recent contribution to the understanding of learning was coming not only from psychology, but from neurology, chemistry, physics, and sociology, as well as other disciplines. In this light, the Report argued for the establishment of learning as a distinct discipline of its own, to be called *Mathetics*.

While the latter has yet to be realized, many Canadians and others have enlarged the exploration of the study of learning as a basis for determining the nature of the educational system. Increasing contributions are being made to the concept of "learning styles", as being characteristic of different individuals at different times and under different circumstances; styles that mediate whatever teaching style may be in use. More is being understood about learning from new and different media of communications, leading to arguments that there are several forms of literacy in addition to that associated with extracting information and truth from the printed word.

In addition, new ideologies emerged. Paulo Freire, working in the poorest parts of Latin America and Africa, asserted a dialetical metaphor for learning, rooting his teaching of literacy in an oral and political context. The Canadian Government experimented some years ago with the use of the Bulgarian theory of "Suggestology", based on an analysis of conditions of the brain, and the receptivity to the careful planning of total learning environments. The method was reported to be especially useful in the teaching of languages, a matter of high priority in official bilingual Canada.

It is an exciting time to be active in adult education, and it would take a much longer survey to identify all of the ideologies and theories that are claiming attention.

> *Whether it is necessary to continue to argue for the absolute difference between adult education and the education of the young remains a question.*

With the two sectors (Andragogy and Pedagogy) drawing together, it may be that something more closely resembling a continuum will appear. However, the continuum can be analyzed in terms of two principal factors: individual development, and the basis of participation.

For individual development, puberty appears to be a fundamental watershed. Once that passage is complete, varying stages of growth and development, and relentlessly varying experiences, appear to be the dominant factors. In any group of seventeen year olds it is possible to find some who, in terms of some characteristics, more closely resemble thirty year olds than they do other seventeen year olds and vice versa.

> *From puberty onward, chronological age becomes less important, while experience, circumstance, and condition become primary.*

However, there are some generalizations that can be made on the basis of socially and culturally defined "life-stages".

The importance of volunteer adult participation

The other major factor is that participation by adults in education is basically voluntary, and that fact dominates recruiting, teaching, administering, and all other facets. It has, more than any other factor, given adult education its dominant characteristics.

To watch even young children participating voluntarily in some form of learning, is to anticipate the basic pattern of adult education, allowing for the importance of variety in experience.

When large scale training and education in non-educational organizations is studied, it is possible to draw some conclusions (see Thomas and others, 1980). They are associated with four principal circumstances, entry to the organization, advancement in that organization (promotion or job change), major technological changes in the organization's activities, and special individual problems. These same four categories would appear to apply to the society as a whole. Entry is of course manifest in the education of the young, but as a continuing immigrant society, we have been and will continue to be concerned with the special circumstances of adult entrants, under the general rubric of citizenship education.

It might also be argued that entry involves re-entry and that this characterizes the millions of women moving into the labour force. Many of the same needs seem to exist as in the case of new citizens. It used to be thought that entry education, plus "learning by example" was sufficient for advancement through the society, and perhaps it was. By and large this is handled within the employing organizations, but increasing cooperation is developing between them and educational agencies. A great deal of care and thought will be required in the development of those relationships, not to damage either them or the potential student.

Major technical change is clearly beyond the scope of any formal entry education program. In the words of an African leader, we cannot wait for the children to grow up in order to maintain our nations.

Massive changes occur, with widely differing and uneven effects on the society. This is most often cited as the basis for adult education, and while it is not the only one, it is a principal one and will remain so.

Special aspects of adult education planning

In general, it calls for educational planning quite unlike that associated with normal systems of education. It calls for short term and widely varying responses in contrast to the more stable and predictable responses associated with traditional programs and agencies.

Individual problems exist wherever education is an alternative, and must be associated with the same practice common to formal education including counselling, coaching, and the chance to fail and to try again. Despite the image of ruthlessness associated with large non-educational organizations, the amount of response to individuals is remarkably high. It may be so because adult education, voluntary as it is, has always been obliged to make responses to individuals. And it may be because it is cheaper to respond in that way than to hire someone new.

We are also witnesses to the shift of special individual problems from that category, such as women re-entering the work force, older workers moving into retirement, or into everyday passages that are part of promotions and coped with by a reasonably effective system of continuing education.

The Present Period

The overwhelming characteristic of the present period is the steady and explosive growth of adult education, however defined. The resources of adult education, and its practices, develop so differently in comparison with the child and youth-centred sector, that such development is not always visible to the untrained eye.

Such growth has occurred despite the equally steady decline of the child and youth-centred educational sector. While available resources appear to have been drying up in that sector, they have been doing the opposite with respect to the education of adults.

Who participates in adult education?

In terms of the participation of adults as individuals, demand has simply gone on increasing over the past three decades. In 1974, Waniewicz reported that nearly half the adult population in Ontario reported either being engaged in some recognizable form of part time learning or having just finished such an engagement and preparing for another. These adults were characterized as being in the upper levels of income and educational achievement, a fact constant in every industrial society in which such research is done. The disturbing aspect of this information is that it is equally constant in industrial societies that individuals with less educational success, and less income (the lower half of the population) hardly participate in adult education. This seems to be true despite the fact that they pay for many of the available resources through their taxes. At the present time, equity with respect to the education of adults seems roughly comparable to the equity with respect to children before the passage of the compulsory attendance laws: the rich take care of themselves privately; the middle class try to provide for themselves through various means including the use of publicly provided resources; and the poor get little or nothing.

Despite this fact, a fact of very great importance to School Board adult educators, growth has been impressive. It has spread through most of the organizations of the society: voluntary, government,

> *quasi-government, military, and industry, as the rate of change and technical growth has surpassed any preparation that schools for the young can anticipate or provide.*

One recent example, indeed the largest public contribution to systematic adult education during the early seventies has been the financial support of the Federal Government for "labour education". In this case, over a seven year period, the Federal Government contributed just under twenty million dollars to the organizations of the labour movement for the purposes of training their officers and members. The expenditures of these organizations on education has also increased, making it possible for thousands of Canadian workers to acquire skills of management, decision making, and knowledge about the society that otherwise would have been very hard to achieve.

It is of special importance to note that the money was given not to educational agencies, but to the labour organizations themselves. Most of these latter established their own educational programs, seeking only occasional assistance from the formal educational agencies. It is of equal interest to note that this Federal intervention into adult education was accomplished without a trace of complaint or objection from the provincial governments.

Educational agencies versus labour organizations

> *Participation in adult education must be viewed from two points of view: that of individuals who participate as students, and that of the agencies that provide the courses and other educational opportunities. In both cases, participation is voluntary; with few exceptions neither party is required by law to engage in the activity.*

This is in sharp contrast to the formal educational system in which the dominant agencies are designed only for the purpose of providing educational services, and in which a large segment of the student population participation is required by law. In recent years, primarily among the professions, experiments have been undertaken in making participation in continuing education compulsory. There is a fierce debate now raging over whether such compulsion actually contributes to the development and maintenance of more competent and responsible professionals.

The great variation of agencies and their style of participation in adult education gives rise to questions of quality. Which ways are better? There is no simple answer, and hopefully both research and debate will continue. Rivalries exist, and such policies as diverting money from educational agencies to labour organizations serve to increase those rivalries. The traditional educational agencies tend to believe that all or most of the educational activities should be entrusted to them, but there is evidence that different educational tasks are better performed by different agencies, not all of whose principal task is education.

Illiteracy remains a serious problem despite nearly a century of compulsory schooling. Despite the evident successes with the upper half of the population, it is now clear that exposure to schooling for the minimal number of compulsory years, is not sufficient to ensure that many people can have a decent chance to succeed in this society.

The largest increase in the labour force for the past few years has come from women, many of whom did not get or have lost the necessary skills for entering reasonable jobs. Since intelligence is distributed normally in a population without regard to gender, it is apparent that the need to provide adequate opportunities for these adult women is a matter not only of individual justice, but of economic and social necessity.

Realities for You, the Instructor and the Priceless Resources of Adult Education

Overall, there are some simple realities that everyone who has worked or is working with adults as learners knows, but sometimes forgets to convey. There is the special and exhilarating tension associated with working with adults.

> *The experience of society that they bring is fresh, and intensely real and authentic to them; the decisions they make after leaving an educational event, perhaps influenced by what happened during the encounter, are authentic and immediate to them, and perhaps to many other people.*

The encounter with you is only a brief shelter. The students know it and value it, the teacher must do likewise.

The reasons for their attendance are often inscrutable even to them. Sometimes it is because they happen to be free at that time, and you are as reasonable an opportunity as several others. Sometimes it is because you represent the educational agency they last attended and the one that they think will make them feel the most welcome. To discourage them inadvertently, may discourage them from any further educational effort for a long time.

> *Sometimes, they are less interested in receiving new information, new knowledge from you, than they are in trying to understand their experience, to articulate it, examine it and share it with others.*

Under these circumstances, the other students present are at least as important as any instructor, and their experience must be sought after, listened to and treated with respect.

When adult Canadians tell you what they are or have been learning, they tell you very important, indeed intimate, things about themselves. They reveal to you information about their hopes, their plans, their ambitions, their very images of themselves.

When we examine patterns of participation by adults in adult education, we can draw some conclusions about the lives of the adults involved. First of all, we are witnesses to a lot of hard work. Imagine the determination involved in attending courses in motor mechanics, two night a week, three hours a night, for thirty weeks. Lots of adults do that many times over. These same adults are also telling us something about their beliefs in their families, their communities, and their country.

> *To be a witness to adult learning, to adult education, is to be a witness to the quality of everyday life. This seems to scare the new adult educator rather than being seen as the priceless resources of adult education.*

All of these are simple things, but it has sometimes seemed to adult educators that they are the very things that teaching in a compulsory system makes one insensitive to.

> *If a student comes freely, feels free enough to share experience, and believes that that experience is not only welcome but important, then that individual will offer his or her attention, will, and imagination to whatever is the developing objective of that particular educational enterprise. That is the essence of adult education.*

Teachers, providing agencies, educational systems, indeed whole societies, must be good enough, sensitive enough, sincere enough, and exciting enough to win, to deserve, that attention.

REFERENCES

Clark, H.F. and Sloan H.S. (1953) *Classrooms in Factories.* Rutherford, N.J.: Research Institute, Fairleigh Dickinson University.

Department of Adult Education (1981) *New Reflections on a Learning Society.* Toronto: OISE Press.

Kidd, J.R. (1973) *How Adults Learn* (1st edition, 1959). New York: Association Press.

Ontario Ministry of Education (1981) *Continuing Education: The Third System.* Toronto.

Thomas, A. and others (1980) *Learning in Organizations.* Toronto, Department of Adult Education, OISE.
Tough, A. and Associates (1971) *The Adult's Learning Projects: a Fresh Approach to Teaching and Practice in Adult Learning.* Toronto: OISE Press.
UNESCO (1973) *Learning to Be: Report on the Faure Commission.* Paris
UNESCO (1980) *Occasional Paper No. 34.* Ottawa: Canadian Commission for UNESCO.
Waniewicz, I. (1974) *Demand for Part-Time Learning in Ontario.* Toronto: OECA-OISE Press.

Chapter 2
We Have with Us Yesterday: Teaching Lessons from the Past

Michael R. Welton

Practitioner's Summary

Because of the dramatic nature of this chapter, we have not added marked highlights to the chapter's text. But we do attempt to condense the highlights in this section. The characters are from the first half of the 20th century in Canada and depict the early adult education "pioneers."

Alfred Fitzpatrick: Pioneered initiatives in the first three decades of the 20th century to found Frontier College in 1918 and to invent the idea of the labourer-teacher. He believed that education was the right of every person and that the "healthy growth of the brain" was concurrent with "the work of the hands": the integration of learning with life.

Jimmy Tompkins: Indelibly associated with the Antigonish Movement (the Nova Scotians who attempted to institute social and economic reforms through adult education), Father Jimmy was the movements' inspirer. He recognized that education was the answer to the people's lethargy and despair after the first World War. "Adults were suffering because nobody believed they could learn!" He believed that "if people learned to be helpless, they could learn to be active!"

Guy Henson: This adult education visionary established The Division of Adult Education in Nova Scotia in 1945 and launched numerous projects to awaken people to their true potential. Especially he was concerned about adult education for the Blacks, worker's groups, credit unions and folkschools for farm people. He said, "... it is adults who make and change the world, and the children largely fit into it."

Violet McNaughton: The legendary social-activist educator who embraced the values of the co-operative, women's and reform movements in Canada, encouraging women to be active participants in shaping the world.

Moses Coady: From the late 1920's to his death in 1959, his vision of becoming "masters of our own destiny" fired the imagination of thousands of Canadian and American adult educators. "Children do not control the world. Children do not change it;" and "without some form of economic democracy, life is not worth living" – were his bywords.

Watson Thomson: From the mid 1930's to the mid 1940's, Watson was a key player in many prairie and national adult education innovations in community (film circuits) and national education (Citizens' Forums). He helped establish government policy for adult education in Saskatchewan with two main objectives: to support people's needs and to awaken them to unresolved world issues.

Alexander Laidlaw: Began as a teacher in Nova Scotia, later (in the 1940's) becoming the premier philosopher of the co-operative movement in Canada.

These were among the pioneers in adult education in Canada, though by no means all. Yet their devotion, actions and philosophies continue to "speak to us in plain language about their understanding of the potential liberating role of adult education" in any society.

Chapter 2
We have with Us Yesterday: Teaching Lessons From the Past
Michael R. Welton

The Setting: A Great Institution of Higher Adult Education

The characters:

The Moderator: The moderator, Michael Welton, is a Canadian historian who believes that the historian's task is to open up a conversation with the past. In our present conversations about the craft of teaching adults and the social purpose of adult education, we must invite our forefathers and foremothers to join us in the dialogue. What questions do they bring to us, and we to them?
Alfred Fitzpatrick: He is best known in Canada for his pioneering initiatives with the bunkhouse men of the frontier camps of northern Canada in the first three decades of the 20th century. He invented the idea of the labourer-teacher, and founded Frontier College in 1918 to serve the neglected citizens of the camps.
Jimmy Tompkins: His name is indelibly associated with one of Canada's most lauded adult education movements, the Antigonish Movement. Father Jimmy was the movement's inspirer in the dark days after World War I. It was he who understood that real adult education sprang from the pain of people's lives.
Guy Henson: The Centre for Continuing Education at Nova Scotia's premier university, Dalhousie, bears his name. But few people know of this brilliant man's encompassing vision for adult education. He established the Division of Adult Education in Nova Scotia in 1945, and launched numerous projects to awaken people to their true potential.
Violet McNaughton: She was a legendary social-activist educator in numerous Canadian organizations such as the Saskatchewan Grain Growers Association. She embraced the values of the co-operative, women's and reform movements in Canada. Through her teaching and journalism, she encouraged women to be active participants in shaping the world.
Moses Coady: The name of Moses Coady is, perhaps, the most famous in Canadian adult educational history. From the late 1920's until his death in 1959, Moses Coady's vision of becoming "masters of our own destiny" fired the imagination of thousands of Canadian and American adult educators.
Watson Thomson: Watson Thomson shone like an incandescent light on the Canadian prairies and national scene from the mid 1930's until the mid 1940's. He

was the first director of the Division of Adult Education in Saskatchewan, and was a key player in numerous experiments in community (film circuits) and national (Citizens' Forums) adult education.

Alexander Laidlaw: Alex Laidlaw began his educational life as a teacher in Nova Scotia. He worked with Coady as Assistant Director of St. Francis Xavier University Extension in the 1940's, and later became the premier philosopher of the co-operative movement in Canada.

Moderator: I have heard it said that educators choose to teach because they cannot handle the rough and tumble of the real world of hard decisions and tough bargaining. Tonight, however, we will dispel this facile image of educators as we listen to a cast of characters who dreamed big dreams and taught in the turbulent decades of the early to mid 20th century, a time when people scarcely imagined that adults were capable of learning anything much beyond the age of twenty-one. Alfred Fitzpatrick once wrote in a book that never saw the light of day, *Schools and Other Penetentiaries [sic],* that adult education was the 'day-dream of visionaries.' The great German philosopher, Ernst Bloch, spoke of the utopian impulse in daydreams. These are his words:

> *Dreams come in the day as well as the night. And both kinds of dreaming are motivated by the wishes they seek to fulfill ... The content of the daydream is not, like that of the night dream, a journey back into repressed experiences and their association. It is concerned with, as far as possible, an unrestricted journey forward ...*

Fitzpatrick: I did write in my unpublished book that adult education was the "daydream of visionaries." Thinking about it now, I would probably have added, and the nightmare of reactionaries! (Raucous laughter is heard in the background, but the moderator continues.)

Moderator: For this grand occasion, we have invited some of our great visionary Canadian adult educators from yesterday. They have been watching us with hope and trepidation for many decades now, decades which have seen adult education become a huge and controversial enterprise throughout North America. Much has been written by modern adult educators on the craft of teaching adults. But tonight we want to hear from these voices from yesterday.

Let me introduce our guests to you now. That imposing bear of a man gesticulating in front of an audience of eighty fishermen in Havre Boucher, an isolated village in Nova Scotia, is Moses Coady. Over there is Alfred Fitzpatrick, standing next to a tent in some lumber camp in Northern Ontario. It has a sign on it called "Reading Camp Association." Can you see that short woman standing next to her husband outside a sod house in Saskatchewan? That's Violet McNaughton, the most prominent prairie radical woman in our history. In the distance, seen through the mist, is Jimmy Tompkins. He is standing on a wharf in Canso, a desolate fishing village in eastern Nova Scotia, and lecturing the men. His pockets are stuffed with pamphlets. Look closely and you can see Watson Thomson. He is sitting in a living room in a large house in Winnipeg.

Many young people are gathered around. They are talking about how adult education can change the world and usher in a new day. There, walking down a dusty road in the Black communities of Nova Scotia is Guy Henson. He is meeting with community leaders to see what can be done about the serious problems amongst oppressed Blacks. And see that man, sitting with friends in a hotel room drinking rum after organizing a local credit union in Cape Breton, that's the legendary philosopher of the co-operative movement, Alexander Laidlaw.

I believe we are all anxious to hear our guests tell us about their struggles on behalf of the adult as learner in the early and mid-decades of the 20th century. As moderator, I have selected several salient themes to focus our discussion.

- What obstacles did they face?
- What vision animated their heroic efforts on behalf of the neglected adult learner?
- What projects did they shape within their vision of human possibility?
- What methods did they invent to achieve their purposes?
- What secrets did they unlock about the meanings and complexities of teaching adults?

Let us begin by asking our guests to tell us about the plight of the adult learner in the early 20th century. Alfred Fitzpatrick, why don't you begin?

Fitzpatrick: As some of you may know, I was a Presbyterian minister from Pictou County in Nova Scotia, and started a Reading Camp Association around the turn of the century. All of my life I railed against establishment Canada – the elites who ran our universities, our churches, our trade unions, our government bureaucracies – for ignoring the plight of the men in the camps, the bunkhouse men. I always believed, even to the day I died of a broken heart, that education was a God-given right of every man, not the exclusive privilege of a few favoured persons. When the education of the masses was spoken of, some said,

> *You are on dangerous ground. Education breeds discontent. If educated, the masses will become lazy and lawless. No educated man will work in the woods, or handle the pick and shovel in mines and on railway construction.*

But the remedy for this discontent, in my view, did not lie in keeping the masses in ignorance, but in educating them, while at the same time improving their environment. The men who produce the wealth do not get any educational benefits! (He is now pacing around, his fingers stabbing the air) ... The toilers of forest, mine and railway construction were being robbed! Their treatment was nothing short of criminal! They were the utterly neglected citizens of the camps!

Tompkins: I was known during my time as excitable of temper with a mind like a jack-rabbit. I was born in 1870, two years later than Alfred, in the lovely Margaree Valley of Cape Breton, the home also of my younger cousin, Moses Coady, who came into the world in 1882 if I am not mistaken, and who was a Catholic priest like me. The fire that burned in Alfred's heart for the neglected learner blazed in mine for four decades of the 20th century, until I lost my mind and had to have those sisters watch my faltering steps. I was almost beside myself trying to figure out why we were spending so much time and energy on the children and youth ...

Coady: Yes, yes, if we waited for the slow evolution of our educational institutions it would be too late. Our situation in Nova Scotia was desperate ... children do not control the world! Children do not change it ...

Tompkins: By the end of the first World War, after experimenting with various schemes to create a civic boostering spirit in my sleepy town of Antigonish, it dawned on us that there was a deep hunger for knowledge amongst our adult population. The whole world was alive with questioning. What role should labour play in the new scientific world of production? What role should women play in the new age of human rights? What role for the Church in the new industrial and secular age of efficiency?

We begin to see glimmerings of what adult education might do in resolving economic and social problems. (Shaking his head slowly and speaking softly.) Our people had abandoned their farms, left our province, and seemed to have sunk into a deep lethargy. I didn't know what the hell to do. At one point, I even wrote letters to the federal Department of Agriculture asking if it were possible to raise goats in Canso to feed the almost-starving people! (The guests laugh loudly.)

But it was dawning on us that the idea that you could not teach old dogs new tricks was a load of malarky. Dr. Thorndike's research gave scientific impetus to the idea that the average adult was educationally worthy of his or her place in the sun. The old saying 'Childhood is the time for learning' was being replaced by the new slogan 'The time for learning anything is the time when you need it.' As you may know, the Antigonish Movement is the story of a group of Nova Scotians who attempted to institute social and economic reform through adult education. Those of us in the early days of the adult education movement believed that fossilized education was the opiate of the people because it kept them from getting the truth about the condition they were in. Adults were suffering because nobody believed they could learn!

Coady: Cousin, I remember the letters you wrote to me while I was studying at the Catholic University in Washington, D.C. You were always several steps ahead of me in seeing the possibilities of adult education. But even when I was teaching math and organizing the Nova Scotia Teacher's Union it became clearer to me that our schools were biased toward urban values and needs, and skimmed the top for elite professional training. The deepest obstacle we faced was ideological.

Thomson: Ah! Moses, there is more dynamite in adult education than any government can handle. I heard you say over and over at the Canadian Association for Adult Education (CAAE) gatherings that your mass meetings were organized to explode "intellectual dynamite to shatter the old mind-sets that had become as rigid as cement and encrusted with tradition." But you must know where to begin and how to proceed with those who may have come to believe that they can't learn to be masters of their own destiny.

Henson: I want to leap in now. Joseph Howe and Moses Coady were my two heroes. I first met Coady as a nineteen year-old cub reporter in 1929 at a meeting in Halifax. Howe and Coady's dream of a people controlling their own destinies kept me going through good and bad times. I was not as excitable as old Jimmy over there, but in some circles I was called a 'renegade bureaucrat' who knew what he wanted. In the end, I simply called myself a "footsoldier in the Antigonish Movement."

In the mid 1930's I was a *de facto* organizer for the Movement in Halifax and Dartmouth, and used whatever vehicle I could find to rouse the people. So I formed a chapter of the Workers Educational Association (WEA) in Halifax and began organizing study clubs. In 1936 the School Board refused the WEA the use of classrooms on the pretext of danger from venereal disease. In the late 1930's I helped organize over twenty credit unions in Halifax and central Nova Scotia. This kind of activity was much criticized by people concerned with education. When folkschools for farm people were created in the late 1940's, there was much breast-beating that "real farmers" didn't think much of them. Some people regarded the work I did with Black groups in the 1940's and 1950's as useless, believing they were a shiftless and hopelessly depressed people.

McNaughton: I have been listening patiently to the men. (Laughing). I had much practice in my almost sixty years as a farm organizer and co-operator in Saskatchewan. I arrived in Canada from England in 1909 and quickly plunged into the farm and women's movements. You might say that I floated around the Prairies on a tide of reform! I believed that men and women could work together, but they had to learn to organize.

I agree with Jimmy that adult education springs from suffering ... A familiar sight for years on the Prairies was the barrel on the stoneboat covered with an open grain sack held in place by an old tire, or stave from a discarded barrel, carrying the precious water over many a hummocky trail. I suffered so much from carrying those pails of water, even after I had a hysterectomy, that they were seared into my mind.

My involvement in farm and women's movements always linked practical problems with my unshakeable belief in the ability of education to make Canadian institutions responsive to our needs and interests. As women learners we faced more obstacles than the men. Our ruling elites had little faith in the masses of men to learn anything; they had even less in the masses of women!

We women were learning all the time as we shaped our beautiful prairie land. We banded together to overcome the pain of our isolation and loneliness, and literally revolutionized Canadian community and political life.

It is just that your fancy university academics haven't quite understood that yet, and it has taken professors of adult education some time to see how, where and what we women in the early 20th century were actually learning in our women's institutions, clubs, associations and parties.

Moderator: This is a fascinating discussion. I don't think I realized how little faith there was in both elite and common circles in the early to mid 20th century in the learning potential of adults. What was your understanding of the social purpose of adult education in Canadian society?

Tompkins: We in the Antigonish Movement were not so much concerned with setting the yard limits of adult education as we were with throwing the switches which would give the average person unobstructed passage to wider fields of knowledge, self-help, and security. We didn't believe that adult education was for the illiterates alone, nor was it to pap-feed social climbers with appreciations of Shakespeare and Beethoven. We thought it was the duty of adult education to make the mute vocal and to make the blind see. But education that was conscious of its mission had to be free from the patronizing air, from talking down from some lofty oracle, from inventing decoys and sops, handy palliatives and barricades, to fence injustice off from justice. There was more real adult education at the pit heads, down in the mines, out among the fishers' shacks, along the wharves ...

McNaughton ... and in the kitchens and women's clubs ...

Tompkins: ... and wherever you can get the farmers and their wives to gather and sit and talk in the evenings, than you can get from one hundred thousand dollars' worth of fossilized formal courses. It springs from the hearts and pains of the people ...

McNaughton: That is pure poetry, Jimmy. For me, adult education was fundamentally about living a life. Individuals had to live a life as well as earn a living, and develop their higher selves. The importance of human development would be recognized as it took its rightful place beside material development. Adult education ought to be for self-fulfillment and the means of building a new and nobler civilization.

Like everybody here gathered from the past, I believed that adult education was essential to the continued viability of the democratic community. In my speeches and journalism for *The Western Producer* I emphasized the educational value of organization. To produce organized effort one first needed organized enlightenment. Enlightenment and understanding always required people to make decisions for action based on their understanding of the issues.

Coady: I profoundly agree with Violet that education must enable a person to realize his or her possibilities, and to live fully. Violet speaks of "earning a living" and "living a life." What we discovered in the Antigonish Movement was that the starting-point for democratic adult education must be the learning and action process of shared responsibility for the creation and distribution of wealth. Without some form of economic democracy, life is not worth living. Violet and her agrarian radical friends would no doubt agree.

In the dawning decades of the 20th century, we had to challenge 'highfalutin' aristocratic educational philosophy that saw no relation between food, shelter, clothing and adult education. A person learns best when his or her interests are keenest, and no one will deny the urgent economic needs of the masses, then or now! We thought that good pedagogy began where the people's interests lay. From there we could lead them to other fields initially thought unattractive. To the extent that people realize their possibilities, to that extent do they extend and transform their culture.

We never intended to create a nation of mere shopkeepers. We simply desired above all that all human beings would discover and develop their own capacities for creation ... (long pause)

When I died in the summer of 1959, my heart was almost cracked in pieces ... Canadians seemed almost resigned to sit in the bleachers and let the few run the show ... I almost thought our dream had slipped away from us. I tell you, friends, I know something of St. John of the Cross's "dark night of the soul ..."

Fitzpatrick: Perhaps we all know something of this dark night.All of my life I wanted ordinary men and women to be able to integrate study and work, head and hand ... But the universities ... (His words trail off in silence)

I was simply an educational radical who stood outside the establishment and cried out incessantly that all people had the right to the cultural resources of our society and were entitled to full citizenship. But my distinctive philosophical contribution to adult education in Canada, one that many scoffed at, was my insistence that there could be no healthy growth of the brain without the concurrent if indeed not previous work of the hands. I invented endless schemes to get schools and colleges and universities to integrate learning with life. Just about everyone turned a deaf ear to me in the 1930's ...

Thomson: Your ideas, Alfred, are a little quirky. But your rejection of "education" as a sphere apart from life is very radical and visionary. Few have caught up with you yet! So take heart. Your preoccupation with the way education runs away from life reminded me of a series of radio talks I gave in Saskatchewan in 1944, called "Power to the People" shortly after I became Director of the first government Division of Adult Education in Canada.

I didn't think that the average person wanted to study the history of medicine, say, in the abstract. When people began to ask why it was not possible to have a decent hospital and to get together with neighbours to figure out how to get one, then they were ready to learn some history of medicine, as well as some social and economic history of Western Canada. I ended my broadcasts with the statement "Education for the people – all the people ... Power to the people." I was riding tempestuous utopian wind ... I believed a new world, built from below by the common people, guided by science and trusted leaders, was flaring into history. Adult education was the spark that fired tinder hearts into study and action.

One of the first moves I made when Tommy Douglas, the first democratic socialist premier of Canada, invited me to launch the biggest adult education program in Canadian history, was to establish government policy for adult education in Saskatchewan. I wrote a brief called *Adult Education Theory and Policy*.

I insisted that the new, liberating theory of adult education was an integral part of just societal organization.

I thought that adult education in Saskatchewan in the mid 1940's had two central objectives: (1) to support people's needs with relevant knowledge in their movement towards the new objectives, whether it be co-operative farms, larger school units, or new public health projects; (2) to waken the people to a sense of the central, unresolved issues of the world crisis so that we can find a clear way ahead for modern society.

Our old friend John Grierson of documentary film-making fame (National Film Board of Canada) was at the centre of much contentious debate about propaganda versus education, and I was accused many times over of being a propagandist and even a communist. But I never believed that it was the business of adult education to recommend specific political programs or party doctrines. I did think it was the necessary business of a socially intelligent adult education to encourage people to play a creative and responsible part in the affairs of the local and wider community.

Henson: Mr. Moderator, it seems fitting that I end the discussion of our understanding of the social purposes of adult education with some of my thoughts. Nova Scotia created the second government Division of Adult Education (Saskatchewan was the first), and I became Watson's counterpart, the director of the Division of Adult Education, in 1946. These were turbulent and conflict-ridden times. The Cold War winds were biting into our resolve and broad social commitment. By the time I launched the division, without much support anywhere in government, Watson was involved in big troubles in

Saskatchewan. This fighter against his times was, tragically, forced to leave his post ...

Moderator: Yes, he was and Watson went to the west coast, where he ended up marking English exams at the University of British Columbia for a time, to make ends meet ...

Henson: Well, I tried to develop a philosophical framework, in difficult times, that maintained the spirit of the Antigonish Movement and Watson's social goal of an activated citizenry. I began my Provincial Report, published in 1946, by saying that adult education had recently emerged as a broad movement; by the end of World War II it was a social force and a personal urge which had never before commanded so much attention and, in many quarters, so much hope ... For the present and the future lie mainly in the hands of the adult population of the Province.It is the adults who make and change the world, and the children largely fit into it.

Like Violet, I insisted that learning should be the process through which we discover how (1) to make a living, (2) to live with others, and (3) to live fully. And like Watson and Alfred, I insisted that learning was inseparable from living at any age or in any state. At every stage in work, citizenship, the home, and the adventure of the inner person, the good life calls for constant growth and readjustment and new ideas, knowledge and skills.

Turning to the realities of Nova Scotian life, I set out the great needs of the Province. First, I argued that adult education had to confront the economic questions that were demanding more all-round intelligence and vocational skill from the average citizen. Second, adult education had to contribute to the enrichment of community life as the foundation of social happiness and progress. Third, a number of special groups (veterans, Blacks, the illiterate) presented opportunities for education designed to meet their needs and interests. Fourth, successful government depended on a widespread civic interest and wisdom.

Moderator: These brilliant minds speak to us in plain language about their understanding of the potential liberating role of adult education in Canadian society. I am deeply inspired by their efforts to articulate a vision of democratic adult education that encompasses all dimensions of human experience – material and spiritual.

Now, for our final theme. I would like all of you to speak, if you so choose, about your understanding of the craft of teaching adults. What are the principles of adult education? What is the relationship between vision and methods?

Coady: This is a subject dear to my heart! We might as well forget all over-refining of method and curricula. Teachers must have an overall philosophy that would supply the dynamics to make their teaching effective in the time and place in which they happened to live. We captured this philosophy with the phrase – "the good and abundant life." Teaching is a slow and difficult process in which learners participate and are encouraged to move along under their own power. I believe that we can comprehend the "scientific" rules for teaching adults; indeed, we in the Antigonish Movement thought we had ... (There is buzzing and some head-shaking in the background).

Tompkins: Teaching is a slow, difficult process, eh? Typical Catholic priest talk! I wanted to find ways of quickening slow learners! My main method was buttonholing the unwary. I think I invented the role of adult educator as pest. I didn't solve people's problems for them, but I kept asking them to read this, or read that ... some of you here tonight would not think that I was a very good facilitator ... (Laughter) ... I was an impatient educator who almost forced my learners to give good reasons for their apathy and hopelessness. I believed in pedagogical seed-sowing and cajoling people into action ... If people learned to be helpless, they could learn to be active!

Moderator: Dr. Tompkins, if Roby Kidd were here, he would probably say, "Well, Jimmy, you may have been a pest, but you were an animateur, a catalyst."

Thomson: I always believed that we had the responsibility to actively and educationally intervene in the life-situation of those who the system had rendered helpless and inactive ... we thought we could be both a catalytic presence and deeply respectful of those we were working with ...

Laidlaw: Moses Coady, with whom I worked as assistant director of St. Francis Xavier University Extension Department in the 1940's and 1950's, spoke of the active participation of the learner in the educational process. We believed that voluntary adult education must spring from within the learner and from his or her motivation. The educator of adults should try to discover the matters of greatest need for the learner and the educator must accept where the learner is. Because we believed that learning took place best in a social environment, emphasis was placed on discussion and open dialogue. But all of us believed that the question – Adult Education for what? – was of far greater importance than all the foregoing principles ...

McNaughton: I want to comment briefly, on Laidlaw's observation of how important the group experience was for the adult education movement. Well, in the agrarian farm movement we discovered early on that face-to-face study circles were the key to building a participatory democratic culture. There, in the everyday activity of the locals, men and women learned democracy by actively participating in meetings that were relatively free and egalitarian places to build self-confident persons and collectivities ...

Henson: We were all searching for pedagogical practices that were in harmony with our commitment to developing democracy through an enlightened citizenry ... All of my projects – the folkschool movement, library development, leadership training classes, artistic activities, actions in the Black community – involved people organizing around a common need and action for community betterment. We never imposed our views or programs on communities.

When I was sorting out the way I wanted our Division to work, numerous organizations were present in the rural communities – Farm Radio Forums, Citizens' Forums, co-ops, labour unions, Women's Institutes, Home and School Associations, and churches. I believed that the local and voluntary group was the natural carrier of adult education; the Division's role was to stimulate and support these groups. I supported study groups by training study group leaders in discussion methods. I chose fieldworkers to work closely with communities throughout Nova Scotia. Our community-based adult educators had to know how to get people together to talk about common interests and what they needed to accomplish their purposes. Today, our popular educators would speak of coalition-building skills ...

Fitzpatrick: In Frontier College we discovered that an effective teacher of oppressed or marginalized adults had to try to share the life of those he was teaching. I tried to recruit empathetic young men (and later, women) from the universities to travel into the camps to work with the labourers by day and teach them by night. You could say that we invented a new type of educator – the *labourer-teacher*. Empathy was the primary characteristic of the kind of adult educators we needed ...

Thomson: In all of my experiments in group living and adult education, we chose methods that would help people to discover their own power to re-fashion the institutions in which they were enmeshed.

And as self-motivated individuals, to build co-operative institutions in local communities, the region, the nation, and the globe. For me, the small study group was the indispensable context for learning to transform self and society through dialogue and action. As I listen to my old colleagues, I think it is safe to say that our vision of a revitalized and participatory democratic society drove us to discover new methods of teaching adults.

For example, the National Film Board's rural and industrial film circuits was an innovation that, like Frontier College, created a new form of teacher, the *projectionist-animator*. If we had more time, all of us could tell many stories about these projectionists ... dragging their heavy projectors and films by stoneboat in -30 degree Prairie weather to some small hotel at 3:00 a.m .... in preparation for the next day's showing of films in schools and local community halls ...

McNaughton: Yes, sometimes it is easy to forget how inventive we were, and how many different kinds of teachers of adults there really are! My sister in struggle, Beatrice Brigden, the socialist-feminist activist, used to teach adults by giving oral recitations in labour halls and community centres throughout western Canada. She was theatrically trained in Toronto, and used to recite progressive literary works for audiences numbering in the hundreds!

I was a *journalist-educator.* Our farm newspapers were absolutely crucial educational vehicles, ways of reaching and teaching farm women about the important issues of the day. Ah! I used to end all my columns, 'Yours in the struggle.'

Coady: Indeed ... the Antigonish Movement used the *Maritime Cooperator* as its written voice ... it was produced by the women leaders in our movement ...

Thomson: The Canadian Farm Radio and Citizens' Forums are quite well-known ... they were very bold endeavours to invent ways of engaging vast numbers of adults in learning that combined listening (radio), studying (reading and reflection) and action (creating projects). Those of us who were involved in these great national projects had to think seriously about new dimensions of teaching adults. How did one teach adults effectively through the radio medium? How did one write effective curricular materials for adults? One might say that those of us who were adult education daydreamers were in the beginning stages of discovering what it really meant to create a learning democracy ... (At this point, the lights begin to fade and a rustling of wind is heard in the background).

Moderator: We could go on very much longer. But our time is almost up. Our visitors from yesterday must return to whence they have come. But we have had a grand opportunity for them to continue to live in our memories. Someone has said that our struggle today is also a struggle of memory and forgetting.

Sources

This imaginary dialogue does not conform to standard historical writing. But the words of our characters have been largely taken from archival sources. We are hearing authentic voices. But I have taken liberty to capture the spirit of their lives and thought, as I have imagined how they might have spoken to one another and reflected on their work. You will notice that I have assumed that our male voices from yesterday are aware most of the time of the sexism of their earlier language, and have changed their words where it seemed appropriate. I assume that even the dead can learn which is, of course, decidedly unorthodox.

SUGGESTED READING

Boyle, G. (1953) "Selected writings of Father Tompkins." In *Father Tompkins of Nova Scotia.* New York: P.J. Kennedy & Sons.

Coady, M.M. (1939) *Masters of Their Destiny.* New York: Harper & Row.

Fitzpatrick, A. (1905) "The neglected citizen in the camps." *The Canadian Magazine.* Vol. 15.

Fitzpatrick, A. (c.1936) "Schools and other penetentiaries [sic]" Unpublished manuscript.

Henson, G. (1946) *A Report on Provincial Support of Adult Education in Nova Scotia.* Halifax: Department of Education.

Henson, G. (1956) "Letter to Dr. A.E. Kerr, President, Dalhousie University, October 15, 1956." In author's possession.

Laidlaw, A. (N.D.) "Some principles of adult education." Aexander Laidlaw Papers, Vol. 9, file 9-54, Public Archives of Canada.

Laidlaw, A. (Ed.) (1971) *The Man from Margaree: Writings and Speeches of M.M. Coady*. (1992) Toronto: McClelland & Stewart.

Sangster, J. "The making of a socialist-feminist: The early career of Beatrice Brigden." In M. Welton (Ed.) *Educating for a Brighter New Day: Women's Organizations as Learning Sites.* Halifax: Dalhousie University.

Steer, S. (1992) "Violet McNaughton and the struggle for the cooperative society." In M. Weldon (Ed.) *Educating for a Brighter New Day: Women's Organizations as Learning Sites.* Halifax: Dalhousie University.

Taylor, G. (1991) "A personal tragedy shapes the future" (Part 2, " Violet McNaughton: History of a Remarkable Woman") *Western People.*

Thomson, W. (1944) Adult Education Theory and Policy. Brief to Saskatchewan government.

Welton, M. (1987) "Mobilizing the people for socialism: The politics of adult education in Canada, 1944-46." In M. Weldon (Ed.) *Knowledge for the People.* Toronto: OISE Press.

Welton, M. (1991) "Amateurs out to change the world." Unpublished paper.

Chapter 3
Valuing What We Do As Practitioners

James A. Draper

Practitioner's Summary

Draper's chapter draws us to a topic that educators rarely consider: philosophy. He explains that philosophy "encompasses the principles, values and attitudes that structure our beliefs and guide our behaviours in work as well as in the whole of our daily life." By providing a capsule view of five general philosophical orientations evident in the practice of adult education, this chapter encourages us to reflect and articulate our own personal philosophy.
Questioning our own values and beliefs and their reflection in our work as adult educators, this chapter helps us to understand why we behave and think as we do.

Draper provides a brief description and comparison of five philosophical stances and their link to adult education:

1. Liberal philosophy:
Intended to "liberalize" the human spirit through the development of rational and critical thinking capacities", it is teacher-centred, with lectures as the predominant teaching method.

2. Progressive philosophy:
The intent is to free students from the predominance of objective or scientifically rational thinking and to value their own experiences thus making education relevant. The teacher is seen as the organizer and the guide. Education is given a pragmatic thrust through individual and group projects and field trips.

3. Behaviourist philosophy:
"Growing from the stimulus-response work of B.F. Skinner and others ... the intent is to change behaviour in terms of stated predetermined goals." This sequenced, task-oriented approach to education may not take account of the student's choices or previous experiences. The teacher's role is to see that

learning modules are followed and successfully completed towards an ultimate goal of measured achievement, sometimes with tangible rewards.

4. Humanist philosophy:
The intent here is to focus on the social context and the individual's ability to promote social change through recognizing the potential of personal growth and self actualization. The teacher is seen as an empathetic facilitator who is himself or herself on a quest of self-discovery.

5. Radical philosophy:
Initially based on Marxist-socialist ideology, focuses on producing"free and autonomous persons by liberating them from their oppression", and begins by "raising their consciousness" about everyday experiences The intent here is to change power relationships between individuals and groups. The teacher is a participating facilitator who engages the students in "dialogue" and the development of a "critical consciousness" as essential elements.
Draper notes that in actual practice, there are seldom "clear and rigid boundaries" between the philosophies, each may be useful for differing aspects of an educational program and therefore "each orientation should be determined by the purposes to be achieved."

He provides provocative lists of questions to enable the adult educator to place his or her own philosophical preferences, and notes how our daily language and behaviour displays our philosophy. He highlights the importance of "generic principles" in all teaching and learning and concludes by emphasizing the need for open dialogue on philosophy.

Chapter 3
Valuing What We Do As Practitioners
James A. Draper

Editors note: This chapter has been adapted from Draper and Taylor (Eds.) (1992) Voices from the Literacy Field. Toronto: Culture Concepts Inc. Reprinted with permission.

Why Should We Consider Philosophy?

A discussion of our values or philosophy of practice is more than an academic exercise. We may not be conscious of it but each day we live our philosophy.

> *Philosophy encompasses the principles, values and attitudes that structure our beliefs and guide our behaviours in our work as well as in the whole of our daily life.*

But to what extent do we articulate and understand these values, assumptions, beliefs and attitudes which guide us? Our individual or collective philosophies are the basis upon which we defend and practice what we do. The way in which we perceive and deal with issues are determined by our philosophy.

Many questions which practitioners ask challenge their beliefs. For example:

- On what basis do we argue that one teaching method is preferred over another?
- Why do we believe that developing curriculum materials with the involvement of students is better than the development of textbooks written by experts?
- Why does the criteria for evaluating our programs, imposed upon us by a funding agency, sometimes conflict with our feelings of how our student-centred program should be evaluated?
- What determines the type of relationships we wish to develop between instructors and students? Between our agency and its surrounding community?
- In our training programs, what determines what we will teach?
- What criteria do we use and what qualifications do we look for when selecting instructors to work in our programs?
- What determines the words we use to describe our programs?

What this chapter is about

This chapter begins by looking at how our behaviour raises philosophical questions and encourages us to reflect on and articulate our personal philosophy. And how this is expressed in our work.

This is followed by a description and discussion of five general philosophical orientations, all of which are evident in the broad field of adult education: liberal, behaviourist, progressive, humanist and radical. The relevance and practice of these in education is then illustrated. The next section discusses how our values as educators are expressed in our daily behaviour and language. The importance of language and the need to take our words seriously follows. Finally, we see that values and assumptions are integral to the way in which we plan, implement and evaluate our programs.

What Do We Mean When We Talk About Philosophy?

It is a human tendency to feel that what we do is rational, that there are reasonable explanations for our behaviour, that we are right in what we think and do. We do not usually articulate these feelings. We just take them for granted. Our philosophy of life, those beliefs and values which guide us in our work and our relationships with others, are an integral part of our identity that we seldom question. But can they also limit our perceptions? Are there other views to listen to and benefit from? Are the assumptions we make about the educational needs of others really a projection of our own values? How do we know? And how shall we do it?

All of these are philosophical questions.

> *Being able to answer these and many other questions helps us to understand and implement the programs in which we are involved, including the identification of training needs, curriculum planning, delivery, evaluation and the selection of teaching materials. Philosophy affects them all.*

The Random House Dictionary (1987) defines philosophy as "a system of principles for guidance in practical affairs; the rational investigation of the truths and principles of being, knowledge, or conduct." Articulating our personal philosophy helps us to understand why we behave and think the way we do.

Furthermore, it helps us to understand the consequences of our behaviour and the influence our philosophy has upon others. It helps us to be consistent but also challenges us to question our inconsistency. It can help us in communicating with others, providing we take care to openly express our values and assumptions. It may help us defend our actions. "I use this teaching approach because it expresses the philosophy I believe in."

Being able to articulate our preferred philosophy also helps us to be more professional as adult educators. That is, it helps us to describe our behaviour through a thoughtful and theoretical point of view. The generalist practitioner is often only able to describe what is done, not why.

> *Articulating our beliefs and values also helps us to bridge theory and practice; to more clearly see the relationship between education and society, and the various social, economic, political and cultural forces which influence education.*

Our philosophy influences our practice, and practice illuminates our philosophy. Rooted in our individual history and the history of our society, our philosophy is always personal yet it identifies us as members of a group. Focusing on our explicit beliefs helps us to both utilize and create knowledge, especially when we are open to the beliefs of others.

Labelling our Philosophies

In their book, *Philosophical Foundations of Adult Education,* Elias and Merriam (1984) discuss five philosophies: liberal, behaviourist, progressive, humanist, and radical. What follows is a brief description and comparison of each and their link to adult education.

Looking at a liberal philosophy

Arising out of early Greek thinking, the purpose of liberal education was to develop a person's intellect and morals (the distinction between right and wrong) and to develop the ability to make wise judgments.

> *The intent was to liberalize the human spirit through the development of rational and critical thinking capacities. This is still the intent of liberal arts programs in universities today. The student was usually guided by an authority figure, a teacher who was conversant with the content. Being teacher-centred, the dominant teaching method was the lecture. The liberal tradition was intended to be a discovery of the self with external assistance, and what a person learned was expected to be reflected in their everyday life. The early history of Western education for instance, often had a moral overtone, focusing on the reading of the holy scriptures or the classics.*

The relevance of this orientation to adult education programs is the value which it places on the quality of the 'philosophical' content which is being read, presenting to the reader new and relevant ideas which often go beyond the classroom.

> *The liberal tradition attempts to teach people to think, to reason, to question, and to engage in timeless reflections and discussions about justice, truth and goodness.*

Looking at behaviourist philosophy

> *Growing out of the stimulus-response work of B.F. Skinner and others, this philosophical orientation aims to change behaviour in the direction of pre-determined stated objectives. The goal of behaviour modification or conditioning is teacher-directed and teacher-rewarded.*

The student is led through a sequencing of learning modules toward an ultimate goal which can be measured. Competency based training is a prime example of this philosophical orientation, where the outcome and the means for reaching it are pre-programmed. Reaching this end goal is all important. This philosophical orientation is sometimes criticized since the student gives up a degree of freedom, putting himself or herself in the hands of another person in order to reach a predetermined goal which, it is presumed, has some value to the student. While the student and the teacher enter into a kind of contract with one another, this task-oriented approach to education often ignores the previous experiences of the student and the choices of learner response may be limited.

This approach to education is practised in many traditional programs where, for example, the student's goal is to prepare for an examination leading to a formal certification or where one is taught to master specific sequentially arranged skills such as learning to use a computer.

Looking at progressive philosophy

Beginning in the early part of this century, this philosophy grew out of a sociopolitical North American context characterized by industrialization, utilitarian values, the expansion of vocational training, capitalism, citizenship education and language training of new immigrants, as well as the increasing predominance of the scientific method and rational thinking (left brain) in objectively explaining human behaviour. These values were reflected in the public schools which were often isolated from the daily life of the community and characterized by an authoritarian approach to education, focusing on facts and memorization.

A reaction against this was an attempt to progress towards an education which would introduce new attitudes, ideas and teaching methods.

> *The intention was to free students to value the experiences they already had; to make education relevant and applicable by developing skills of problem solving and by using a scientific method to discover knowledge through field trips and projects.*

The teacher became the organizer and guide. Education became more democratized and more focused on the pragmatic, and was seen to be both experimental as well as experiential.

This progressive approach had a profound influence on the practice and theory of adult education. Individual experiences were valued and encouraged. Participation in one's own learning, with degrees of control over what is learned, and the idea of human developmental potential took on a new depth of meaning.

This philosophy also helped to raise questions about the social responsibility of institutions such as schools and private industry. Beginning with an assessment of learner's needs, this approach to education was seen as an instrument of social change. Much of the spirit and practice of this progressive philosophical approach is seen today in many adult education programs, especially those which are community based.

Looking at humanist philosophy

The progressive philosophy focused on the social context of individuals and their ability to promote social change. The humanist philosophy differed because it focused on personal growth and self actualization. It arose out of an 18th century reaction against the authority of traditional institutions and the anonymity of industrialization which was thought to dehumanize the individual.

> *Viewing individuals holistically, humanistic philosophy valued the intrinsic, intuitive (right brain), ethical sense of people and their willingness and ability to take responsibility for their own learning through a process of self-direction, self-evaluation and self-actualization.*

This approach focused on encouraging people to explore the depths of their feelings, building self-concept, and valuing human life. The goal was to maximize human potential, building on the innate goodness of the individual, with the support of empathetic teachers as facilitators and partners in learning who were themselves on the quest of self-discovery. This philosophy is especially evident in adult education programs today which value learning as a process (see Barer-Stein and Connolly's chapter) and which encourage discussion and self-discovery.

Looking at radical philosophy

Based initially on Marxist-socialist ideas, the radical educational philosophy set out to produce free and autonomous persons by liberating them from their oppression. The first step is to 'raise their consciousness' about their daily life experiences. In doing so, people describe their 'world' (their community and surroundings), exposing those forces which they believe prevent them from reaching their potential.

To free themselves from oppressive elements, it is important for people to discuss these elements in groups. First they articulate and critically examine their "world" (for example their workplace), then they plan actions to gain greater control (power) over their lives, thus changing the system which they believe to be the cause of their oppression. Being involved in the process of change provides people with a shared vocabulary.

> *The radical philosophy more than any of the other orientations, acknowledges that it is a political one. The goal is to change the power relationships between individuals and groups.*

Groups which gather to discuss their social issues are examples of this philosophical orientation and out of this process people may realize the need to develop various skills. On the other hand, such programs are sometimes used to bring people together to discuss political and economic issues and education becomes a secondary focus. This philosophy attempts to democratize and humanize society by questioning its assumptions and myths. The process is often guided by a participating facilitator-teacher. Dialogue and the development of a critical consciousness are essential elements in the process. Improving the quality of life and extending the choices in people's lives is another goal.

This philosophy is one that is frequently misunderstood in both its interpretation and application. Too often people think of this as a method only and not as a philosophy. In fact, it is both. One can practice radical philosophy in any human situation, for example, in examining the sources and form of power in one's family or one's workplace. Depending on the tolerance level of those who have power, this process can lead to mutually constructive and peaceful changes, which in themselves may extend the tolerance for change.

The radical philosophy makes reference to the 'colonizing of the mind' which refers to the labels which are often used to describe people, such as troublesome, inferior, un-intelligent, lazy, immoral, stupid. Frequently internalized by those who are labelled, these often result in negative self-concepts. Sadly, there are all too many examples of the dehumanizing effect of blaming the victim, of labelling people who are on welfare, illiterate, unemployed, poor or disabled. Often the first task of an educational program is to begin, not with the teaching content or skills but to focus on eliminating negative internalized labels, in order to revive individual self-esteem and dignity. Only then can education provide an open door to learning.

Philosophically Where Do We Stand?

Given the above descriptions of the five philosophical orientations applicable to education, an adult education instructor in a program might begin by asking which one best describes my approach to education? "Do the methods I use in my work match with what I say I am doing?

A similar question can be posed as well for the employers, planners and managers who are associated with these programs. Quite naturally, these persons may see themselves in more than one of the philosophical orientations, depending on the context in which they are working. "Sometimes I do things this way but at other times another approach seems more appropriate."

> *In practice there are seldom clear and rigid boundaries. The application of these philosophies are situational, often determined by educational goals (which may conflict with each other), the resources and time available, and especially by the content, skills or attitudes to be learned.*

The comparative value of the five orientations can be useful to those responsible for the different parts of an educational program. Each orientation is determined by the purposes to be achieved. There are specific expectations of students and teachers in each orientation. Each is also characterized by predominant methods for teaching and learning and is described by key concepts.

Understanding Our Own Philosophical Orientation

In an attempt to understand the essence of each philosophical orientation and as a way of assessing our own teaching philosophy, the adult educator might ask:

- What is the role of social change in each orientation?
- Does our philosophy focus on perpetuating the status quo or in bringing about constructive change? Change from whose point of view and to what ends?
- Does the program value experiential learning, questioning and exploration, and the interaction with others in working toward the achievement of educational goals?
- Are these processes stated explicitly as intended outcomes of the program? Or is the program focused on the achievement of pre-determined end goals, such as in a behaviourist philosophy? Or both?
- How is the individual (as compared with the group) valued in the program? Is the focus of the program on individuals competing with each other or are individuals encouraged to interact, share, cooperate and support each other in their learning?
- Is individual learning assessed consistently with the stated goals of the educational program? Is the evaluation done by the student or by an authority figure? Or is evaluation a cooperative effort?
- Finally, is the program built on a model which Barer-Stein (1992) calls Rote Internalizing as compared with Reflective Internalizing? That is, are individuals expected to learn solely through rote memorizing, (expected to repeat what has been presented to them) or are they encouraged to submit their accumulated learning to a process of critical reflection?

Gaining a familiarity with the alternative philosophies, educators can understand more clearly what they are doing and why. They may become more aware of and value alternative approaches to planning educational programs. If nothing more, an awareness of these orientations might minimize contradictions while at the same time clarify goals and outcomes of a program.

> *Each philosophical orientation has its place within the rich diversity of educational practice. With experience, the educator will know when to use a particular method or practice a particular philosophy.*

Sometimes it might seem that there is a contradiction between a person's general philosophical approach to teaching (which may be humanistic) and the need to apply a different philosophical approach (behaviouristic) for a particular situation. Sometimes short term goals such as acquiring basic knowledge and preliminary skills can be achieved best through "behavioural objectives" yet the long term goal may be to make use of those acquired skills in creative ways.

Flexibility is more important than rigid adherence to a particular philosophy or method. The effective educator is able to orchestrate all the variables of a program without losing sight of the overall goal of holistic human development.

The Importance of Language in Expressing a Philosophy

> *A philosophy is expressed through people's attitudes and behaviour but also through the language which they use to describe what they do.*

Is the practitioner's language genuine? That is, are current terminologies being used but neither understood nor practised? For example, it is relatively easy to use current terminology, such as "learner centred" or "community based" or "self directed learning" without really knowing the meaning of these terms or the implications of practising them. The words used by the radical philosophical orientation, words like "power", "social change", and "critical consciousness" are in vogue today but are they understood in the context of local action?

An adult education program might encourage its participants to become more self-directing, to offer their suggestions on how things might be done differently, to value and encourage creativity (which begins with constructive criticism about how things are currently done), and to build a "team environment". The achievement of such goals exposes the power and political relationships between people and nurtures individual critical faculties, helping to bring about degrees of social change.

Each philosophical orientation has key words that describe its main focus. For example, what are the different meanings of such words as facilitator, instructor, teacher, guide and tutor?

Much of the vocabulary used today in adult education is now taken for granted. Some has been rediscovered from past usage and some has come from a radical philosophy within a Third World or developing nations context. For example we speak of equity and justice as the real end goals of education. Value laden words such as freedom, exploitation, struggle are also used. The end goal of education may be the empowerment of the individual, or education may be seen as a synonym for self-reliance, for liberation, for independence. Although seldom stated explicitly, all educational programs are expressions of an ideology, a philosophy, and a kind of vision .

From the language we use and from the goals we develop, we can speak of generic and philosophical goals for education. In an educational program, not only content and subject matter are being taught. We know that adult students are also reacting to the program environment, developing attitudes about the subject matter, reacting to the teaching methods being used and becoming aware of how they are perceived and treated.

A Generic Approach to Training and Teaching

In the midst of this discussion of philosophical stances in education, it may be useful to pause and describe some generic educational goals which transcend all educational programs.

- The development of communication skills of listening, speaking and writing.
- The valuing of learning as a lifelong process.
- The development of skills to retrieve and store information.
- The building of positive attitudes about oneself as well as developing the skills of critical thinking.

The practitioner needs to consciously teach for these goals. They will not automatically come about. All too often the absence of an articulated philosophy tends to narrow rather than broaden the stated goals of education. Comparing the different approaches to education, the practitioner can imagine:

- Perceiving the student learner as one who is dependent on others for direction, compared to one who is interdependent/independent and self-directing.
- An educational program which is subject matter centred compared to one which is task, problem or self-centred.
- A program which students enter because of external or imposed forces as compared with one in which the student voluntarily and enthusiastically participates.
- A program which has been planned by an authority figure or expert, such as a teacher specialist, as compared with one in which the planning is democratized and includes wide participation, and involvement of the students.

Which philosophy does your program portray? How do we balance short term and long term goals? Our philosophy of teaching and learning can be enhanced by being more precise with the vocabulary we use to describe what we do.

The Need for a Dialogue on Philosophy

A number of questions further help to focus on the need for a dialogue on philosophy. For example, how do we account for differing cultures which provide differing orientations, differing perspectives and perhaps differing philosophies in any organization and in any classroom? Where is the place of the educator as learner in the educational program? Is education to focus only on learning immediate skills or does it include goals which help people become more socially responsible and more critically reflective? Does our educational philosophy help people to reflect on possibilities and to make choices?

We know that education is not a neutral enterprise but involves both political and philosophical decisions, and influences all aspects of an educational program from its original inception to the teaching and evaluating. We know that particular philosophies, based on particular assumptions about human nature, can help to democratize an education program and society. There needs to be a compatibility of management and infrastructure with the philosophy which we expound and want to emulate in the classroom.

We know that our philosophy, like culture and values, is learned. Our philosophy may encourage us to seek partnerships with student learners, with the community, and with other organizations. Or it may encourage us to remain closed. We know also that the forces which influence our behaviours are real and may conflict with our preferred way of behaving. For example a funding agency may impose a quantitative model of evaluation upon a program which values qualitative outcomes of learning. Similarly, organizational policies may be incompatible with the philosophy of a workplace education program. How do we philosophically handle these and other contradictions?

Finally, we know that our philosophy is an expression of an ideology.

> *By understanding our values we maximize the rationality of our behaviour. Our philosophy is the foundation upon which we act.*

These are the rudders which steer us through our daily life and which determine how we will teach and behave in countless other ways. A philosophy is not a theoretical thing that other people possess. It is the profound understanding which provides meaning for each individual.

REFERENCES

Barer-Stein, T. (1992) Learning about Learning. In J. Draper and M.T. Taylor (Eds.) *Voices from the Literacy Field.* Toronto: Culture Concepts Inc.

Cross, P. (1981) *Adults as Learners.* San Francisco: Jossey-Bass Publishers.

Elias, J.L. and Merriam, S. (1984) *Philosophical Foundations of Adult Education.* Malabar, Florida: Robert E. Krieger Publishing Co.

Random House Dictionary of the English Language. (1987) Second Edition. Unabridged. New York: Random House.

SUGGESTED READING

Bergevin, P.A. (1967) *A Philosophy for Adult Education.* New York: Seabury Press.

Darkenwald, G. and Merriam, S. (1982) *Adult Education: Foundations of Practice.* New York: Harper & Row.

Lawson, K.H. (1979) *Philosophical Concepts and Values in Adult Education.* Milton Keynes, England: The Open University Press.

Lindeman, E.C. (1989) *The Meaning of Adult Education.* Oklahoma: Oklahoma Research Center for Continuing Professional & Higher Education. First Published 1926.

Merriam, S.B. and Cunningham P.M. (1989) *Handbook of Adult and Continuing Education.* San Francisco: Jossey-Bass Publishers.

Patterson, R.W.K. (1979) *Values Education and the Adult.* Boston: Routledge & Kegan Paul.

Chapter 4
Women as Learners

Dorothy MacKeracher

Practitioner's Summary

This chapter is about women as learners, but even more specifically, it provides insightful commentary from feminist research to illuminate every adult educator's teaching with all adults.

While most adult educators incorporate humanistic principles, women have become aware that such planning and facilitating approaches may be insufficient in several important ways: small groups do not always confer equity, even a so-called supportive environment may not lead learners to feel empowered, the relative independence of self-directed learning may not be appropriate for all learners, learning skills may not be adequate.

Beginning with an explanation of Gilligan's (1982) comparison of the traditional Justice Model with a developed Care Model of moral reasoning, MacKeracher points out the lack of responses from women in the Justice Model development – which is based on equality, fair rules and moral contracts – does not take into consideration the typical moral reasoning of women which is based on concerns for connectedness to others and responsiveness to the needs of others. This is not to say that one model depicts men and the other depicts women, it is just to point out that at least two models of moral reasoning exist and should be considered.

Self identity and self development also emerge as important considerations in the different ways that learning may be affected. The traditional view of self development, for example, describes the emergence of a separate or autonomous self which is separate from others and independent in its relations. Other differences emerge from research by Lyons (1987, 1990) to distinguish this type of development from the connected or relational self development in which interdependence and interactive relationships are deemed dominant.

Other factors that emerge from feminist research, particularly from the work of Belenky and associates (1986) revolve around shifts in thinking. These are shown to move from Dualistic Thinking dominated by a belief in the certainty of truth and knowledge, towards Multiplistic Thinking which permits the notion of the uncertainty of truth and knowledge with the concommittant necessity of encouragement to hold ideas and opinions differing from authorities, and to identify one's own ideas through independent thinking. Finally, Relativistic

Thinking describes a contextual perspective of thinking where ideas can be understood in relation to their context, where anyone can contribute to a knowledge base, and where truth relies on what makes sense within each context.

Another contribution emerges from the work of Lyons (1987) and Wingfield and Haste (1987) helping to distinguish and to understand learners with the notions of 'separate' and 'connected'. MacKeracher provides an intriguing table to document and summarize these characteristics. For readers involved in research, separate and connected ways of learning will also echo objective and subjective modes of research.

MacKeracher defines Feminist Education as being concerned with the content of what is taught in the formal education of girls and women, while Feminist Pedagogy to be concerned with the processes and the teaching methods used. She lists nine clear ideas emerging from study and research which inform feminist pedagogy and concludes with a plea for the sensitive integration of this knowledge into all adult teaching and learning.

Chapter 4
Women as Learners
Dorothy MacKeracher

What Makes Women Feel Left Out?

This chapter is about women as learners and about how we, as adult educators, can make the educational programs and activities we plan and implement more responsive to women's styles of learning.

In the field of adult education, most educators believe in humanistic values in dealing with all learners. They plan programs which strive to maintain equity among learners, introduce content which is relevant to the needs of the learners, provide opportunities for learners to be self-directing, create an environment which supports and values individual learners, and implement activities which encourage the development of learning-to-learn skills.

Women have become aware that such planning and facilitating approaches are sometimes not enough. For example, we know that:

> *small group discussions do not confer equity on all members of a learning group; a supportive environment does not lead all learners to feel empowered enough to share what they know; the relative independence of self-directed learning is not appropriate for all learners; and learning-to-learn skills may help in learning through thinking but not necessarily in learning through doing.*

What is it about women's learning which makes them feel left out of many educational endeavours? Such knowledge might help us understand other groups in our society, such as the poor and minority racial or linguistic groups that have been left behind by the educational system.

In this chapter, I'll begin by considering how and why women's experiences must be reclaimed in order to expand our understanding of human behaviour in general. Then I'll review some of the ideas which have emerged recently from feminist research and commentary about women as learners. At the end I'll return to the issue of how we, as adult educators, can use these ideas to expand our understanding of human learning and to improve our approaches to facilitating the learning of both men and women.

Reclaiming Women's Voices: The Justice Model and the Care Model of Moral Reasoning.

> *Much of the literature on adult learning and development is written by men about male behaviours which are described as "normal" for all humans both men and women.*

To help us understand how the female voice has been left out of our traditional understanding of adult learning and development, we'll look at the work of Carol Gilligan (1982) who draws our attention to the development of moral reasoning and how this may help us to understand adult learning and development. Traditional opinion about morality tells us that, in order to become morally mature, we should develop and use ideas which focus on justice, equality among persons, the value of fair rules, and setting, maintaining and abiding by moral contracts between persons and social groups.

However, we find that the research upon which this *justice model* was based either did not include any females as participants, or the caring responses that were gathered from girls and women did not fit into the justice model and were ignored. Yet written reports about the justice model explicitly state that it describes the full range of moral behaviour and is equally true for girls and boys, women and men.

Gilligan (1982) proposes a second, equally valid approach to moral reasoning, described as a *care model,* which focuses on concerns for being connected to others and the value of responsiveness to the needs of others. These two models of moral reasoning focus on different moral concerns, moral problems and moral ideas as outlined in Table 1.

Gilligan (1990) reports that while most of the men and women in her studies were able to utilize both models of moral reasoning, two-thirds of them focused on one model, elaborating one set of concerns and minimally representing the other. She also reports that the tendency to focus on one model was equally characteristic of both men and women but the care focus was almost exclusively a female phenomenon. Further, if girls and women had been eliminated from her studies, the care focus in moral reasoning would virtually disappear.

The justice model of moral reasoning is not the only theory which describes human behaviour on the basis of male examples. Such an approach is also found in Piaget's model of cognitive development, Freud's model of sexual development, and Erikson's model of psychosocial development. Since such theorists have dominated our thinking about human behaviour, women have consistently been excluded from the development of the knowledge base which guides our behaviour in everyday life. When women have been included it has been because of unusual abilities or circumstances and not because they are representatives of their gender. In the social sciences, therefore, the experiences and opinions of

Table 1
Comparison of Justice & Care Models of Moral Reasoning
(Based on ideas described in Gilligan, 1982,1990)

	Justice Model	Care Model
Focus of concern	Equality among persons Fair rules Moral contracts Reciprocity Rights of individuals & society	Being connected to others Being responsive to the needs of others Understanding others Needs of individuals & society
Moral problems defined in terms of	Oppression Inequity Exploitation	Detachment Abandonment Neglect
Moral ideals defined in terms of	Respect Equality Honour	Attention Regard Care

women rarely are included in our understanding of human behaviour. Gilligan's work helped women to understand how they had been left out of one theoretical explanation of human behaviour and challenged all of us to examine other models more carefully.

Questions which remain to be answered include: How are other descriptions of human behaviour inaccurate with regard to girls and women? What must we understand about the behaviour of girls and women to develop a more integrated view of human behaviour? How is the well-being of girls and women affected when they are left out of descriptions and explanations of human behaviour? In this chapter we will address these questions in terms of adult learning.

Four Lines of Inquiry: Knowing and Thinking about Women as Learners

Our knowledge about women's learning is based on research published since 1975 and emerges from the intersection of four lines of inquiry. The first line examines the experiences of girls and women within the educational system. The second comes from studies on the development of self; the third from studies on the nature of the content and processes which appear to dominate the learning of most girls and women; and the fourth from feminist pedagogy and concerns about the education of women, particularly in relation to Women's Studies Programs. I will consider each of these lines of inquiry separately and then attempt to integrate the dominant themes.

1. Women's experiences in the educational system

Since the women's movement began, female educators have scolded the educational system for failing to meet the needs of female learners. (Spender & Sarah, 1980)

Gloria Steinem (1992) suggests that one factor which prevents women from knowing that all is not well for them in the educational system, is that women get good grades, often better than their male counterparts.

> *Since grades are the measure of academic life, they obscure the larger question of what is being learned: that a female student may be getting an A-plus in self-denigration. (Steinem, 1992)*

Steinem reports that research shows that the self-esteem of girls begins at relatively high levels in the elementary grades, begins to fall off in the secondary grades, and declines with women's successful passage through the various levels of colleges and universities.

Joan Gallos (1992) describes the fear and self-doubt that women experienced when they participated in a graduate program on management development, in which they were asked to answer the question "Who am I?"

> *The women felt deep terror that they would not be able to understand, that they wouldn't know what to do, that they would demonstrate that they did not belong (in the college), that they would show everyone their "dumbness." They felt self-doubt that they wouldn't have anything important to say, that their fears about themselves and this undertaking were justified, and they would be lost. (Gallos, 1992)*

Gallos goes on to state that women approach learning with more self-doubt and experiences of alienation than their male counterparts. Because cultural and personal experiences support women's silence, we should not wonder at women's doubts about their ability to make a valued contribution to educational discussions.

Gallos believes that the alienation women experience in the educational system stems from two sources. First, there are important developmental differences between men and women which can effect how each think, know and learn. Second, the basic structures of our educational system – teaching methods and knowledge – are informed by male-based ideas and experiences which may undermine women's approaches to learning.

2. Development of self in two modes: Autonomous and Relational

Gilligan's work on the development of moral reasoning identified a "different voice" in women's conceptions of self and introduced the concept of the "connected self" to expand our understanding of human development. Other writers echo Gilligan's theme in describing the nature and development of a

Table 2
Comparison of Two Modes of Self Definition
(Based on ideas described in Lyons, 1987,1990)

	Separate/Autonomous Self	Connected/Relational Self
Major focus of self definition	Autonmous in relation to others Independence	Connected in relation to others Interdependence
Basis for self definition	Through seeing oneself as if through the eyes of significant others	Through interactive relationships with significant others
Relationships between self and others	Experienced through reciprocity Maintained through impartiality, objectivity and increasing distance between self and others Others are assumed to be more similar than different in comparison to self (making reciprocity possible)	Experienced through interdependence Maintained through concern for other's well-being, understanding needs and contexts of others, and reducing distance between self and others Others are assumed to be more different than similar in comparison to self (making responsiveness necessary)

"separate" or autonomous self and a "connected" or relational self. A comparison of these two forms of self definition is provided in Table 2.

Separate/autonomous self

The traditional view of self development describes the emergence of a separate or autonomous self which is separate from others and independent in its relations with others. Through these predictable sequences of behaviours, the individual moves from an immature self (participating in unequal relationships, feeling powerless and using dependent behaviours) toward a mature, equal, empowered and independent self. Since other persons are assumed to be similar to oneself, the individual is able to understand the others' points of view without much difficulty. Reciprocity allows the individual to be impartial and objective and to maintain a distance between self and others.

Connected/relational self

Women's views of self development (Gilligan, 1982; Miller, 1986) describe, in addition to the separate or autonomous self, the emergence of a connected or relational self that is linked to others yet *interdependent* in relationships. The development of this self is viewed as a multi-dimensional and complex process, emerging through life's expected and unexpected experiences and changes. (Schlossberg, 1984) It is defined and discovered through interacting with others around mutual concerns for each other's well-being and of responsiveness to the needs of others. (Lyons, 1990)

Since others are assumed to be different than self, mutual relationships are maintained and sustained by considering others in terms of their specific contexts and needs, but not necessarily in terms of strict equality.

> *To be responsive implies seeing others in their own terms and being open to different ways in which others make sense of their own situations and experiences.*

These two different forms of self development are described as being gender-related but not gender-specific. Most of us define ourselves in terms consistent with both the connected and separate self. Men and women who have reached maturity in their self development are able to use and combine both ways of defining self, more or less equally.

> *Since we know that an individual's self-concept is a central factor in learning, we can assume that the manner in which learners describe themselves becomes a crucial element in how they go about learning.*

Understanding changes leading to maturity as learners

Ways of thinking: dualistic, multiplistic, relativistic

What changes do women and men go through as they become more mature and more competent as learners? Much of this research began as a re-examination of the ideas of William Perry (1970) who reported that, during their undergraduate years, the thinking of male students shifts from a reliance on dualistic thinking to multiplistic thinking and then to relativistic (or contextual) thinking. Beyond the relativistic phase, the changes that occur in thinking are found not so much in the processes, as in the learner's commitment to ideas and the learning done as a consequence of these commitments.

> *In dualistic thinking, students believe that knowledge is either right or wrong, that the truth of knowledge is certain, and that authority figures cannot (should not) be questioned about truth and knowledge.*
>
> *In multiplistic thinking, students discover that truth and knowledge are sometimes uncertain, that authority figures sometimes disagree with each other about what is true, that students are (sometimes) encouraged to hold ideas and opinions which differ from those of*

> *authorities, and that one can (should) identify one's own ideas and opinions through independent thought.*
>
> *In relativistic thinking, students discover that knowledge can only be understood in relation to the context in which it was developed, that anyone can contribute to the knowledge base which is used in each context, and that truth is what makes sense within each context.*

These shifts in thinking are also found among women. Mary Belenky and her colleagues (Belenky, Clinchy, Goldberger & Tarule, 1986) report that as college women move away from dualism, they need to understand the ideas and opinions of others (e.g., authorities, classmates) by hearing about the situations which give rise to these ideas and opinions. That is, women appear to introduce a form of relativism into their thinking much earlier than men. One conclusion from this finding is that the early introduction of relativism occurs because most women are more likely to rely on a relational self when they enter formal learning activities.

Based on other studies which re-examined Perry's ideas, Marcia Baxter Magolda (1991) reports that some students, men more often than women, learn most effectively in activities which involve mastery of the material, individual achievement, working with others to challenge one's thinking, and focusing primarily on self-directed learning even in collaborative learning activities. When these learners move to multiplistic thinking, they advocate the use of research and logic to resolve questions where knowledge is uncertain. They view discrepancies between opinions as resulting from the selection of different facts to support their logic, and evaluation as an opportunity to correct both the selection of facts and the logic used.

Some students, more often women than men, learn most effectively in settings which involve connecting what one is learning to one's own experience, establishing connections with other learners, and focusing on a collective or collaborative perspective even in individualized learning situations.

When these learners move to multiplistic thinking, they advocate listening to the ideas of others when knowledge is uncertain as a means for expanding their understanding and reconciling differences. They view discrepancies between opinions as resulting from a different interpretation of the facts, and evaluation as an opportunity to demonstrate their understanding of the different sides of an issue. These differences, which appear once the learners move beyond dualistic thinking, are consistent with the concepts of separateness and connectedness which we examined in relation to self development.

Describing "separate" and "connected" learners

Nona Lyons (1987) describes both "separate" and "connected" learners. Her description can be expanded by drawing on the work of other writers (Wingfield

Table 3

Comparison of Two Types of Learners

(Based on ideas described in Blenky & others, 1986; Lyons,1987; Wingfield & Haste, 1987, Magolda,1981)

	Separate/Autonomous Learner	Connected/Relational Learner
Learning concerns	Mastery of content. Individual achievement. Ask questions to prove truth or worth of ideas. Identifying truth.	Establishing connection to other learners. Ask questions to understand situations, contexts, & ideas of others. Identifying differences in ideas and opinions.
Learning activities	Challenging ideas of others. Convincing others through logic ,order maintained through agreement to abide by rules. Conflicts resolved through detached imposition of existing rules. Involves doubting or excluding ideas until their worth has been proven. Attempts to reveal truth that is general, impersonal & grounded in rational, logical thought or generalized perception of reality. Prefers self-directed activities; competition in group activities. Objectivity maintained through adopting frame of reference of discipline (e.g. biology,history) or authority(e.g. the law, the instructor). Prefer to hold thought & feeling separate.	Listening when knowledge is uncertain. Convincing others through sharing particulars of personal experiences. Order maintained through implicit agreement to avoid conflict. Conflicts resolved through reconciling differences. Involves believing other's ideas in order to expand one's understanding. Attempts to create truth that is personal, particular & grounded in firsthand experiences or unique historical/ personal events. Prefered collective or collaborative group activities or learning partnerships. Objectivity maintained through under-standing frame of reference of other person(s). Prefer to keep thought and feeling together.
Preferred thinking styles	Analytical. Based on patterns & exemplars.	Holistic. Based on narratives & metaphors.
Nature of truth& knowledge	Truth resides in reliability & validity of knowledge. Knowledge separate from knower.	Truth resides in believability of meaning given to experiences or interpretation of facts.
Nature of evaluation	Opportunity to correct errors in selection of facts and logic used. Individual accountable for own learning.	Opportunity to demonstrate understanding of different sides of an issue. Individual accountable to others for learning.

& Haste, 1987) and these are presented in Table 3. Separate learners are autonomous. They tend to use analytic thinking styles, test for truth by looking for consistency and logic in knowledge, and prefer to hold thought and feeling apart from each other.

> *When* separate learners *ask "Why?", they want an answer which will justify the logic or worth of an idea.*

Connected learners are interdependent. They tend to use holistic thinking styles, test for truth by looking for believability in knowledge, and prefer to integrate thought and feeling.

> *When* connected learners *ask "Why?", they want to know how the idea was developed or constructed, preferably by hearing a description of the specific situation or activities in which the idea emerged.*

These writers also remind us that separated and connected approaches to learning are gender-related but not gender-specific.

> *Many men and women are capable of using both approaches. However, more men than women use the separate approach as their dominant way of thinking and learning, and more women than men use the connected approach as their dominant way of thinking and learning.*

4. Feminist Pedagogy: processes and teaching methods

> Feminist education *is concerned with the* content *of what is taught in the formal education of girls and women;* feminist pedagogy *with the processes and teaching methods used.*

Feminist educators are committed to the development of women-centred teaching methods, knowledge sources and materials. Processes and teaching methods which are most often associated with feminist pedagogy have been derived in part, from the research we have considered in the first part of this paper and in part, from the experiences of students and instructors in Women's Studies Programs, in using women-centred teaching methods and knowledge. (Schneidewind, 1983; Hayes, 1989)

Nine ideas which inform feminist pedagogy:

1. Women-only programs are recommended for women who are re-entering the educational system, who are entering a new field of study or training, or whose

self-esteem is low. In mixed-gender groups, women tend to speak less frequently and feel less empowered. (Tannen, 1990) Women-only groups are more supportive and less risky than mixed-gender groups. (Spender & Sarah, 1980)

2. Women-centred content, in which the knowledge and experience of women are the central theme, is recommended in order to correct the fact that women have been excluded from the knowledge base in most areas of study. Women-centred content includes both knowledge created by women and knowledge about women and their concerns and interests. (Smith, 1987)
3. A connected learning environment is one which utilizes small groups to foster the development of trust, thus allowing for self-disclosure; of mutual respect, thus allowing each woman to share her experience and knowledge comfortably; and of connectedness among learners and instructional staff. (Schneidewind, 1983)

> *A connected learning environment allows for the sharing of the knowledge derived from personal experience and collective searches for shared meaning and knowledge.*

4. Cooperative and collaborative learning structures, such as small groups and learning partnerships, help to minimize hierarchial relationships and equalize power relationships among learners and between learners and instructor. (Schneidewind, 1983)
5. Cooperative evaluation techniques encourage all the learners in each small group to be accountable both for their own learning and for the learning done by others. (Hayes, 1989)
6. Cooperative communication styles occur when each speaker recognizes and builds on the contributions made by other speakers. Turn taking is encouraged with a Talking Circle, in which an object is passed and the only person who may speak is the one holding the object. (Hayes, 1989) Belenky and others (1986) refer to the process of recognizing and augmenting the ideas brought forward by others as the "believing game." They compare it with the "doubting game" in which each new speaker attempts to find errors in the logic of the ideas proposed by previous speakers or ignores these ideas by introducing new ideas.
7. Shared leadership works best in cooperative learning structures. Leadership tasks include sharing the responsibilities for listening to others, being patient, synthesizing ideas, facilitating interpersonal interactions and so on. (Lyons, 1990)
8. Holistic approaches to teaching and learning are perceived as better for female learners than analytical approaches. (Hayes, 1989) These focus first on the global aspects of a subject before examining its various parts; and involve

moving back and forth between the whole and the parts. Unlike analytical approaches, holistic approaches provide opportunities to integrate thoughts and feelings, theory and practice, to bring together and find connections between specific, concrete experiences and generalized or abstracted versions of experiences. Appropriate activities might include: consciousness-raising, journal-keeping, group discussions, case studies, experiments, simulations, and so on.

> *Holistic approaches also call on the instructor to engage in passionate teaching rather than the objective and distanced teaching typical of analytical approaches.*

9. Teaching for transformation and emancipation is implicit in feminist pedagogy. (Weiler, 1988) Through the use of the previous eight techniques, women develop the attitudes, abilities and knowledge they will need to work individually and collectively for improvements in their homes, educational institutions, communities and workplaces.

> *Feelings of empowerment emerge as women share their experiences and establish connections to other women through connected learning processes.*

To become more mature as learners, women need to construct their own ideas and opinions, make commitments to an idea or action, develop strategies for defending this choice and for acting congruently with it. This step in the learning process requires that individuals be able to integrate separate learning with their connected learning processes as they move toward a more integrated approach. When women begin to use constructed knowing, they begin a process of personal transformation. At this stage, their knowledge becomes an integral part of their self definition; and further changes in knowledge and self definition continually transform and reconstruct each other. (Hayes, 1989)

Women as Learners: A Summary of Ideas

Ways to increase women's active participation

When we integrate the ideas which have been presented in this paper, we find some consistent themes. We know that self-esteem and self-confidence are crucial to active participation in learning activities. Women's self-esteem is generally lower than that of their male counterparts and this difference increases at higher educational levels. Since adult education theory prescribes active participation as a means for improving learning, our educational practices should include ways to increase the active participation of women. Three suggestions for doing this are found in the feminist literature:

1. include women in the development of the knowledge base used in the learning activities as both sources and creators of knowledge;
2. include information about and of interest to women in the learning materials to be used in any program; and
3. include teaching methods which are consistent with women's dominant forms of self development and learning.

We know that the nature of the self which enters into the learning process affects what and how an individual learns. Our knowledge about the forms which this self might take has been expanded by feminist writers. We now know that both men and women use both separate and connected definitions of self; and that women are more likely than men to describe a connected self, while men are more likely than women to describe a separate self. We now know that both men and women develop through dualistic, multiplistic and relativistic ways of thinking; but the nature of the knowing and learning processes in these three types of thinking may differ for separate and connected knowers.

Effects of "separate" and "connected" knowing on learning

Separate knowing and learning can be understood as the preferred way of knowing for the separate self. Separate knowers and learners prefer knowledge which presents an objective, generalized and logical version of reality, which holds thoughts and feelings separate from each other; and which can be presented by an expert or authority figure through presentation-based techniques, such as lectures. Separate knowing calls for discussions in which learners can distance themselves from each other and ideas can be challenged and debated, processes which involve the potential for interpersonal conflict.

Connected knowing and learning can be understood as the preferred way of knowing for the connected self. Connected knowers and learners prefer knowledge which presents a personalized, specific and particularized version of reality; which connects thoughts and feelings; and which can be presented by co-learners through discussion-based techniques, such as consciousness-raising. Connected knowing calls for discussions in which learners can connect to other learners and ideas can be shared, processes in which the participants would prefer to avoid interpersonal conflict.

Integrating Women's Learning, Feminist Pedagogy and Adult Education Practice

Finally, it is time to think about how we, as adult educators, can integrate the ideas encountered in this chapter with our current educational practices in order to equitably support the learning of both women and men.

> *A sensitive reader may have decided, by now, that the description of feminist pedagogy does not differ that much from good adult education practice.*

In fact, adult education and feminist pedagogy appear to share values and approaches related to establishing an environment of mutual trust and respect; the provision of learning materials which centre on the learners and their concerns and interests; the use of co-operative learning structures, communication processes and shared leadership.

Some differences between adult education and feminist pedagogy

There are also some important differences between adult education and feminist pedagogy, particularly with regard to the emphasis placed on various aspects of the learning process. The first difference relates to the focus of our attention.

> *Feminist pedagogy calls for a focus on the individual and her personal experience as both an initial learning activity and as an ongoing part of the entire learning process. This approach is seen as important in building self-esteem and empowering the learner. In adult education, such a personal focus is often used for climate setting purposes but may not be considered to be an integral part of all learning activities.*

In a world in which time is money, many adult educators do not want to be seen as wasting a learner's time by encouraging them to engage in the kind of personal talk which best supports women's learning.

> *I believe that from such talk, important learning emerges and the men are equally likely to benefit from having opportunities to talk about knowledge derived from personal experience, compare this knowledge with theoretical knowledge, and construct integrated knowledge as an integral part of all learning activities.*

A second difference lies in the manner by which individual learners establish personal learning objectives.

> *In the feminist approach, individuals are encouraged to identify the personal connection between who they are and their personal concerns, and what they want to learn (that is, issues to be inquired into, skills to be mastered, problems to be solved).*

In adult education, learners may be encouraged to set their own learning objectives, but these objectives are often stated in terms which are more consistent with separate knowing and learning, rarely identifying the means for building specific connections to the learner's personal identity.

> *A third difference focuses on the emphasis placed, in the feminist approach, on maintaining a holistic connection between thinking*

and feeling, experience and ideas, theory and practice, reflection and action.

Holistic connections are often missing in adult education., Good adult education practices encourage instructors and learners to attend to feelings when these interfere with learning or teaching activities. The feminist approach would encourage instructors and learners to consider how their feelings are connected to the ideas they are discussing, as a means for furthering their understanding and knowledge.

A fourth difference concerns the emphasis placed, in feminist pedagogy, on cooperative and collaborative learning.

Feminist pedagogy hopes to facilitate "other-connected" learning as the primary objective; with self-directed or autonomous learning as an objective once the learner feels empowered and ready to make a commitment. On the other hand, adult education has traditionally placed a strong emphasis on self-directed learning as the primary objective; with "other-connected" learning as an objective only when it seems necessary or appropriate for reaching the primary objective.

A fifth difference lies in the use of cooperative evaluation techniques in which learners are accountable for their own learning and that of others.

That is, individual achievement is less important than group progress. In most educational institutions, the use of cooperative evaluation techniques may be perceived as denying individuals the right to be evaluated on the basis of personal achievement.

A sixth difference concerns teaching for transformation and emancipation as a value which should present few problems to adult educators since good adult education practice encourages such teaching in all groups of learners.However, as a practice, such teaching is hard to accomplish. Many adult learning programs operate under time constraints and institutional expectations. Transformative learning takes time and may not occur within the time frame imposed by the institution (or the next instructor). Designing learning programs to deliberately accomplish transformative learning objectives is difficult.

Transformative learning objectives may be more easily accomplished through the indirect influence of the instructor's behaviour on the learner. If the instructor models competitive or authoritative behaviour, then the learners will respond with very traditional, even passive participation and little transformative learning is likely to occur. If the instructor models collaboration, trust, respect for others, recognition of the contributions of others, the sharing of knowledge derived from personal experience, the integration of thought and feeling, separate and connected knowing and learning, and so on, then transformative learning is more likely to occur.

We, as adult educators, can make programs and learning activities more responsive to the needs of both men and women. It's up to us.

REFERENCES AND SUGGESTED READING

About Women

Smith, D.E. (1987) *The Everyday World as Problematic: A Feminist Sociology.* Toronto: University of Toronto Press.

Steinem, G. (1992) *Revolution from Within: A Book of Self-Esteem.* Boston: Little, Brown & Company.

About Development

Gilligan, C. (1982) *In a Different voice: Psychological Theory and Women's Development.* Cambridge: Harvard University Press.

Gilligan, C. (1990) Preface: "Teaching Shakespeare's sister." In C. Gilligan, N.P. Lyons, and T.J. Hanmer (Eds.) *Making Connections: The Relational Worlds of Adolescent Girls at Emma Willard School.* Cambridge: Harvard University Press.

Miller, J.B. (1976, 1986) *Toward a New Psychology for Women.* Boston: Beacon Press.

Perry, W. (1970) *Forms of Intellectual and Ethical Development in the College Years.* New York: Holt, Rinehart & Winston.

Schlossberg, N.K. (1984) *Counselling Adults in Transition: Linking Practice with Theory.* New York: Springer Pub.

About Women's Learning

Astin, H. (Ed.) (1976) *Some Action of Her Own: The Adult Woman and Higher Education.* Lexington: D.C. Heath & Company.

Belenky, M.F., Clinchy, B.M., Goldberger, N.R. and Tarule, J.M. (1986) *Women's Ways of Knowing: The Development of Self, Voice and Mind.* New York: Basic Books, Inc.

Gallos, J.V. (1992) "Educating women and men in the 21st century: Gender, diversity, leadership opportunities." *The Journal of Continuing Higher Education,* Vol.2, No. 8.

Hayes, E. (1989) "Insights from women's experiences for teaching and learning." In E.R. Hayes (Ed.) *Effective teaching styles, New Directions for Continuing Education,* no. 43. San Francisco: Jossey-Bass Inc.

Lyons, N.P. (1987) "Ways of knowing, learning and making moral choices." *Journal of Moral Education.* Vol. 16, No. 3.

Lyons, N.P. (1990) "Listening to voices we have not heard." In C. Gilligan, N.P. Lyons, and T.J. Hanmer (Eds.), *Making Connections: The Relational Worlds of Adolescent Girls at Emma Willard School.* Cambridge: Harvard University Press.

Magolda, M.B. (1991) *Knowing and Reasoning in College: Gender-Related Patterns in Students' Intellectual Development.* San Francisco: Jossey-Bass Inc.

Schneidewind, N. (1983) "Feminist values: Guidelines for teaching methodology in women's studies." In C. Bunch and S. Pollack (Eds.), *Learning Our Way: Essays in Feminist Education.* London, England: The Women's Press.

Spender, D. and Sarah, E. (Eds.) (1980) *Learning to Lose: Sexism and Education.* London, England: The Women's Press.

Tannen, D. (1990) *You Just Don't Understand: Men and women in Conversation.* New York: William Morrow & Company.

Weiler, K. (1988) *Women Teaching for Change: Gender, Class and Power.* South Hadley: Bergin & Garvey Publishing Inc.

Wingfield, L. and Haste, H. (1987) "Connectedness and separateness: Cognitive style or moral orientation." *Journal of Moral Education.* Vol. 16, No. 3.

Chapter 5
The Health Educator: Nurturing the Learning Link

Thelma Barer-Stein
and Carmen Connolly

Practitioner's Summary

Since the theory and practice of "adult education" is not usually a part of the education and training of health professionals, this chapter provides a brief introduction of adult education principles laid against the framework of a Learning Process that emerged from recent research. Beginning with the explanation that adult education as a specific field of study, research and practice developed from the recognition that adults differ from children in terms of their extensive life experiences, their relationships, their interactions, their responsibilities and their potential to make choices, the authors note that none of these factors can be ignored in helping adults to learn.

Emphasis is placed on "nurturing the learning of adults" rather than the more commonly used term of "facilitating" because of the holistic nature that it implies. Further, 'nurturing' assumes that each person has the potential to develop and to eventually shift towards independence from that nurturing. The holistic nature of nurturing mirrors the holistic nature of learning itself.

To do more than merely disseminate information on health, requires both a reactive and a proactive approach. The health professional's concern of how to provide health information and skills that can be made into effective and meaningful daily practice becomes the core of this chapter. How, indeed.

Some key questions are posed: How can we nurture change? What motivates adults to learn? How does information become transformed into habitual behaviour? To help with a response, the authors provide reflections of both a client and a dietitian as they move through the five sequential steps of Barer-Stein's Learning Process:

"Learning as a process of experiencing the unfamiliar:"

Step One: Becoming Aware
Step Two: Observing
Step Three: Participating
Step Three A: Rote Internalizing
Step Four: Confronting Perceived Risk or Perceived Challenge
Step Five: Reflective Internalizing

The answers to the posed questions emerge gradually as the reader moves through the summaries of each of the five Steps together with the accompanying thoughts, feelings and behaviours of both the professional and the client.

Understanding change and tackling it effectively involves an understanding of learning from the learner's viewpoint. Confronting problems, decisions, dilemmas and perceiving these as challenges to be reflected upon, integrated and acted upon, help both the learner and the health educator to understand and to predict their own roles, behaviours and feelings and later to assess how they progressed.

We find that knowledge and skills can become habits either through being Rotely Internalized or Reflectively Internalized; and we discover from the outset that Curiosity, Relevance and Enticement are the components of all motivation.

What seems most important for health educators (and most health professionals are educators whether they recognize this or not) is to engage the client or patient in all aspects of their own learning: the planning, the teaching methodologies and materials, and the eventual assessing of their own progress. What emerges most distinctly is the radical difference between communicating information and understanding it. A potent lesson for all health professionals.

Chapter 5
The Health Educator: Nurturing the Learning Link

Thelma Barer-Stein
and Carmen R. Connolly

What's adult education about?

Helping adults learn and providing opportunities for them to do so is what adult education is all about.

> *Adult education is a specific field of study because adults differ from children in terms of their extensive life experiences, their relationships, their interactions, their responsibilities and their potential to make choices. None of these can be ignored in helping adults to learn.*

Adults learn because they want to, as they need to, and only what is relevant. But we shall see that the degree and the extent of learning may vary from a superficial awareness to a profound and creative understanding.

'Learning' describes both the outcome of a process as well as the process itself. Helping adults to learn is not only the goal or outcome of adult education, it is also the process through which all knowledge and skills are gradually acquired, eventually understood and possibly formed into habits. Nor does learning take place in isolation; learning is always entwined into the human complexity of daily living with its attendant feelings, emotions and activities.

How can health professionals help to nurture learning in adults?

> *Nurture ... to support and encourage, as during the period of training or development; educate...(Random House Dictionary, 22nd edition)*

We have deliberately chosen the notion of 'nurturing' instead of the more commonly used 'facilitating' when speaking of adult health education because we feel that this implies more. The holistic nature of nurturing assumes that each person has the potential to learn and to develop, and eventually to shift towards independence from that nurturing. The very nature of nurturing itself is to provide a supportive, nourishing context for that potential development. The holistic nature of nurturing mirrors well the holistic nature of learning. (Griffin, 1988, 1993; Boud and Griffin, 1897; Miller, 1988)

> *When we speak in terms of nurturing learning, we also imply the drawing out of personal potential, and we imply the teaching to show what is needed for personal growth, development and health.*

We find ourselves thinking about other aspects that impact on learning and not just what information or advice we can offer. Such aspects as the context or the environment of the learning, the feelings and the emotions that attend the learning, and how the content of the learning should be planned with these factors in mind. In short, we realize that learning is much more than the giving and receiving of information.

And while traditional tenets of humanistic adult education seek out and respond to individual and communal needs, this is not enough. For where health is concerned, responding to needs is a reactive approach. To disseminate health information and develop habituation requires more than pamphlets and lectures. To determine from past experiences and research what may be required for future health practices requires a proactive approach. (Clark,1986; Boshier,1985) Could we do this more effectively if we understood more about learning?

As health professionals, we frequently provide current scientific information to individual clients, patients and to the general public as well as to our colleagues. But often what is really needed is an interpretation of that scientific information to make it practical and relevant for the intended audience. Where does such skill enter our professional training? Exchanging information with colleagues is easier because we have similar interests, we 'speak the same language' and we have a common goal to maintain our professional expertise. We are already 'close' because we share the same culture. We are already involved.

> *But how can we provide health information and the skills needed to make that information effective and meaningful in daily practice to our clients and patients?*

How can we nurture change? What motivates adults to learn? How does information become transformed into habitual behaviour? Change, motivation and eventual habituation of new information and skills are all part of the process of learning. Let's look at this more closely.

From the Learner's Viewpoint

Aside from those characteristics which we have inherited, the daily knowledge and skills, values, beliefs and assumptions that form our culture have all been learned. From this learning emerges the behaviour that forms the patterns and habits of daily life. Much of this learning is absorbed through imitation, repetition, and rote learning and is sustained through acceptance, rewards and continual reinforcements that confirm each of us as members of a group. In short, cultural learning provides us with identity, esteem, confidence and acceptance.

> *We are concerned here not with the actual content of the learning, but rather with the sequence and the form of the personal experience of learning.*

Learning is always attended with emotions, feelings, interactions and relationships; learning is always tugged by past experiences and pulled by anticipation, curiosity. Learning is affected by individual and contextual factors such as personal learning styles and preferences, external responsibilities, committments, and the whole realm of cultural and socio-economic factors.

> *Learning is a human experience and therefore it's obvious that the whole of daily living impacts upon learning and that what is learned impacts on daily living.*

Understanding learning in this holistic way can provide the needed framework upon which to base program planning, teaching methods, considerations of place, timing and even assessment of the learner's progress. Understanding learning in this way can also help the learner to plan, to appreciate the teaching methodologies, and to support those educative efforts. With a better understanding of the learning process and its place in daily life, the learner will recognize choices within that learning sequence, and will have a vocabulary to discuss their learning process as well as the learning content with others.

Learning as a Process of Experiencing the Unfamiliar

A sequential five-step Learning Process has been identified. (Barer-Stein, 1985, 1987a, 1987b, 1989) The steps not only indicate shifts in behaviour and feelings, they also provide for choices of movement such as remaining on a step, regressing, progressing or exiting from the Process. Each step is summarized below, with the highlights of typical behaviours and accompanying feelings. This provides a predictive framework and vocabulary to comprehend the human learning process. Of course it is important to recognize that any model of a human experience can only be a reified example of a dynamic spiralling process.

> *Using this Learning Process as a framework to understand health program planning, methods of teaching, and assessment of the learning, is something that can be shared among professionals, and*

between professionals and clients as a basis for discussing and developing the most relevant forms of knowledge and practical skills and recognizing at which point each should be integrated.

Such sharing can initiate a nurturing relationship in health and nutrition education. It minimizes the distance often perceived between professional and client and increases the sense of individual comfort and self-worth. The Learning Process is the same for both professional and client, as each move through the steps of learning, from their own viewpoint and needs. Their learning goal is congruent: to share and to learn for personal development and health.

Learning is always a process of experiencing the unfamiliar. Each one of us is engaged in countless Learning Processes at any one moment, and likely at differing steps of each.

The steps of Learning: A Process of Experiencing the Unfamiliar include:
1. Being Aware
2. Observing
3. Participating
3a.Rote Internalizing
4. Confronting Perceived Risk or Perceived Challenge
5. Reflective Internalizing

We will examine each of the steps of the Learning Process and provide examples of both client and professional feelings, thoughts and behaviours. While of course the content of the learning will vary, the affective reactions and the behaviours will be similar enough to be readily identified.

Step one: Being Aware - What is this?

Summary of characteristics of Step I:
• Begins with a flicker of attention.
• Span of attention is determined by inner responses of Curiosity, Relevance and Enticement.
• The learner is (safely) distanced from the object of attention.
• Engagement of a mode of thinking called the Reflective Pause: a brief and superficial collecting, questioning, comparing and selecting of information.

What is important here is to note that motivation is driven by Curiosity, Relevance and Enticement. Like a troika of three horses pulling a carriage, it is impossible at any given moment to determine which of the horses is working the hardest! Should the 'strength' of any one aspect of motivation be undermined or lessened for whatever reason, the progress will be lessened, impeded or eventually halted, and the now un-motivated individual will opt out or exit from the Learning Process. *(Does our program entice all the components of motivation?)* But what has been learned so far remains, and it is always possible, as one or more of the motivating factors returns, for the individual to enter that particular learning process again. (*Do our programs provide for such re-entry?*) It is also important to recognize that although the Reflective Pause is a common thought process, it is essentially based on and accepting of external authority. Probably it is commonly employed because it is brief, superficial, and usually provides immediate satisfaction.

Client

Mary was aware of the importance of healthy eating from materials that her son brought home from school and from articles in magazines. Nutrition didn't really mean too much, it seemed boring. But this week her physician suggested nutrition counselling to reduce fat intake and Mary found herself trying to recall some of the information she had scanned so quickly and wondering what might be useful for her.

Professional

Diane recognized that in order to engage Mary in a Learning Process, she had to first determine "where Mary was at". She began by helping Mary to list all that she already knew about healthy eating, asking her questions, and helping her to make comparisons with some of the nutrition materials and her own eating habits. This became the basis for a plan of learning based on what was relevant for Mary. Then Diane piqued her curiosity by identifying further possible ways to gain the necessary knowledge and skills to change her eating habits.

Step two: Observing: What's going on? How does this compare?

> *Summary of characteristics of Step 2:*
> *• Attention of the learner is heightening and focusing.*
> *• The learner remains marginal (at a distance)(Spectator).*
> *• The learner is watchful (moving closer in interest)(Sightseer).*
> *• Previous characteristics of Curiosity, Relevance and Enticement are retained together with the Reflective Pause mode of thinking.*
> *• A learner may decide to regress to the first step and remain there for a longer time, or may decide to exit this Learning Process.*

What's important here is that both professional and client are retaining a marginal but watchful distance to the topic of the learning. At the same time interest and confidence for each are gradually increasing. The importance of this step is that it is non-threatening and comfortable. Little is required and little is given. *(Do we provide opportunities for learners to just be observers?)*

Client:
Mary agreed to attend peer group sessions on healthy eating. While she sat to one side and watched and listened to the others, she kept running over in her mind just how things would be different. She was worried about her limited time and average income. How she would be able to prepare healthier meals for herself and the rest of the family? Would they accept these new ideas?

Professional:
Diane met with the group in a sunny, comfortable room. Posters lined the walls, a small table was brightly set with plates of colourful food models. The groups especially enjoyed sharing the ingredients of their favourite dishes as Diane wrote them on the board. By the time they had viewed a video on healthy eating, she was pleased to observe that Mary had shifted her chair closer to the others and was joining in the discussion.

Step three: Participating - Shall I try it out?

> *Summary of characteristics of Step 3:*
> *• Attentiveness has extended to the learner now taking part and trying things out.*
> *• Watchfulness has shifted to confident appraisal of what's going on.(Appraiser)*
> *• Overwhelming desire/need to discuss and tell everyone.(Missionizing)*
> *• The learner now tends to cluster all others as participants or nonparticipants (Cluster-Judging) in this new learning.*
> *• The learner claiming ownership. ("living like the natives", or "I know how!")*
> *• Reflective Pause is retained as the mode of thinking, and the learner is still strongly dependent on external authority for information, modelling of skills, approval and assessment.*
> *• Some learners may wish to remain for a while in Step 2, or may vacilate between Steps 2 and 3.*

What's important here is that the professional's role shifts from leading discussions and modelling ideas and behaviour, to being responsive, supportive and interacting with others in a decidedly less dominant role. *(As health professionals, can we learn to do this?)* Conversely, the client, with gained confidence now steps into the action, taking part in what others are already doing. Being open to individual diversity in styles and pace of learning are important throughout. There is a tension here on the part of the professional: wanting to let go, but remaining still within the authoritative mode.

Client:
Mary felt that she had now come a long way. She was more confident about reading labels and selecting lower fat foods, and she had tried some of the easy ways for preparing lower fat meals that the whole family could enjoy. She told several friends about the healthy eating group and shared some ideas and recipes with her sister. Mary enjoyed practicing what she had learned.

Professional:
Not only could Diane see that the group was gaining cohesiveness and actually enjoying their collaboration, she noticed the increase in confidence of each of the participants as they counselled and rewarded each other for good ideas about food and individual ways of being active. Now Diane felt more like a member of the group, than a teacher or leader.

Step three-A: Rote Internalizing – Repetition and rewards

> *Summary of characteristics of Step 3A:*
> - *This Step is an extension of Step 3.*
> - *Rote memorizing, copying and reciting are central.*
> - *High sense of confidence and camaraderie prevail.*
> - *Learner dependency on external reinforcements, rewards and assessments still persists.*
> - *Reflective Pause is still the predominant mode of thinking.*
> - *Rote Internalizing leads to copied routines, attitudes and values. There seems to be less conscious effort as all of these melt into behaviours.*
> - *Learners rarely regress from this Step. They may prefer to remain indefinitely.*

What's important here is that both the professional and client realize this is a critically important step for accumulating information and skills as well as attitudes and values that will eventually lead to habitual behaviours. Such habits are derived from the repetitive imitation rather than from any deliberate personal reflection. (*Do we provide opportunities to practice new skills?*)

Throughout the first three steps of the Learning Process, knowledge is transmitted, but is not changed. It may be selectively adopted or adapted in whole or in part by the learner but the learner is still dependent on external authority and external evaluations. As the professional relinquishes 'power', she is at the same time looking for opportunities to begin presenting individual challenges in order to nurture the learners to the next critical steps.

Client:
Mary felt happier, more confident and secure than she had in a long time. Even her husband, Gerald, admitted pride in how well Mary was doing. With the whole family helping with the meals, it even seemed fun to eat breakfast and do other things together like evening walks and weekend outdoor activities.

Professional:
Diane listened and watched each of the clients as they practised routines, collected and shared articles in papers and magazines and enjoyed their newly-gained camaraderie, skills and knowledge. She was always there to encourage, to praise and to listen, but now she carefully planned individual challenges for her learners. Some would, in the course of their daily lives bump against problems and dilemmas regarding their eating, but for others, she may have to stimulate further development towards autonomy and interdependence. She understood this duality in her professional role.

Step four: Confronting: Perceived risk or perceived challenge

> *Summary of characteristics of Step 4:*
> *• Confronting means to 'come face to face'.*
> *• Two main viewpoints: Perception of Risk or Perception of Challenge. The learner's responses and subsequent behaviour are dependent on which of these they perceive.*
> *• Learners perceiving Risk (doubt, dilemma etc.) may engage in Accommodating, Conflicting and/or Withdrawing feelings, responses and behaviours, or they may regress to a previous Step or exit the Process.*
> *• Learners perceiving Challenge will excitedly progress to Step 5.*
> *• Progression to Step 5 may be aided by a Significant Resource.*
> *• For the learner this Step can be a dismaying 'dance' of confusing emotions, fears, even panic which may provoke regression to a previous Step, extension of this 'dance' as a deliberate delaying tactic, or an exit from the Process.*

What's important here is for the client to realize that the confronting of risk or challenge is in fact facing the possibility (or the necessity) of change. A dip in confidence and esteem, feelings of anxiety, fear and even panic may attend any period of change. Unfamiliarity is always attended with some degree of anxiety, which may be eased only as the unfamiliar is dissected and seen to be OK, or may be increased if the unfamiliar remains obscure. Similarly for the professional there is some anxiety in "letting go" and some concern of the sufficiency of the learning. (*How aware are we of such ambivalence? What are we doing about it?*)

Change is necessary when whatever worked previously suddenly isn't working anymore. But it may not always be perceived as "not working". The cause of a dilemma, doubt, or problem, risk or challenge being recognized as "change" may not be clear. Change may be spontaneous, gradual, imposed or invoked. (Watzlawick and others, 1974) All are possibilities. The person needs to feel assured (internal) or to be assured (external) that the attendant feelings are normal, and that time, space and a Significant Resource helps.

This step represents the possible shift from dependency on external authority and evaluation, to an internally-driven effort towards creativity and self-directed action and self assessment. With experience in successfully confronting risk situations and perceiving them as challenges, the experience becomes its own reward.

Client:
So far everything that Mary learned had progressed comfortably. But when Gerald spoke of their upcoming summer vacation in the mountains, Mary felt anxious. She wanted to go, but how would she manage with the necessary changes in her eating patterns? In her nutrition group, Bill worried about how he would manage since the sudden death of his wife, while Frieda felt anxious about planning for the upcoming holiday season. Arguments broke out in the group, and for the first time a few withdrew from the meetings. A few others felt these problems would never happen to them and so ignored what was happening.

Professional:
If these real-life concerns had not emerged from the client or the group, Diane would have tried role playing or other group strategies to present realistic problems and encourage each person to work out plausible solutions. She already knew that within any group, there would be those eager to involve themselves in challenging situations, and others who retreated from what seemed unfamiliar. Diane shared her own experiences in 'breaking down' problems to manageable size, deciding on priorities, and trying out new ideas by writing them down, discussing them, even imagining possibilities and solutions. It wasn't necessary to name these 'devices' as management tactics or critical thinking, her clients found the group itself to be a Significant Resource.

Step five: Reflective Internalizing

Summary of characteristics of Step 5:
• Reflective Internalizing can occur following the Confronting of something abruptly unfamiliar: contradiction, dilemma, doubt, prob-

lem, decision or sudden change. But only when the unfamiliar is perceived as a challenge whose solution will extend the learning and eventually enhance the person.
• It involves deliberate, concentrated effort and a committment to change.
• 'Change' can mean improvization, reorganization, innovation, problem-solving, decision-making, or creativity.
• Whether change is negative or positive, the learning achieved is always an extension to what was previously known and may be excitedly embraced by those with previous successful experience with change.
• The essence of Reflective Internalizing is the mode of thinking encompassed in the four-fold process of The Sh'ma: Listening, Dialoguing, Critical Recursive Reflecting and the Integration and Action that results in changed ways of Doing and/or Being.

The four-fold process of The Sh'ma includes the following sequential steps:

1. Listening: attentive and responsive openness to what is seen and heard. A collecting of knowledge both immediate and past (combining logic and reason with feelings and intuition).
2. Dialoguing: a further opening of oneself to accept and consider (trying out mentally) differing views, underlined by a willingness to see differently and to exchange ideas and to consider each for relevancy.
3. Critical Recursive Reflecting: represents the analyzing (separating) and interpreting (reassembling) of possibilities to discover their personally relevant meaning. This may involve imagining, visualizing, intuiting, inferring, projecting into differing patterns and possibilities of all that has been collected in order to form new meaning.
4. Integration and Action: The changed way of doing or being is the outcome of this last step. This represents the integration of that change as part of oneself and one's identity eventually melt into changed habitual values, attitudes, beliefs and behaviour.

Enhanced self-image and increasing independence result, all with an increased appreciation of internal capabilities and the value of Significant Resources (interdependence).

Client:

Mary felt genuine relief as she realized, with Diane and the group's support, that there were many possibilities of solving the travel issue. Bill listened and shared differing views with the others who suggested ways for him to become increasingly self-supporting. Frieda spoke with her family and guests, telling them of her intention to make the holidays a time for healthy eating and was surprised to see how willing they all were to contribute dishes and help with chores. The problems of a few became lessons for the whole group. The value of reflecting on problems, analyzing them into chunks that were manageable, and eventually recognizing them as challenges that provoked further learning and possibilities for change became exciting rather than fearful.

Professional:
Diane now saw that people in the group listened more carefully to each other and seemed more willing to talk over differing views within the atmosphere of trust and genuine care that had emerged over their time together. They not only recognized Diane as a Significant Resource, but also saw themselves and their peers as sources of support and information. People seemed less reliant on her for planning, for appraisal. There was a palpable increase in confidence and independence.
The challenge for her was to nurture this new-found independence. Most importantly, she confirmed again for herself that the profound reflection on dilemmas and problems was really the beginning of relevant personal learning, appreciation and understanding. This surpassed the mere acquisition of skills and knowledge in a rote way.

How Does Change Happen?

> *Change, innovation, reorganization, creativity, improvization, can only occur when previous knowledge and skills are confirmed and then enhanced, extended or transformed in some way.*

This requires the concentrated effort to expose the need or the cause for change, to recognize previous and possible solutions, to be able to describe desired or needed change and to develop a plan of action that is relevant and makes sense. ("Meaning" and "making sense" as the goals of learning are discussed in detail by Frankl (1978) and by Daloz (1986) among others.) A base of foundational knowledge and skills, attitudes, values, and behaviours are required.

Any perceptible change within the learner that occurs during the first three steps is due only to the learning that has been rotely accumulated. But that accumulated knowledge has not been changed in any way; the learner has acquired (added on) what seemed useful, relevant. The actual *transformation* of previously acquired knowledge and skills can only occur in Step 5 through Reflective Internalizing. It is in Step 5 that acquired knowledge becomes shaped and transformed, becoming personally meaningful and relevant. *(How can we incorporate this into health programs?)*

Often such progress and enhancement of learning – any learning – requires or is supported by a Significant Resource, which may be within the learner (the enhanced ability to research and reflect critically and recursively) or external (searching out and collecting information from other sources).

Such extension of learning is often accompanied by increased appreciation of one's connectedness with others, and the necessary interdependence of most human activities.

What's Important Here for the Health or Nutrition Educator?

Several questions were posed at the outset of this discussion. We cited our dilemma of how to interpret current scientific information so that it is practical and relevant for the intended audience. With a deeper understanding of what learning means for the learner and how learning progresses through five steps,

we can see that we need to dialogue with representative members of our intended audience, moving through the Learning Process and sharing ideas of what might be the most effective means to learn.

The learning and the teaching have to become a collaborative enterprise in order to be practical and relevant.

We asked, How can we nurture change? And in a similar way, we saw that the illumination of the steps within the Learning Process provided a sense of pacing, and of what kind of learning opportunities best aided each learning step. We saw that the professional (the teacher, the nurturer) played many roles: dialoguing, presenting, lecturing and demonstrating, and only then providing an opportunity for others to participate in non-threatening clearly modelled ways. At each step, learners felt encouraged to progress (or regress) as they felt comfortable to do so because they too, understood what learning steps lay ahead.

We asked What motivates adults to learn? And not surprisingly, we saw that the three inner responses of Curiosity, Relevance and Enticement (which could be internally or externally stimulated) clearly drove the Learning Process.

Motivation is composed of Curiosity, Relevance and Enticement.

From this research in learning, two "paths" to habit formation emerged: through Rote Internalizing and through Reflective Internalizing.

Rote internalizing is important for the accumulation and mastery of skills and basic knowledge. Reflective Internalizing is important to personalize that rote learning and if possible, to enhance, to transform, and even to transcend it through creativity and the further discovery of personally relevant meaning.

Similarly, there are here two predominant modes of thinking, and each serves a purpose. Within each, many other aspects can be considered; Mackeracher's chapter on women's learning exposes many of these. For example, engagement in the Reflective Pause seems to occur with little conscious effort and can be expanded with considerations of Perry's (1970) descriptions of dualistic, multiplistic and relativistic modes of thinking which were later examined to understand shifts in women's thinking. (Belencky and others, 1986) The development of thinking from an early dependence on the rightness or wrongness of facts and ideas and the authorities who enunciate them (dualistic), to a later development recognizing the uncertainty of facts and authorities and the concommitant possibility of one's own thoughtful contributions (multiplistic), blends into a gradual development of a concurrent need to recognize context and its place in assessing knowledge and truth (relativistic). Dualistic thinking and Rote Internalizing provide a foundation for more complex thinking.

Engagement in the Sh'ma (Reflective Internalizing) encompassing both multiplistic and relativistic thinking as well as deliberate creativity (Edwards, 1989) and improvization (Nachmanovich, 1990) requires effort and practice and in itself can become habitual. The very ability to reflect on modes of thinking indicates that the learner has experience within the fifth step of learning and has successfully navigated through the dilemmas of Step 4. Yet with each new Learning Process, the attendant feelings and behaviours may impede or accelerate progress accordingly.

The following table condenses the key outcomes of the five steps of the Learning Process for both the professional and the client:

1 Being Aware 2. Observing	"Communicating"	Awareness
3. Participating 3a. Role Internalizing	Participating	Knowing
4. Confronting 5. Reflective Internalizing	Involving	Understanding

Collected Reflections

For the health professional (the teacher, counsellor, facilitator – the'nurturer') the Learning Process helps to make adult education philosophy and practice explicit. When the educative aspect of the professional's role is practiced as a nurturer of lifelong learning, the relationships and the interaction with the learner enhances confidence and self-image. The enhancement is mutual.

Using the Learning Process helps in many ways to set goals, plan programs, and allow for client's exits and lingering plateaus based on the client's styles and preferences of learning. It helps both the professional and the client to understand learning not just as an outcome but also as steps of a human process. In this way a sense of direction, predictability and personal control emerge in the interactions of a nurturing relationship. Using the Learning Process as a tool facilitates planning in ways that permit the client to sometimes feel OK about being "stuck", regressing, exiting or possibly re-entering at a later time.

Professionals need to forget about feeling responsible for other's learning. Learning is not something that can either be done to a person or for a person. Communicating information is only the beginning of the Learning Process. The development of lifelong healthy behaviours can only come with sustained effort. This includes nurturing the learning of others, developing an attitude and an environment that nurtures clients and patients to develop increasing responsibility for and committment to their own health and to progress in learning what is relevant for themselves.

> *When health professionals and their clients recognize the experiences, knowledge and skills that can be shared, the steps for learning that can be planned, the teaching methodologies and materials that can be used, and the possibility of personally assessing their own progress, then an understanding of the Learning Process will be validated.*

The supportive, nurturing context for that potential development provided by the health professionals in collaboration with their intended audience will – unquestioningly – prove to be practical and relevant.

REFERENCES

Barer-Stein, T. (1985) Learning as a process of experiencing difference. Unpublished doctoral (Ph.D.) thesis. Ontario Institute for the Studies in Education, University of Toronto.

Barer-Stein, T. (1987a) "Learning as a process of experiencing the unfamiliar". *Studies in the Education of Adults (UK).* Vol. 19, No. 2.

Barer-Stein, T. (1987b) "Who needs teachers?" *Australian Journal of Adult Education.* Vol. 27, No. 3.

Barer-Stein, T. (1989) "Reflections on literacy and the universal learning process." In M.C. Taylor and J. Draper (Eds.) *Adult Literacy Perspectives.* Toronto: Culture Concepts Inc.

Belencky, M.F. and others. (1986) *Women's Ways of Knowing: The Development of Self, Voice and Mind.* New York: Basic books Inc.

Boshier, R. (1985) "Proaction for a change: Some guidelines for the future." *International Journal of Lifelong Education.* Vol. 5. No. 1.

Boud, D. and Griffin, V. (Eds.) (1987) *Appreciating Adults Learning: From the Learner's Perspective.* London: Kogan-Page.

Clark, J. (1986) "Community education and the concept of need." *International Journal of Lifelong Education.* Vol. 5, No. 3.

Daloz, L.A. (1986) *Effective Teaching and Mentoring: Realizing the Transformational Power of Adult Learning Experiences.* San Francisco: Jossey-Bass.

Edwards, B. (1989) *Drawing on the Right Side of the Brain.* Los Angeles: Jeremy P. Tarcher Inc.

Frankl, V.E. (1978) *The Unheard Cry for Meaning.* New York: Washington Square Press.

Griffin, V. (1988, 1993) "Holistic learning/teaching in adult education: Would you play a one-string guitar?" In T. Barer-Stein and J. Draper (Eds.) *The Craft of Teaching Adults.* Toronto: Culture Concepts Inc.(2nd edition)

Mackeracher, D. (1993) "Women as Learners."In T. Barer-Stein and J.A. Draper (Eds.) *The Craft of Teaching Adults.* Toronto: Culture Concept Inc. (2nd edition)

Miller, J.P. (1988) *The Holistic Curriculum.* Toronto: OISE Press.

Nachmanovitch, S. (1990) *Free Play: Improvisation in Life and Art.* Los Angeles: Jeremy P. Tarcher Inc.

Perry, W. (1970) *Forms of Intellectual and Ethical Development in the College Years.* New York: Basic Books Inc.

Watzlawick, P. and others. (1974) *Change: Principles of Problem Formation and Problem Resolution.* New York: W.W. Norton and Co.

Suggested Reading

Carter, R.E. (1992) *Becoming Bamboo: Western and Eastern Explorations of the Meaning of Life.* Montreal and Kingston: McGill-Queen's University Press.

Marton, F. and others, (Eds.) (1984) *The Experience of Learning.* Edinburgh: The Scottish Academic Press.

Chapter 6

Holistic Learning/ Teaching in Adult Education: Would You Play a One-String Guitar?

Virginia R. Griffin

Practitioner's Summary

The author compares the playing of a guitar with only one string to the use of the human mind with only one capability: the rational mind. Her intent in this chapter therefore, is to explore the "often-overlooked capabilities" with a view to exposing the ways in which these may enhance the learning and teaching process.

The six strings which provide the beauty and complexity of the human mind in its fullest capability include: emotional, relational, physical, metaphoric or intuitive, spiritual and of course the rational. Each are discussed in turn with clear and expressive arguments for their presence in any learning situation. The resultant discussion is one that will strongly challenge any complacent instructor.

It is this chapter that explains and illustrates what others may refer to merely as 'care' or 'sensitivity' in helping adults to learn.

Emotions, whether negative or positive, play a crucial role in enabling the process of learning to take place. What is most important is to encourage the identification of emotions by naming them and then accepting them in order to take the sequential steps required to "change or change the situation". Griffin identifies Menlo's competencies for a successful teacher of adults as having a sensitive awareness of the learner's responses and being able to deal with these without defense or judgement. Here the open reciprocity between teacher and student's emotions promote understanding and enhance further learning.

Dealing with the 'relational' capability, Griffin notes the interplay of our five senses (taste, touch, sight, hearing, smell) together with tension and energy, each representing signals rooted in some emotional source. When these are recognized, we are enabled to deal with them, whether pleasurable (such as excitement) or negative (such as frustration).

The left-brain capacity that educators give most of their attention to, is here made use of as "thinking games" for adults that might include question formation, pattern detection, thinking of possibilities, logical relevance and representations. Similar games may also be used to help adults reinforce cognitive skills while learning other skills.

The metaphoric or intuitive capability is the one that "rounds out" the crucial and central one of rationality. Griffin shows that this capability is only released by "quieting the rational mind, relaxing and moving into another state of consciousness". She notes in particular three techniques which may aid this process:

1. knowing with certainty that learning will occur;
2. temporarily suspending or quieting the rational mind;
3. remaining open to the expected, but more especially to the unexpected.

Griffin notes that the 'spiritual capability' is not intended here, necessarily, to denote that which arises from a religious background, but rather to denote an awakening to the self and "a transformation in how we manifest our special qualities in the world".

While research in this area is increasing, this chapter stresses not only the importance of understanding these aspects of mind, but also of recognizing their inter-relatedness. Such recognition and the gradual building of confidence and trust is readily conveyed to the learners, especially with the realization that these are everyday experiences which we can control. Recalling the obvious usefulness of the 'one string rationality' it is encouraging to imagine what might be achieved if all the other 'strings' could be employed as well.

Chapter 6
Holistic Learning/Teaching in Adult Education: Would You Play a One-String Guitar?
Virginia R. Griffin

Playing a guitar with just one string would soon become monotonous, and the music would be limited in scope. Playing a guitar with six strings allows beautiful and complex music, limited only by our skill to use the six strings and our imagination.

> *Learning is like playing a guitar. Most of us have been trained by our schooling to play one string - our rational mind. However, we have at least five other strings, and if we learn to play them well and keep them properly tuned, we can make limitless music in our learning and can then go on to help our students do the same.*

> *What are the other five strings in this analogy? They are the other capabilities we have as human beings, in addition to our rational, logical minds. They are our (1) emotional, (2) relational, (3) physical, (4) metaphoric or intuitive, and (5) spiritual capabilities.*

My intent in this chapter is to invite you to consider the learning potential in these often-overlooked capabilities, to take a fresh look at the familiar one of rational mind, and to suggest ways you might help yourself and your learners make your learning richer, fuller, more exciting and beautiful by using all of the strings of your guitar.

As Jean Houston (1981), one of my favourite authors and a leading thinker and researcher in education, has written:

> ... *the human brain is incredibly endowed. We use about ten percent of our physical capacity, and far less of our mental capacity. With holistic/integral education it is quite possible that many students can learn to use a much greater range of their innate capacity.*

In the dictionary holistic is defined "emphasizing the organic or functional relation between parts and wholes." There is a growing body of literature about holistic education. (J. Miller, 1988; J. Miller, Cassie, and Drake, 1989; R. Miller,

1990) One major part of holistic adult education is the whole person. My metaphor for the whole person is the person who uses all six strings of his or her guitar for learning. Let's look at these innate capacities (strings of the guitar) and how we can help ourselves and our learners use a much greater range of them.

Emotional Capability

Recently one of my students wrote in her paper:

> *During the past semester I have lived my way through a constellation of feelings ... (In the fourth session) I feel tremendously anxious, suspicious, and just plain fearful ... (After the eighth session) exhilaration gives way to serenity and ease. (Ross, 1984)*

She explains in her paper how she made use of her emotional conflict (in a different kind of course than she had ever experienced) to undergo an important and unforeseen change in her view of herself, and of what learning and teaching is. The particulars of what happened to Lorna aren't important here; what is important is that negative or positive emotions can play a crucial role in enabling our learning.

Negative emotions

> *Frustration, fear, guilt, hurt, rejection, confusion, anger often serve as blocks to learning.*

They do if we (the teacher or the student) don't recognize them and do something about them. Neither recognizing nor doing something about them is easy. If the emotion promises to be too painful, and something we want to learn is sure to raise that emotion, we avoid the desired learning. We stay away from a class in which we fear we will fail. I avoid learning about how to handle group conflict because I fear and dislike conflict so much.

But not all negative emotions are strong enough to disable us completely. We can defuse, overcome, and use many of them to our advantage in a learning situation.

An important early step is experiencing, rather than denying the emotion. Then we have to acknowledge that we are feeling something. Next comes accurate naming of the emotion. Emotions are interrelated and easily confused. What feels at first like anger may be hurt pride or fear. Another aspect of naming emotions is not to confuse opinions or evaluations with emotions. I'm grateful to Don McFadyen (1983) for pointing out to me how we distort the situation if we say "You shouldn't work late so often" rather than "I'm lonely for you". Such substitutions of opinion for emotion often generate intense feelings of anger or anxiety.

Once emotions are experienced, acknowledged and named they should be accepted. If we accept them for what they are, without judging them or being judged by them, we are free to move to take steps to change, or change the situation.

For example, we may find the courage to say to our learning group "I feel abandoned by the group because no one even acknowledged my comments, I want to feel a part of the group, can you help me"? In most cases, such a comment will lead to discussion that will enable the group to become stronger and more effective, and enable the individual to get back on track in her learning.

In addition to letting others know their effect on us, our emotions help us know ourselves better:

Accepting our emotions means accepting the message they are giving us about ourselves in our present situation. A painful emotion tells us that we put a negative value on the situation, but it also gives us an opportunity to reconsider our values, attitudes, beliefs, etc. since every valuation conveys an implicit message about our stance in the world. (McFadyen, 1983)

Thus, negative emotions can lead to important learning and change.

Chief among negative emotions in adult learning is one often labelled as resistance to accepting new ideas or change. Al Menlo (1979), an educational psychologist, has clearly stated one of his basic beliefs as one that applies to this emotion.

Persons do not resist change; they seek it as part of their inherent nature. What persons do resist are expected consequences which will diminish their self or social esteem.

He further reminds us that in instances in which learners experience the fear of such consequences, we need to encourage them to be active in their learning and we need to reassure them that they have the power to decide whether or not and how to act.

Positive emotions

Through attending to our positive emotions, we can become aware of what has meaning for us and how our learning can have personal meaning. Since I feel so happy and energized when I am reading gardening books, I know that gardening has meaning for me, even though the actual work of gardening is difficult. When I read transpersonal psychology books, I feel excitement and energy. When I read cognitive psychology books, I get bored and fall asleep. These two observations tell me that transpersonal psychology, at this stage, has more meaning to me than the other. If my job requires me to read cognitive psychology, I have to concoct some purpose for the reading that has special meaning for me so that I can stay awake.

Another way to say that positive emotions can give us guidance and direction in our learning comes from Castaneda (1968):

> *Any path is only a path, and there is no affront to oneself or to others, in dropping it if that is what your heart tells you ... Look at every path closely and deliberately. Try it as many times as you think necessary. Then ask yourself, and yourself alone, one question ... Does this path have a heart? If it does, the path is good, if it doesn't it is of no use.*

> ***Positive emotions are the rewards we give ourselves when we are "on track" in a project or when we have successfully learned something.***

In addition to affirming ourselves to ourselves, we could at a time of feeling the high of accomplishment, reflect on what enabled it to happen, what we've learned about ourselves in the process and how we like to learn.

The teacher's role

Those of us who want to help learners recognize and use their emotions for more effective learning have few role models. We see the traditional school as one that functioned not by creating healthy emotional learning environments, but by advocating that "Students are best governed by being kept in an intermittant or constant state of fear." (Rogers, 1977) Wanting a different emotional climate, we have to invent ways to create it.

> ***The extent to which you can create a more open climate will depend on the subject matter you teach, the size of your class, and how secure you feel. But acknowledging and dealing with emotions in learning can be an important part of even the hardest sciences and the largest classes.***

Menlo (1979) identified awareness, skills, and behaviours that a teacher of adults needs to have to be successful. Some of these competencies are relevant to helping students benefit from the emotions in the classroom:

1. awareness of existence of communication nuances
2. scanning acuity
3. ability to be supportively invitational
4. ability to be non-intrusively encouraging
5. ability to be authentically self-sharing
6. ability to be non-defensive and vital.

One of these competencies, scanning acuity, deserves elaboration. The less you become concerned with agendas and content and your own self-esteem, the more you notice what there is to observe in a group of learners, both verbal and non-verbal clues to emotions that are being felt. We can never be sure what the clues mean. A frown can mean "I disagree", "I'm frustrated", or "My shoes hurt my feet". We must ask. If several people are frowning, we had better stop to ask what the frowns mean.

A teacher who is herself non-defensive will be able to encourage the expression of emotion without feeling judgmental and without giving lengthy justification of the activity that stimulated any negative emotion. She can also share with the learners what her emotions are when she hears theirs, and share with them how she will handle hers and use hers to enable further learning.

Another source of help for understanding and dealing with emotion in adult learning is William More's excellent book, listed under Suggested Reading.

Relational Capability

Since much of our time is spent in relationships with others, we tend to take them for granted, not realizing our teachers, our classmates or learning partners deserve a great deal of credit for whatever learning we achieve. (Lavery, 1983)

> *Do we need others in order to learn? My contention is that we do, although the interactions with others cannot be constant. We need a "being with" and a "being alone" in a rhythmic pulsation to learn best.*

Teacher-learner

It is easy to see that a teacher is helpful in learning situations. But the quality of the relationship between the teacher and the student, if significant learning is to result, is more difficult to identify and to create. Carl Rogers (1967) names what to him are the most important attitudinal qualities for the teacher to have: congruence, empathy, and positive and unconditional regard for learners. As the learner perceives this genuineness, empathy, and acceptance, a climate of trust grows between the teacher and the student that is more important than all the scholarly knowledge and technical skill a teacher can have.

Even if we have developed trusting relationships with our students, we often find them staying more dependent on us than we would like. Many adults tend to have too much faith in the teacher's wisdom and omniscience, and too little faith in their own wisdom and experience. They often need lots of encouragement and guidance in making decisions about their learning. We all have times when we need to be dependent, other times when we need to be independent. The more of our learning we can undertake in an interdependent or mutually cooperative way, the more satisfying our learning will be. A partnership between the teacher and the students, and among the students, has many advantages for all persons involved. If this topic intrigues you, you will find Gwenneth Griffith's (1987) work a helpful source in learning more about interdependence.

As learners make more and more decisions for themselves, with the teacher and other students, they become intrigued by what they are learning about themselves and how they like to learn, and learn best. Learning how to learn is the subject of an excellent book by Smith (1982). It is well worth reading.

Co-learners

How can other learners help us so that we don't become as Cyril Houle used to say, "the bland leading the bland"? Again, trust is a necessary element. Trust between co-learners is not automatic – it has to be nurtured gradually and carefully. When people first meet in class, they find it difficult to be themselves. They try to impress others and/or hide their uncertainties and fears. But once trust starts to grow, important discoveries are made:

> *1. Others can give needed support and encouragement.*
> *2. Others often have similar feelings in the situation, so you are not alone; together you can do something about any problem.*
> *3. Talking to someone often helps you sort out your emotions, and find ways to deal with them.*
> *4. Finding someone who thinks as you do about a certain topic or learns the same way you do can be very affirming.*
> *5. Finding someone whom you trust and respect but who thinks differently about a topic or who learns differently can help you understand yourself more clearly and perhaps alter your perspective or enlarge your learning style.*
> *6. Someone who knows you, can help you find the personal meaning in an idea that at first doesn't seem to fit.*
> *7. By talking to others you sometimes discover what you think. By helping someone understand what you are trying to say, you clarify it for yourself.*
> *8. Others can give you personal feedback that is either very confirming or may lead you to explore some aspect of yourself to which you have been blind.*

Marilyn Taylor (1987) in her research into the experiences of learners in one of my courses, found that learners experience phases in their growth, their emotions, and their involvement with content and resources, and with the other learners in the group. There were times when they yearned to talk to others; at other times they needed to be alone, and avoided discussing their learning. I have since become aware that there are times in each class session when people need to talk to others to explore their feelings and ideas, and times when they need silence to centre themselves, to knit together their thoughts, and to reflect on personal meanings in the experience. And then often they need to tell someone about the insights that have come. This is what I mean by rhythmic pulsations in learning with others.

The stages of group growth and ways to help learners develop skills for relating well to others are readily available in other books. Gibb (1967) and Johnson (1981) are two I find helpful.

Learning partners

Very often a class is too large to allow each person "air time" for exploring his ideas, emotions, experiences of the course. Then we use small groups. But we still run out of time for each person to deal with their feelings and explore their learnings. To overcome this problem, we have in recent years urged students in classes to find a learning partner in the class – someone with whom they can spend time outside the class on a regular basis – to help each other in their learning. Ross Keane (1985), one of my students, identified four ways his partnership with Casey Gehrels helped him: deepening insights and converting feelings into learning, expanding insights through sharing, opening new directions in reading and learning and forming new perspectives through challenge or confrontation. Casey (1985), his learning partner, as well as talking about changes in his perspective of self, said:

> *We started to be able to take risks with our ideas and behaviour, we ... developed the confidence to play with images and visions of a different world. This, in turn, created such an energy that we often became caught in a surge of enthusiasm and excitement. Learning and changing became joyous, where before it has often been threatening.*

Because a significant number of our students have found having a learning partner such an enrichment of their learning, we created a monograph on the idea and the experiences we have had with it. Two students, Joan Robinson and Sharon Saberton, gave leadership to this project with my help. (Robinson, Saberton and Griffin, 1985)

Physical Capability

Have you ever been so tense you had to ask people to repeat important information? Or have you looked at the clock after being immersed in some project and realized that you had worked most of the night without getting tired? Or you may have at times been so tired you couldn't read even an interesting book. Most people have had these experiences and thus are aware that our physical state and our minds are inevitably linked. Our physical state can both help and hinder our learning.

Five senses

Our senses, sight, hearing, smell, taste, and touch, are the only normal ways we take in any information from our surroundings.

> ***The more of these senses we can use in learning something, the more likely we are to understand and remember it.***

If I can see your name on a name tag as well as hear you say it, I'm more likely to remember it. If you also smell of cigars and have a strong, calloused handshake, I'm even more certain to remember you, as well as your name.

If all our senses are working properly, we are indeed fortunate. But as adults get older, we tend to lose our sensory acuity, and appreciate a teacher who speaks loudly enough for us to hear and who uses print and visual aides that are clear and easy to read and see.

Tension

Some tension and stress are necessary. Too much is a hindrance in our lives, and too much stress in learning is no exception. The late Beverley Galyean (1981) described what happens as "intellectual shutdown in the face of high anxiety". As she explains, what happens in the brain is this: Information from the senses enters the brain at the tip of the spine, and must pass through the lower central region of the brain (called the limbic region) to get to the upper and frontal part of the brain (the neo cortex) for processing. Within the lower central region are five glands (including the thalamus and pituitary) that serve as a gateway.

> *These glands operate on the basis of emotional preference. If the learner has a negative attitude, or is bored, threatened or overly fatigued by outside stimuli ... the thalamus secretes a series of hormones called endorphins which anaesthetize the other glands thereby blocking the passage of new information into the neo cortex (Galyean, 1981).*

> ***Learners therefore learn better if they have a positive attitude, are interested in what they are learning, and are relaxed and rested.***

Teachers can do many things to bring about positive attitudes and higher self-esteem in learners. A learner who has helped plan what and how he is to learn is more likely to be interested in what he is learning. A relaxing learning environment can be created with colour, softer lights, music and rearrangement of furniture. A number of relaxation exercises are available (see White and Fadiman, 1976) to use with learners, and are activities they can use by themselves at other times to reduce stress in their lives.

Energy

Some experiences stimulate high energy in us, and some seem to drain us of energy. Are you aware of what kinds of learning experiences energize you? What de-energizes you? The students with whom you work probably would have similar descriptions. Lee Davies (1987) studied learners who had experienced a high energy class and others who had had a low energy class experience.

An important idea he proposes is that the learner's skill and the challenges in the learning situation have to be at an optimum balance: too much skill and the learner is bored, too much challenge and the learner is frustrated. (Davies,1976)

Characteristics (or skills) associated with high energy learning in Lee's study were:

> *a strong internal sense (being optimistic) but also a move towards sharing with others (letting go and risk taking) and a willingness to receive from others (getting feedback). The high energy experience is where personal internal energy is used and evaluated.*

The characteristics, according to Lee, associated with low energy experiences were "holding on, not risking, being a follower, and being pessimistic".

> *Groups may be thought of as having an energy level and a flow of energy. Experienced teachers learn to be sensitive to that flow, and respond to it.*

As one has said:

> *Submitting to whatever is happening will give us a surge of renewed energy in any unfamiliar situation. If we stop running "against the tide", if we stop being so "set" and "rigid" in our habits, we can adapt much more easily to change. (Davies, 1987)*

I have found as a teacher and as an individual that the suggestion that you "get in touch with your energy and go with that" is a freeing one, and allows you to tap into your inner wisdom. If you have no energy for a learning task, there may be a good reason. Identifying and dealing with the reason often pays rich dividends in clarifying or redirecting the task.

Body reactions as signals

We all know that our bodies reflect our emotions. Anxiety turns into tense shoulder muscles or knots in the stomach; embarrassment turns into a blush on the cheeks. Sometimes however, we feel the bodily reaction without having noticed the emotion. Sometimes we ignore the emotion, sometimes we deny it or repress it. The body knows it is there however, and expresses it in some way.

For example, when I feel my shoulders feeling very tense I know to look for areas in which I am feeling inadequate. When I have identified the area, I can then do something about it. I can either become adequate or adjust my standards to something less than "perfection". If I have been accurate in my diagnosis, my shoulders soon relax, and I have learned something.

My suggestion here is that we pay attention to body signals, examine our lives to find the emotional source, and cope with the triggering situation as best we can, often through learning.

Signals from the body are not always saying that something is wrong. Excitement and pleasure are perhaps more important signals; their source is to be cherished and nurtured.

Rational, Intellectual Capability

Our ability to use words and sentences to convey our ideas; to read a book and understand its ideas; analyze a problem situation, gather information, decide on a logical solution and evaluate its effect, all come from our rational or intellectual capability.

I think of this capability as residing primarily in our left brain hemisphere. The left hemisphere "analyses, abstracts, counts, marks time, plans step-by-step procedures, verbalizes, makes rational statements based on logic". (Edwards, 1979)

I say "resides primarily" in the left hemisphere because the two hemispheres are connected and interact in every activity we do. (Hart, 1983) This is the capability that adult educators give most of their attention to, it is the one our school system spends most of its energy to develop. We tend to equate its development and use with "learning". We use it and are aware of it daily.

We have had much experience using the rational capability, and have had years of opportunity to watch our teachers use various means to help us to develop it. We cannot assume, however, that we know the best ways to help our learners use it. Maybe we weren't very observant as we watched our teachers, maybe they were using a limited range of methods or methods that weren't appropriate for use with adults.

Let's identify some of the methods that can be used to help learners use this capability.

Lecture

The most often used method is the lecture. Its use is based on the perspective that learning means acquiring information from an authority who has more information than the learner and can better help the learner find meaning and a structure to understand and remember it. The lecturer most often finds the structure form within the logical organization of the subject matter being taught, but other and often better organizing schemes for a lecture are available. Ausabel (1968) proposes making the new material meaningful and related to material the learner already knows. Miller (1983) provides us a good overview of Ausabel's work:

> *Ausabel's approach to teaching tends to be deductive, that is, he recommends proceeding from general ideas to specific information. He calls this "progressive differentiation", which means that the teacher should develop new concepts that are closely related to the ideas that have been presented previously ...*
>
> *Advance organizers facilitate progressive differentiation and integrative reconciliation. Advance organizers are concepts that are abstract and inclusive and prepare the student to learn new information. Advance organizers should use ideas and terms that are already familiar to the learner.*

He developed his ideas for education of children but they are equally useful for adults and parallel the common statement in adult education: "You must start where the learner is".

Other ways to make lectures more interesting and useful for adults include orienting the lecture to specific interests or problems that the learners recognize and want to solve, including visuals and illustrations, relevant humor and wit, and ideas for application of the information being presented. Also, giving the learners time to think about and discuss how they might make applications from the lecture material.

Demonstrations with practice

Much of adult education is helping people develop skills, learning how to do something. Therefore we often show them how to do it, explaining the process as we go, and helping them know why we do it as we do. Then we must remember that the learner needs an opportunity to practice the skill, have any mistakes corrected, and then have the correct way affirmed so that she has the correct action and steps clearly in her mind.

Experiments, research, discovery learning

Some adult learners want to become informed and competent in an academic discipline, such as history, physics, chemistry, sociology, psychology. Teachers in these areas often help the learner become engaged in some form of discovery learning, so that the adult can begin to develop a conceptual framework of the field and skills in the method of inquiry used by scholars in that particular field.

Problem-solving

Adults sometimes turn to adult educators for help in solving problems. Adult educators often believe that the way to help learners is not only to provide some needed information, but to help the adult develop problem solving skills such as identifying the question (an inquiry-oriented question), identifying alternatives, collecting data, drawing conclusion, expressing (or applying the conclusion), and evaluating the results (Miller,1983).

I feel compelled here to state my belief that this very rational problem-solving method omits very important human aspects such as emotions. I am grateful for an article by Kneeland (1979) in which he suggests a concrete way to consider emotions in problem-solving.

I don't want to leave an impression that Miller limits his interests to the rational mode. In his discussions of the educational spectrum, he describes a broad range of orientations to learning and curriculum - including humanistic and transpersonal.

Other ways of helping adults learn

Debates, seminars, and guided discussions are sometimes used to help learners develop the skills of forming logical arguments, of seeing something from different points of view and other cognitive skills. Thinking games are available for use with children to help them develop cognitive skills (Bereiter,1972). I don't know anyone who has applied these ideas to adult learners, but I think if we as adult educators are alert to these cognitive skills (such as pattern detection, formulating questions, thinking of possibilities, using logical representations, determining relevance) we will find ways to reinforce adults in keeping their cognitive skills sharp as they go about the business of learning other content.

Hart (1983) who gives more attention in his writing to current brain research than do most cognitive psychologists, defines the process of learning as the "extraction from confusion of meaningful patterns". He makes an interesting and convincing case that methods used in most schools are antagonistic to what we now know about how the brain functions, instead of being "brain-compatible". His theory of learning is clearly spelled out as are his implications for how teachers of children can better facilitate learning. Those implications: rich input, effective and extensive communication between learners, immediate feedback from reality, and learner-selected risk rather than imposed threat seem relevant for adult learning as well. I think you will find it stimulating reading.

> ***As you will have gathered by now, I regard the rational capability as crucial and central in adult learning and functioning, but incomplete.***

The next capability we will examine helps to round it out.

Metaphoric or Intuitive Capability

The role of metaphoric thinking is to invent, to create, and to challenge conformity by extending what is known into new meadows of knowing. (Samples, 1979)

> ***The metaphoric mind is a partner to the rational mind. It is different in the way it perceives information, the information it perceives, the way it processes information, the way it retrieves information, and the way it expresses itself.***

I have a friend who many times does not hear the words you say to her – she is busy attending to the tone of your voice, the rhythm and pitch of your speaking, and is intuiting what all of the information means about the quality of your present experience so she can choose how to relate to you. She has a strong metaphoric capability. She is artistic, creative, intuitive.

The metaphoric mind is this, and more; it

> *... is the reservoir of the intuitive simultaneous, spontaneous, diffuse, and non-linear functions of thinking. It is voiceless but adds emotional color to language, it accommodates inexactitude as it works figuratively, linking dissimilar objects to develop an unrelated third. Above all it is a pattern detector. (Conway,1983)*

Brain hemisphere research (Orenstein, 1977; Sperry, 1973) suggests that what I have described so far is housed primarily in the right brain hemisphere. For my purposes here I'd like to call the metaphoric mind that which is beyond what is usually described as right brain functioning, and to include what is often described as the subconscious. The two have many similarities, and are "tapped" with similar techniques for learning purposes, so I find it difficult to separate them. Perhaps the subconscious is the right brain's storage and reprocessing of all past experience. For example, imagery is a right brain activity. For many it is visual, has no sense of time, is without words. (Williams, 1983)

> *But the specific image comes out of the workings of the subconscious, and is released only by quieting the rational mind, relaxing and moving into another state of consciousness.*

The specific image is the result of creatively reprocessed past experiences – our "inner wisdom's" attempt to make sense of all the input without resorting to the pros and cons and words of rational problem solving.

I recently was reminded of the power this version of the metaphoric mind has when I had hypnosis to lose weight. The process was one of deep relaxation, dredging up and focusing on an image of myself when I was at my ideal weight, and knowing that I would want to eat only that amount of food that would allow me to lose 1-2 pounds a week, so that I could again look like my ideal image. I was amazed how easy it was to lose 50 pounds. Dieting has never been so easy. My doctor who hypnotized me did not control my mind; he helped me release my subconscious mind and use its power to control my eating. Prior to hypnosis, I attempted a rational approach, identifying all the reasons why I should lose weight, and planning low calorie meals; but I gained, instead of losing. Rational mind by itself was not enough but it did lead me to seek the help I needed. And my knowledge of nutrition provided essential help along the way.

Rational mind and metaphoric mind are necessary partners.
There are many activities described in the literature that you can use to get in touch with your metaphoric mind, and to help your learners do the same.
Common elements in all of them:
- *Knowing with certainty that learning will occur.*
- *Temporarily suspending or quieting rational mind.*
- *Remaining open to the expected, but more especially to the unexpected.*

You don't have to be a hypnotist. These techniques have been used in just about any subject matter area from physics and chemistry to personal problem solving, from tennis to cooking, from typing to self understanding. Some of the techniques are centering (Hendricks and Roberts, 1977), visualization (Samuels and Samuels, 1975), guided imagery (Sheehan, 1972), meditation (Miller, 1982), dream analysis (Garfield, 1976), synectics (Gordon, 1961) and psychosynthesis (Assagioli, 1965). Entire books have been written about each, as you can see from my references.

I owe thanks to Marge Denis for these statements, drawn from her list of basic processes of intuitive learning. Marge also makes the point, and many people's experience verifies it, that you cannot will the metaphoric mind to function. You have to let it function, relax so that it will, and trust that it will. Artistic endeavours emerge from the metaphoric mind, too. Drawing, painting, sculpting with clay, weaving, creating music, poetry, all allow the right brain to function and reveals to us what we can be and how we can integrate and synthesize ideas, as well as create.

I have never used my metaphoric mind to create music or poetry but I have used it to synthesize ideas. Several years ago at the end of a course, I listed the major learning processes I had experienced during the course, as I had asked students in the course to do. I had a list of about 30 processes. Understandably, no one was particularly interested in my list. After class was over, I decided I needed to do more work with the list, to see if I could find a way to make it more meaningful and interesting to myself and others. I first cut the list into individual processes. Next I grouped similar processes together and gave each grouping a name (a rational, cognitive process identified by Taba, 1967). By then I had no further ideas of what to do, but was not yet satisfied. So I went to bed, but did not sleep.

Suddenly an idea came – a metaphor to represent the grouping of process. I grabbed my tape recorder which was by my bed, put in a blank tape, and described the metaphor. (I knew that if I got up and got pencil and paper, I would lose the idea in logic and rational structures.) I talked into the recorder until the idea was exhausted, shut off the recorder and tried to sleep. About 30 minutes later, more ideas emerged, and I talked them onto the tape until I felt finished. This cycle occurred at least three more times. I was awake and productive nearly all night, and by morning I had synthesized ideas that have served me well in my teaching for five years, and were the beginnings of this chapter. It was a most exciting night.

> *Had I sat at my desk with a blank page in front of me, and tried to create the metaphor and the synthesis of ideas I would have given up in frustration or something very boring would have come from my rational mind.*

I recognize how incomplete this section is. I take comfort in my knowledge that you will be able to create ways to use the metaphoric mind in your teaching. But the metaphoric mind works better if you give it some input from the rational mind. I hope you are able to find, read, enjoy, and profit from some of the suggested readings I have listed.

Spiritual Capability

Our spiritual capability that helps us in learning is not necessarily one that grows out of a religious background. The spiritual is difficult to define. I can only make some statements about some of what it includes:

Spirituality involves an awareness of all there is and an openness to what is not. It is the strength and fearlessness to allow ourselves to transcend reality and ourselves. (Buscaglia, 1978)

> *Spirituality is an awareness, wonder, deep sense of awe of the present, the potential, of persons or nature. It is an awareness and awe of connectedness of what is and what could be. It includes your vision of what could be for yourself – your purpose in life – for others, for nature.*

The fact that I can plant a seed and it becomes a flower, share a bit of knowledge and it becomes another's, smile at someone and receive a smile in return, are to me continual spiritual exercises. (Buscaglia, 1978)

Aldous Huxley (1975) quotes a poem by Wordsworth, in which he writes impatiently about books:

Enough Science and of Art;
Close up those barren leaves;
Come forth and bring with you a heart
That watches and receives.

I like the phrase "a heart that watches and receives" but do not feel we have to set aside our spiritual capability while we are reading a book or engaging in a rational mind, scientific experiment. As Buscaglia (1978) says:

> *The scientific answer had not taken the mystery from the experience. Because something can be explained need not affect its wonder.*

As I think back about teachers and learners whom I have known who have allowed their spiritual capability to develop even to some extent, their way of expressing themselves in everyday conversations reveals the awe they feel about life, learning, and the deep (or higher) sources of meaning. They recognize each other and have an immediate sense of trust in each other as co-learners about life. We can begin to understand why this is so as we take in the words of Molly Brown (1983) as she describes spiritual awakening and transformation:

> *Spiritual experiences are those which give us new expansive perceptions about our relationship to the cosmos, which allow us to glimpse a reality beyond the logical, rational, physically bound world we usually consider to be our home. These new perceptions are naturally accompanied by strong emotions of fear, joy, hope, and even despair. Our thinking may become confused, disjointed, and at the same time expansive. We may create whole new patterns of understanding from this seemingly mental chaos ... When we undergo such experiences, our values change. We become more open to 'transpersonal' values: ethical, aesthetic, heroic, humanitarian, altruistic, and creative ...*

Many adults have had such experiences without thinking of them as spiritual. Brown goes on to explain:

> *Spiritual awakening takes many forms, compatible with the qualities and characteristics of the individual. It may be an artistic urge, a strong impulse to express one's self in colour, shapes, textures, or music. It may come as a vision to create something of service to the world ... Many people speak of "being guided" in their lives by a wisdom beyond their consciousness.*

Some of the adults who come to our classes may be there to gain information and skill needed to fulfill a spiritual urge or "obsession". What a privilege we have to help them fulfill their vision.

Brown describes how the metaphors and procedures of psychosynthesis can help people develop and express their "Higher Selves" or spiritual capability. Using these procedures requires special training, but students who take the training often subsequently reveal how important it has been for them in their lives.

There are surely many paths to becoming aware of our spiritual capabilities and using them in our learning. I again turn to Brown for another thought that enables me to feel that I am on the journey and am able to support others on their journeys:

Spiritual awakening is an awakening to who we really are and a transformation in how we manifest our special qualities in the world ... When we free ourselves of inhibitions, distortions, and fear which block our self-understanding, how rich and beautiful are our gifts, how joyful their expression, and how awesome the impact they can have upon the world.

The Whole Picture

I have described these six capabilities as separate phenomena, but they are not separate; they are very much inter-related. In some, perhaps most, learning projects all are operating, sometimes even simultaneously. For example, meet fictional Ann. She is meditating one day; an image appears in her metaphoric mind. It suggests that she wants to make a major change in her life. But thoughts of major change stir strong emotions, taking form in physical agitation and sleeplessness. She talks with a friend (relational) about the image, finding it somewhat difficult to express the image in words, but explains it and her feelings to her friend. She then identifies all the pros and cons of the change (rational) and still feels indecisive (emotional) to find another way of making the change that would not be so disruptive in her life. The answer she finds fits in beautifully with her vision of her life's purpose (spiritual), so she makes the decision to make the altered change, and learns what steps to take to do so (rational). She is now happy (emotional) and full of energy to begin (physical). She is convinced she has made the right decisions because her whole being feels in harmony (spiritual).

The research dealing with the relationships between capabilities is sparse. There are two studies I can report, however. One deals with the emotional and the rational. Common belief is that a highly emotional person is also chaotic, diffuse, and disorganized. However, in one study it was shown that this is not so. The study demonstrates that the wider the range of one's emotional expressions, the more complex is one's intellectual expression. The research, done by Summers, suggests:

A person who is capable of shifting viewpoints and considering a situation from its multiple perspectives is especially likely to rapidly alter his or her initial evaluation and to transform the corresponding emotions. (Brain Mind Bulletin, 1982)

This research is seen as strongly supporting a theory of emotional-cognitive structures, proposed by Gray and LaViolette (Brain Mind Bulletin, 1982). The theory maintains that thoughts are embedded in emotional codes in our brains. Gray gives educators some hint about how to use this information:

We are feeling beings before we are thinking beings. Emotional nuances play the primary and organizing role, and the cognitive structures are more passive. Therefore, the ideal transmission of knowledge should start with an emotional nuance.

Another combination which research helps us understand a little more is the rational-metaphoric. Samples (1979) watched children of various ages work through learning sequences in physics, natural science, and astronomy. Teacher interventions were not allowed, so the children were following their natural inclinations. They spent most of their early time in a problem sequence in play (metaphoric). When they tired of that they switched to the rational. When they had had enough of that, they switched back to play. They alternated back and forth between the approaches. About two-thirds of the way through the sequence, they became more rational, "constantly choosing linear and logical explanation and routes for exploration ... The closer the children got to a rational solution, the more difficult it was for them to return to the metaphor". He also reports that at that stage the children's appearance changed, they became more serious, didn't smile as much, their body movement diminished, and they seemed to be looking for approval from nearby adults.

The research reporting how children play at various stages of learning reminds me of the important innovative research of Melamed (1987) on the role of play in adult learning. She states:

> *During the course of my study, five areas emerged as particularly compatible with a playful approach to living and learning. Although play is not an isolated phenomenon in these themes, its threads intertwine, enrich and humanize each of them. The areas are:*
> *Relational - the capacity for cooperation and connectedness.*
> *Experiential - validating and learning from experience.*
> *Metaphoric - intuitive and right-brain thinking.*
> *Integrative - valuing a holistic and organic connectedness to people and things.*
> *Empowering - facilitating transformation in ourselves and the world(s) we inhabit.*

We can also look at personal experience and historical evidence to see the interrelatedness of the six capabilities. Instances of high level creativity and inventiveness show us several capabilities at work. Gray (Brain Mind Bulletin,1984) gives us two instances: Kekule's deciphering of the benzene ring after being moved by a dream of a snake swallowing its tail, and:

> *Einstein's repeated statement that ideas came to him first in the form of vague and diffuse bodily sensations that gradually refined themselves into exact and reproducible feeling-tones. Only when this process was completed could Einstein mathematically define the new concept.*

Few of us are Einsteins even in our own field, but we can use all of these capabilities for a more creative life through richer, fuller learning.

Keane (1987) in his research, has documented and illustrated how men who were not Einsteins, did use all of the capabilities as they worked their way through long periods of self-doubt in their lives to emerge into fuller, more integrated selves. They experienced phases of disorientation, self-acceptance and integration in their search for meaning and peace. These men used all of their capabilities in very crucial times during their journeys out of doubt.

> *I have a hunch that if we have more or less equally developed all of these capabilities, they will serve as checks and balances on each other, and keep us from going overboard in one direction. The whole has a wisdom beyond the sum of the parts.*

Learners' Awareness of Capabilities

An increasing number of people are becoming aware of this enlarged view of the potential of humans in learning. It is compatible with the new paradigm or world view Marilyn Ferguson (1980) describes in *The Aquarian Conspiracy.* Several assumptions will change in education as this new paradigm becomes more prevalent. Some of the newer assumptions that are emerging:

• Learning as a process, a journey.
• Relatively flexible structure. Belief that there are many ways to teach a given subject.
• Priority of self-image as the generator of performance.
-Inner experience seen as context for learning. Use of imagery, story-telling, dream journals, centring exercises, and exploration of feeling is encouraged.
• Strives for whole-brain education. Augments left-brain rationality with holistic, nonlinear, and intuitive strategies. Confluence and fusion of the two processes emphasized.
• Concern with the individual's performance in terms of potential. Interest in testing outer limits, transcending perceived limitations.
• Concern for the environment of learning: lighting, colors, air, physical comfort, needs for privacy and interaction, quiet and exuberant activities.
• Human relationships between teachers and learners are of primary importance.
• Teacher is learner, too, learning from students. (Ferguson, 1980)

She also states: " ... we are capable of imagination, invention, and experiences we have only glimpsed."

There are other writers who describe what they see emerging as a new paradigm: Schwartz and Ogilvy, 1980; Jantsch and Waddington, 1976; Lemkow, 1990.

I don't claim that the view of learners that I have posed here captures all the characteristics they see emerging, but it is compatible with them.

Nonetheless, it has been my experience, even recently, that most adult learners are not aware of the potential of all of these capabilities in their own learning. Once they become aware of them by experiencing them in their own learning, they feel greatly empowered and eager to learn more and experience more of their own resources.

> *When first introduced to these ideas, learners seem to react in one of two ways: (1) resistance and disbelief based on fear; or (2) relief that at last the way they have learned all their lives is being recognized. More express resistance than relief.*

Helping Learners Learn How to Learn More Fully

So how do we help learners recognize they have been playing only one string of their guitar and are missing out on music that is fuller and more beautiful? None of us would advertize ourselves as guitar teachers if we could play only one string, regardless of how many notes we could play on that string. We could get a lot further if we could play a few chords, at least, using three or four strings.

> *I'm suggesting that before we attempt to help learners use any of the capabilities other than the rational, that we become comfortable and confident of our own use of the capability that we want to introduce into our classroom.*

I think my own progression through them has been: (1) rational, (2) relational, (3) emotional, (4) physical, (5) metaphoric, and (6) spiritual. I have not developed as fully as I want to in the final two – metaphoric and spiritual, and am continually learning more about each of the six.

If we have used a particular capability in our own learning, and know one or two techniques we are comfortable using, our confidence and trust is communicated to our students, and they become willing to risk or experiment.

A technique that I have learned from my doctor (Dr. Charles Bill) will serve well in this context, too. He does a lot of hypnosis, and finds most people are afraid to undergo hypnosis. He thus explains hypnosis as moving to another state of consciousness, a phenomenon that we all experience hundreds of times a day. We sometimes are very intensely focused on something, then we drift on into daydreams, we relax, then we become very busy, thinking of many tasks at once. All are different states of consciousness.

As teachers, we can help ourselves and our learners become aware of how much of our everyday experience these capabilities are. There is nothing new or strange about them; we are just going to use them in our learning.

My doctor further reassures hypnosis patients that hypnosis can only help them do what they want to do (stop smoking, lose weight, be free of pain). The patient is always in control; there cannot be coercion into doing something he or she objects to.

Learners going through an imagery exercise are always in control. If the directions are not comfortable or helpful, they can change them for themselves. If everyone else is on a fantasy trip back in a dark tunnel, but Sue is afraid of the dark, she could climb a mountain instead.

A final caution is that there are no "shoulds" or "oughts" in emotions, in physical reactions, in intuition, in imagery, in spirituality, in relationships. We must not judge or question what a learner has had as an inner experience. We just accept. If the learner's experience was an unusual one, he or she may want to explore it later with you, but the exploration can never be judgemental.

Think of how much you are as a person because of your rational capability and the training it has had.

> *If each of our other capabilities could add l/10 as much to your experience and your being (and I suspect they can add more than that) think how rich you would be.*

Wouldn't it be worth a little effort and openness to what could be? Wouldn't you rather play all the strings of your guitar and teach others to play more beautiful music on their guitars?

REFERENCES

Assagioli, R. (1965) *Psychosynthesis: A Manual of Principles and Techniques.* New York: Hobbs, Dorman.

Ausabel, D. (1968) *Educational Psychology: A Cognitive View.* New York: Holt, Rinehart & Winston.

Bereiter, C. (1972) "Games to teach thinking". *Orbit.* OISE Press, Vol. 3, No. l.

Brain Mind Bulletin. March 8, 1982 and 1984.

Brown, M.Y. (1983) *The Unfolding Self: Psychosynthesis and Counselling.* Los Angeles: Psychosynthesis Press.

Buscaglia, L. (1987) *Personhood: The Art of Being Fully Human.* New York: Fawcet Columbine.

Casteneda, C. (1968) *The Teachings of Don Juan.* New York: Ballentine Books.

Conway, J. (1983) The Metaphoric Mind: Awakening the Sleeper of the Shadows. Toronto: OISE. Unpublished term paper.

Davies, L.J. (1976) Energy Experiences of Adult Learners in Learning Groups. Toronto: Unpublished dissertation OISE.

Davies, L.J. (1987) "Charting human energy in learning: A path to understanding". In D. Boud and V. Griffin (Eds.) *Appreciating Adults Learning: From the Learners' Perspective.* London: Kogan-Page.

Denis, M. and Richter, I. (1987) "Learning about intuitive learning: Moose-hunting techniques". In D. Boud and V. Griffin (Eds.) *Appreciating Adults Learning: From the Learners' Perspective.* London: Kogan-Page.

Ferguson, M. (1980) *The Acquarian Conspiracy: Personal and Social Transformation in the 1980's.* Los Angeles: J.P. Tarcher.

Galyean, B. (1981) "Brain hemispheric functioning". *Roper Review: A Journal on Gifted Education.* Vol. 4, No. 1.

Garfield, P. (1976) *Creative Dreaming.* New York: Ballantine.

Gehrels, C. (1985) "Learning partners". In J. Robinson, S. Saberton and V. Griiffin (Eds.) *Learning Partnerships: Interdependent Learning in Adult Education.* Toronto: Department of Adult Education, OISE.

Gibb, J.(1967) "Humanistic elements in group growth". In J.F.T. Bugental (Ed.) *Challenges of Humanistic Psychology.* New York: McGraw Hill.

Gordon, W.J.J. (1961) *Synectics.* New York: Harper and Row.

Griffith, G. (1987) "Images of interdependence: Authority and power in teaching/learning". In D. Boud and V. Griffin (Eds.) *Appreciating Adults Learning: From the Learners' Perspective.* London: Kogan-Page.

Hart, L.A. (1983) *Human Brain and Human Learning.* New York: Longman.

Hendricks, G. and Roberts, T. (1977) *The Second Centering Book: More Awareness Activities for Children, Parents, and Teachers.* Englewood Cliffs, N.J.:Prentice-Hall.

Houston, J. (1981) "Education". In V. Alberto and K. Dychtwald (Eds.) *Millennium: Glimpses Into the 21st Century.* Los Angeles: J.P. Tarcher.

Huxley, A. (1975) "Education on the Nonverbal Level". In T.B. Roberts (Ed.) *Four Psychologies Applied to Education.* New York: Wiley.

Johnson, D.W. (1981) *Reaching Out: Interpersonal Effectiveness and Self-Actualization.* Englewood Cliffs, N.J.: Prentice-Hall.

Keane, R. (1987) "The doubting journey: A learning process of self-transformation". In D. Boud and V. Griffin (Eds.) *Appreciating Adults Learning: From the Learner's Perspective.* London: Kogan-Page.

Kneeland, S.J. (1979) "A thinking man's guide to emotional decision making". *Canadian Training Methods.* June.

Lavery, R. (1983) Contacting the Learning Enablers. Toronto: OISE. Unpublished term paper.

McFadyen, D. (1983) Emotions as Enablers in the Learning Process. Toronto: OISE. Unpublished term paper.

Melamed, L. (1987) "The role of play in adult learning". In D. Boud and V. Griffin (Eds.) *Appreciating Adults Learning: From the Learners' Perspective.* London: Kogan-Page.

Menlo, A. and others (1979) Teaching Educators of Adults How to Facilitate Participation in Adult Learning Groups. Ann Arbor, Mich.: University of Michigan, School of Education. Unpublished paper.

Miller, J.P. (1983) *The Educational Spectrum: Orientation to Curriculum.* New York: Longman.

Miller, J.P. (1988) *The Holistic Curriculum.* Toronto: OISE Press.

Miller, J.P., Cassie, J.R., and Drake, S.M. (1990) *Holistic Learning: A Teacher's Guide to Integrated Studies. No. 59.* Toronto: OISE Press.
Miller, R. (1991) *New Directions in Education: Selections from Holistic Education Review.* Brandon, Vermont: Holistic Education Press.
Ornstein, R. (1977) *The Psychology of Consciousness* (2nd edition) New York: Harcourt Brace Jovanovich.
Robinson, J., Saberton, S. and Griffin, V. (Eds.) (1985) *Learning Partnerships: Interdependent Learning in Adult Education.* Toronto: OISE Department of Adult Education.
Rogers, C.R. (1967) "Learning to be free". In C.R. Rogers and B. Sevens (Eds.) *Person to Person: The Problem of Being Human.* Moab, Utah: Real People Press.
Ross, L. (1984) 1110-A Transformative Learning Experience. Toronto: OISE. Unpublished term paper.
Samples, B. (1979) *The Metaphoric Mind.* Reading, Mass.: Addison Wesley.
Samuels, M. and Samuels, N. (1975) *Seeing with the Mind's Eye – The History, Techniques and Uses of Visualization.* New York: Random House.
Sheehan, P. (1972) *The Function and Nature of Imagery.* New York: Academic Press.
Sperry, R.W. (1973) "Later specialization in cerebral function in the surgically separated hemispheres". In F.J. McGuigan and R.A. Schoonover (Eds.) *The Psychophysiology of Thinking.* New York: Academic Press.
Smith, R. (1982) *Learning How to Learn: Applied Theory for Adults.* New York: Cambridge.
Taylor, M. (1987) "Self-directed learning: More than meets the observer's eye". In D. Boud and V. Griffin (Eds.) *Appreciating Adults Learning: From the Learner's Perspective.* London: Kogan-Page.
White, J. and Fadiman, J. (Eds.) (1976) *Relax: How You Can Feel Better, Reduce Stress, and Overcome Tension.* The Confucian Press. (Place not available)
Williams, M. (1983) Images: Towards an Understanding of the Links Between Adult Learning and Image Learning. Toronto: OISE. Unpublished thesis.

SUGGESTED READING

Brookfield, S.D. (1990) *The Skillful Teacher.* San Francisco: Jossey-Bass.
Chopra, D. (1989) *Quantum Healing: Exploring the Frontiers of Mind/Body Medicine.* New York: Bantam Books.
Devereux, P., Steele, J. and Kubrin, D. (1989) *Earth Mind: Communicating with the Living Word of Gaia.* Rochester, Vermont: Destiny.
Edwards, B. (1986) *Drawing on the Artist Within.* New York: Simon & Schuster.
Fanning, P. (1986) *Visualization for Change: A Step by Step Guide to Using Your Powers of Imagination for Self-Improvement, Therapy, Healing, and Pain Control.* Oakland, CA: New Harbinger.
Gardner, H. (1983) *Frames of Mind: The Theory of Multiple Intelligences.* New York: Basic Books.

Heider, J. (1985) *The Tao of Leadership: Lao Tzu's Tao Te Ching Adapted for a New Age.* Toronto: Bantam Books.
Hendricks, G. and Fadiman, J. (1976) *Transpersonal Education: A Curriculum, for Feeling and Being.* Englewood Cliffs, N.J.: Prentice Hall.
Hunt, D.E. (1992) *The Renewal of Personal Energy.* Toronto: OISE Press.
Masters, R. and Houston, J. (1978) *Listening to the Body.* New York: Dell.
McKim, R.H. (1980) *Experiences in Visual Thinking.* (2nd edition). Monterey, CA: Brooks/Cole.
More, W.S. (1974) *Emotions and Adult Learning.* Farnborough: Saxon House
Ostrander, S. and Schroeder, L. (1979) *Superlearning.* New York: Dell.
Purpel, D.E. (1989) *The Moral & Spiritual Crisis in Education: A Curriculum for Justice & Compassion in Education.* New York: Bergin & Garvey.
Ram, D. (1990) *Journey of Awakening: A Meditator's Guidebook.* (Rev. Ed.) New York: Bantam Books.
Rico, G.L. (1983) *Writing the Natural Way: Using Your Right Brain Techniques to Release Your Expressive Powers.* Los Angeles: J.P. Tarcher.
Roberts, T.B. (Ed.) (1975) *Four Psychologies Applied to Education.* New York: Wiley.
Rogers, C.R. (1980) *A Way of Being.* Boston: Houghton Mifflin.
Samuels, M. and Samuels, N. (1990) *Healing with the Mind's Eye: A Guide for Using Imagery and Visions for Personal Growth and Healing.* New York: Summit Books.
Sanders, L.G. and Tucker, M.J. (1983) *Centering: A Guide to Inner Growth.* New York: Destiny Books.
Shone, R. (1984) *Creative Visualization: How to Use Imagery and Imagination for Self-Improvement.* Wellingborough, N.Y.: Thorsons.
Smith, R.M. and Associates (1990) *Learning to Learn Across the Lifespan.* San Francisco: Jossey-Bass.
Vaughan, F. (1979) *Awakening Intuition.* Garden City, N.Y.: Doubleday.
Wilber, K. (Ed.) (1982) *The Holographic Paradigm and Other Paradoxes.* Boulder: Shambala.
Zukav, G. (1989) *The Seat of the Soul.* New York: Simon & Schuster.

Chapter 7
Application of Learning Theory to the Instruction of Adults

Donald Brundage, Ross Keane,
Ruth Mackneson

Practitioner's Summary

It is one thing to state that "people learn in a variety of ways", it is quite another to make clear not only how this is so but also what this may mean to the instructor of adults.

Descriptively and almost experientially this chapter takes the fledgling instructor by the hand. The long-time practitioner may well take a second look here too. From the initial stages of planning an adult program with practical suggestions to ease and solve common problems, as well as pointers that help to maximize learning, this chapter even includes some innovative ways to evaluate "what you have done and what has happened in your class".

For a teacher accustomed to teaching children, what differences will be encountered when teaching adults? And how should these be handled?

The authors point out that increasing age represents increasing life experience and this complexity causes each person to view their learning in differing ways in accord with their own development. It follows then that the teaching itself will have to be modified to accommodate these differing ways and to encourage the continuation of learning long after the program is finished.

Further, it is important that initial planning be flexible enough to accommodate these differing needs. While these thoughts refer to the content and process of the learning within the class, the instructor also needs to be sensitive to the environmental needs of adults while learning: lighting and temperature, and even the placement of chairs all reflect a sincere interest on the part of the instructor to enhance the learning in every way possible.

Beginning contact with the students not only creates opportunities for their input and expectations, but also a chance for general introductions before a brief outline of what the program may include is presented. These are called "processes of climate setting".

Typical problems of adults: tiredness, excessive talkativeness, or retiring shyness, are all discussed together with practical solutions. Exposing the experience and knowledge of those in the group becomes a challenge for the instructor.

Recognizing that the primary purpose of all evaluation is really to "provide information for action", the strategies detailed here are of value to both instructor and institution, but most especially to provide a basis for ongoing learning by the adult student.

The "final words" of this chapter depart from the previous ease of format and thrust deeply into some exciting new findings about learners adapting to "self-directed learning" and just how the instructor can be of assistance by becoming aware of previously hidden difficulties.

This expansion on taken-for-granted concepts such as "self-directed", "climate", "facilitator", "learner behaviour" and even "learning processes", provides the instructor with a tantalizing glimpse of the world of research and theory from which each of these concepts has emerged. Well-practiced adult educators will find refreshing insights here.

Chapter 7
Application of Learning Theory to the Instruction of Adults
Donald Brundage, Ross Keane, Ruth MacKneson

What Do We Need to Know?

People learn in different ways. This simple fact is often not understood or acknowledged by those of us who share the professional task of helping adults to learn. Efforts to learn are also compounded by failure to grasp the facilitative process upon which much learning is based. How do we help others to learn? What are the processes associated with that activity which, if properly understood, could make us much more effective teachers and learners?

This chapter attempts to make explicit the link between what is known about how adults learn and what we can do as facilitators to improve the process. Instead of approaching the subject theoretically and abstractly, we will take you on a personal journey of discovery as you undertake the onerous responsibility of instructing adults. We have tried to imagine you as an instructor preparing to meet a class of adults. This chapter will help you to:

- deal with the essential differences between adults and children;
- plan a course or curriculum;
- enter the facilitation process;
- cope with the fallout of problems;
- maximize the learning process; and finally
- evaluate what you have done and what has occurred in your class.

Design of the Chapter

To do all this, we have chosen a prototype named Lesley, who has been contracted by a community college to teach a new course in Canadian History. (see Fullan (1982), especially Chapters 3 and 7). One of the goals of the course is to help the participants learn about the elusive nature of Canadian identity through an examination of historical events.

Lesley has been a very successful high school teacher, specializing in Canadian History. She has learned over the years to balance the demands of career, family and personal life. She has been impressed by the reports of her friends that somehow teaching adult evening classes is qualitatively different from teaching children during the day. She has accepted the invitation to teach for the community college and she is excited by the possibilities but also somewhat apprehensive about doing it.

What does Lesley need to know? What new skills does she need to learn and what attitudes would be helpful in successfully conducting her courses?

Characteristics of the Adult Learner

Often educators are not convinced of the differences between teaching adults and children, between andragogy and pedagogy, until they grapple with broader experiences of the adult learner.

What are these differences? Lesley will likely be asking herself this question as she begins to plan her course in Canadian History. Her professional career to date has been devoted to understanding children, their learning needs and what they have to do with Canadian History. How will she go about helping her class of adults master the same basic content?

First, she will have to appreciate that her students are older and by the nature of that fact, more complex as learners. Not only could their ages span more than 50 years, but along with that difference and all the life experience associated with it, are all the variations of ability and personality seen in any class of children. Secondly, the adults will also have different expectations of what Lesley will do and should do, and a wide range of reasons for taking the course. Each will be in a different life space and a different developmental phase, so each person will view this learning experience differently. Lesley will want to work with these individuals and their own unique characteristics so that all participants will learn in a manner appropriate to their learning styles and developmental stages.

> *Effective teaching depends on strategies that consider the entire educational situation, the skills and resources of the learners, their characteristics and goals and the requirements of the subject matter.*

Patricia Cross (1981) points out that different stages of life actually call for different learning abilities. She maintains the educational model that would capitalize on the learning strengths of adults, de-emphasize the processing and acquisition of large amounts of new cognitive functions calling for integration, interpretation and application of knowledge. She identifies the greatest problems with memory for older people as occurring with meaningless learning, complex learning and learning requiring reassessment of old learnings.

Planning the Program/Course

With her increasing awareness of the complex forces at work in helping adults learn, Lesley now approaches the central task of planning her program in

Canadian History. Malcolm Knowles (1980) outlines his comprehensive guidelines for shaping a program based on the learning needs of adults. His model contains six steps, each following in a logical order that is at once comprehensive and simple:

> *Knowles' Program Planning Model*
> - *climate setting;*
> - *needs assessment, awareness of expectations;*
> - *objective and goal setting, desired outcomes;*
> - *structure and strategies, methodology;*
> - *implementation, action;*
> - *evaluation, guidance for change.*

Knowles, like any competent adult educator, recognizes the complexities of developing a curriculum based on the systematic integration of content and process. In Lesley's case, the content is the Canadian History subject matter, and the process involves the interaction between Lesley and her adult students, the students with one another and with the content, and the learning environment and the class. (See Brundage and MacKeracher (1980) especially Chapter 5.)

Stages in program planning (Knowles' model)

Knowles begins his model with the assertion that it is essential to discern the needs of the students you will be instructing. In Lesley's case, she will know that the students who enrol in her class will be primarily interested in learning more about Canadian History. But what else might be on their agendas which will affect their learning of history and their satisfaction with the class? Perhaps they want to develop greater expertise in teaching themselves, or to become more specific about what it means to become a Canadian, or to get back to the books after a long interval away from formal learning, or to escape a cantankerous mate in a failing marriage, or just to support the continuing education program at the local community college.

> *The possibilities of student needs are endless. But in her planning before meeting her class, Lesley needs to be open to this range of expectancies and be sufficiently flexible with her plan to respond to many of them.*

At this point, she can only conjecture what these needs might be by becoming familiar with the learning needs of adults in general.

The next step in Knowles' model is to develop objectives for the course to meet as many of the needs as possible. Lesley will then want to elaborate the details of her planning in specific modules for presentation to her class. Finally, she will want to evaluate what she has done in relation to what her students have learned.

Lesley is now prepared to meet her class for the first time. She has conscientiously tried to understand the assumptions underlying the notion of how adults learn, why and how adult students differ from children and what their learning characteristics are likely to be, given their maturity. She has now developed a program plan for Canadian History to meet the learning needs of her adult students.

The First Class: Setting The Climate for Learning

The physical environment for adults may require careful attention. Adults are more likely to need good lighting, accoustics, fresh air and comfortable chairs than children because many more have begun to have sensory impairment and chronic diseases such as arthritis and other effects of the aging process. As well, the facilitator needs to consider room management, arrangements for food and beverages, washroom facilities and so on. Other sources which speak to the need for a conducive physical environment are: Botwinick, 1973; Kidd, 1973; McCluskey, 1970.

The class now sits before her. She has introduced herself to the students as they arrived. This was possible since she has only 20 students. Had the enrollment been any larger, she would have had to wait to introduce herself more formally at the beginning of the class. Lesley may have her students put their first names on cards in front of their chairs or on their desks to help the process of relating names to faces. After calling the class to order and again identifying herself, she sketches in brief detail the nature of the learning experience the class is about to enter. With this done, and having responded to the few questions raised about the course outline, she says she is interested in knowing more about the people in the class, the reasons they have for coming, and some expectations they have for the course. Lesley models the kind of response she is seeking by briefly telling them why she is teaching this course, of her interest in Canadian History and, as this is her first experience of teaching adults, of her pleasure in anticipating such an opportunity.

Each member of the class follows in order until everyone has had a brief moment to say why he or she is present and what he or she would like to learn. Lesley, in the meantime, has been taking notes and encouraging participants by asking questions to broaden their comments.

Now Lesley is in a position to enlarge on the plan for the course. In some detail she reviews the program she has developed and shares with the students what they can expect to cover and why, as well as setting out the requirements for the course, and how student learning will be evaluated. She will also outline the resources students will need for the course.

These processes of climate setting may have exhausted the first class depending on how long the group meets. No matter how long the time, the care that goes into setting an appropriate climate for learning will pay off as the class progresses.

People do like to be acknowledged by name and will respond if properly encouraged with comments about their learning goals. These may not be clearly articulated - in fact, some students may have subconscious reasons for being in class, but fuzzy and ill defined as these goals may be, students like to have a chance to express them.

Common Problems or Challenges in Teaching Adults

Lesley now progresses with her teaching and she is excited about the good things that are happening each time she meets her class. As the weeks progress however, she encounters a series of minor problems common to most teaching situations for both children and adults which are especially critical for the adult learner and now challenge her.

Challenge one: catering for pooped pete

Pete is a very keen student of Canadian History but is a chartered accountant who has already spent a full day at his office. His capacity to stay alert fades as the evening progresses.

> *Lesley comes to appreciate the fact that if Pete is encouraged to move around, to share in the leadership of the group and have a coffee break occasionally, his learning capacity stays fairly constant.*

Challenge two: Catering for talkative tracy

A Tracy and a Sam (who follows as Challenge Three) are a trying pair who seem to turn up in every learning situation. Lesley has had long experience in dealing with such personality types in children, but in this class of adults she observes some differences. Tracy is inquisitive by nature and very long experience has persuaded her that talking about what she knows and asking questions about what she doesn't know is an effective way of learning for her. So over the years she has developed that style which is to the relative disadvantage of other learners in the class.

Lesley recognizes that the challenge to her is not to stifle Tracy's inquiring mind, but to help her see that what she has to offer is related to what other class members may contribute.

> *The technique is essentially a linking one by taking a firm but positive leadership in chaining ideas together so that each member of the group comes to feel that they made a contribution to the growing idea.*

With this accomplished, Lesley discovers that Tracy has become a better listener for she now appreciates that her ideas are seen to have worth and have become part of a larger knowledge base. Since she is already a keen learner, Tracy is now consciously aware that by honing her listening skills she is improving her capacity to learn.

Challenge three: Catering for silent sam

Sam, on the other hand, is a mystery to Lesley. His normal learning style is to participate as a listener and again, he has spent his life learning that way. Shy by nature, he somehow feels his ideas have little merit especially when verbalized, so he keeps his mouth shut but participates actively as a silent learner. Lesley knows that the class would likely benefit from what Sam has to say but doesn't want to upset him by asking a direct question.

> *It occurs to her, however, that if she breaks the class down into small groups that Sam would likely feel more at ease and begin to talk.*

It worked, especially when she began the small group process on a dyad basis and then moved three dyads together to form a small group of six. Having discovered that it is fun to speak in class (as long as there are not too many listeners around) Sam has progressed so that he can make a contribution to the small group which gets repeated to the larger group without being identified as his. Slowly he alters his learning style to be more talkative and feels better for it. So does Lesley.

Challenge four: Sharing the teaching/leadership function

While Lesley is excited about her class, she is getting more fatigued as the weeks go by. As a full-time teacher she has already done a day's work and in addition, has rushed home to tend to her family's needs and hurried back to teach her class. She knows her subject matter so well that she is tempted to simply lecture and let it go at that. However, she soon learns that if she is willing to give up some aspects of her teaching function, her students will quickly pick them up - especially if she had planned well for that eventuality. The power of experiential learning has long been in her arsenal of teaching methods and now she learns how to apply the method to adults.

> *By encouraging her students to become involved in preparing projects for class presentation, she had demonstrated her willingness to share in providing teaching/learning resources for her class.*

She also discovers with increasing pleasure that her adult students are a remarkable learning resource in themselves and have a great deal to contribute to the knowledge and skill of her class.

Challenge five: Channelling new enthusiasms for learning

Like most adult educators Lesley is discovering that her new approach to teaching adults is yielding dividends she had not expected. Some members of the class have begun to develop personal learning projects based on their class experience, and for which they would like assistance from Lesley.

> *Lesley must somehow encourage and focus such learning without being an essential part of it. To encourage but not get directly involved is an art which Lesley has developed in all her teaching.*

But now she senses a difference with her adult students. They expect her to react as a colleague, as an equal. While she knows that her knowledge is respected, it is different.

> *If she responds positively to the collegial expectation, she will not have to become directly involved but will simply suggest direction and expect her students to weigh the value of her advice and move from there.*

In essence, Lesley has moved her students from a dependent stance of learning through independency to interdependency.

Challenge six: Providing for continuous evaluation

Things are going so well for Lesley that she tends to feel that it really isn't necessary to check back with her students for their feedback about the course as a whole and her role as an instructor.

> *She learns, however, that periodic quick checks improve the nature of the learning experience for all, and so makes a point of building such techniques into her planning for the course.*

She knows too, that the College expects an evaluation of her course so she begins to plan how she will do this as the class reaches its final session.

At the end of some of her classes she provides an evaluation check list for her students to complete before leaving. On other occasions she uses the last few minutes of her class for students to reflect on the experience of the class and the personal learning that has taken place. Lesley shares this feedback with her class and modifies future activities so the students will know she is serious about their reactions to the course.

> *She discovers with satisfaction that continuous evaluation of an adult learner's experience helps immeasurably to consolidate the*

learning that has occurred and to build a climate of mutual trust that is shared by instructor and student alike.

A final responsibility Lesley faces is to conduct an examination or provide a means by which she, the participants and the College will know how successful the students have been in achieving their learning goals. The College may have a common format for evaluations which Lesley may be obliged to use but beyond that she can develop her own techniques of evaluation to supplement the one used by the College.

For example, she could ask each student to reflect silently on the major learnings that have taken place for that student. Then students would be asked to share their insights with one another and then with a group of four. At this time, the groups would record their reactions stating what conditions, people or events helped them in their learning and which did not. The groups could then share these findings and this could be followed with a full discussion about the course.

In using such an experiential process of evaluation Lesley would discover that the feelings which surround all learning events can be increasingly articulated, explored and documented to see how they complement and support the content learnings of the course.

Evaluation

Most school oriented institutions require a report from the teachers about each student as the basis for their accreditation. In adult education however, evaluation has a wider application because it is felt that the primary purpose of evaluation is to provide information for action. Thus it is relevant to the goals of all participants, and an integral part of every stage of the program.

In order to fulfil the requirements of the school or College, the adult educator can ask their assistance in developing an evaluation system that both complies with policy and assists their own learning.

There can even be variation in the evaluation formats for various members of a class, where some prefer an examination type of evaluation, and others prefer to write a paper or make a class presentation. Research in adult education has shown that student-referenced evaluations are the most conducive to optimum learning.

Should an examination be required by the sponsoring institution, what type should it be? An open-book type, or one that stresses prepared answers relating to students' own goals or should it be learning-centred evaluations that in themselves can facilitate learning? Malcolm Knowles has championed the practice of learning contracts. Since the goal of adult education is learning, and teaching is but a means to learning, Lesley will want all the evaluations to be congruent with that philosophy, and avoid any notion of an authoritarian position. But some of her students will desire her approval, and will only validate themselves through her criteria. During the time of the course, Lesley will try to help such students to value their own experience, and to see their learning and course goals as worthy criteria for their accomplishments, accepting self-evaluation as valid.

The instructor's evaluative reflection

Lesley has now completed her first course with adults and reflects with some satisfaction on her efforts. She has been consciously aware of the subtle differences between how adults and children learn and has become familiar with the characteristics of the adult learner. In addition, she has mastered the techniques of program planning for adults based on the knowledge of these differences. Her skills in climate setting, working through the common problems that face instructors of adults and developing criteria for evaluation have all made her a promising and effective adult educator.

Some Pitfalls and Some Solutions

The main body of the text of this chapter has been written in a manner which we think will convey to the busy adult educator a sense of how learning theory can be applied to the instruction of adults. But in real life things don't always move smoothly. Let's now direct our attention to some problems experienced by learners as they increasingly share responsibility for program planning and implementation.

In other words, what are some of the pitfalls facing instructors of adults and what are some possible preventions or solutions?

Virginia Griffin is an adult educator who has explored ways of helping learners become more self directed in class groups. The problems and issues she names are different from those cited by Knowles and will need to be considered by facilitators who involve learners heavily in program planning and implementation. She presents, in the context of a learning group, a list of problems facing learners as they try to take greater degrees of responsibility for planning their own programs.

1. *Becoming and staying responsible* for themselves. It is one thing for facilitators and learners to intellectualize about taking responsibility; it is another to immerse themselves in the hard struggle of being responsible.
2. *Maintaining and increasing self-esteem.* Once learners can say "I'm scared about doing well" they develop intense feelings of support and find great bursts of high energy for learning.
3. *Owning one's strengths,* desires, skills, needs. This is necessary for learners to move out of a dependent stance.
4. *Trusting one's own flow,* energies, and intuitions. Learners need to be in touch

with their feelings and their bodies to find where their own energy is. Very often they get caught up in what they assume to be other people's expectations.

5. *Dealing with confusion and ambiguity.*
6. *Clarifying* what they have learned.
7. *Redefining* what legitimate knowledge is. It can be a challenge to the adult educator to help learners capitalize on their experience and regard that as legitimate knowledge. Learners find it difficult to accept that learning from their own experience and reflection is legitimate knowledge.
8. *Relating* to others.
9. *Dealing with content.*

Importance of socio-emotional (relational) climate

The introduction exercise detailed previously about Lesley was one way of showing how to attend to aspects of the social-emotional environment. Alternatively Lesley could have asked the class to break into twos or threes and spend some time talking about themselves. These small clusters could be formed into larger groups or members could introduce each other to the class. Introductions should help to develop a climate that is free from threat and that will allow for interpersonal relationships based on developing trust and openness. These conditions must be nurtured and developed at the beginning of the learning program and then maintained throughout.

> *Climate setting enriches the entire course experience by fostering student-to-student interaction in learning tasks.*

Removing obstacles as a way of improving climate

Obstacles to learning are many and varied. Many students begin courses with anxieties about the facilitator's expectations. These may be reduced if the facilitator makes clear statements about her objectives and intended methods of teaching. It can be helpful to have course requirements available to students as a handout. Also lists of resources, including community based resources, reading materials and cultural resources can be useful here.

A word about motivation

The facilitator could profitably spend some time during the first few learning sessions deliberately lowering anxiety to a manageable level. Sharing and participating in the course plan is helpful in lowering anxiety.

Relationships between facilitator behaviour and learner behaviour

Our present understanding of the relationship between teaching and learning is limited. There may be little direct, causal behaviour but it is hard to reject the idea that facilitators play an important role in adult learning. It is the facilitator who is most likely to focus on maintaining the learning environment and to support the life of the class through wise interventions and suggestions of strategies and resources to help learners make optimum progress toward their varied goals.

Facilitating The Learning Process

Research done at OISE in the department of Adult Education by Marilyn Taylor and Heather Bates shows significant interaction for the individual learner between three processes: first, the ability to make sense of the class experience and to order and label it; secondly, feelings of self-esteem and third, the ability to relate to other individuals in the class. These processes interact and enhance one another. The implications of this finding are that facilitators may need to explore ways of increasing interaction among learners, promoting conditions conducive to trusting relationships, promoting reflection on experiences and encouraging the naming of experience in a way that makes sense to the learner, and finally, of finding ways to enhance the learner's self-esteem.

What would this look like in practice?

A facilitator committed to acting on these findings might

- have small groups of learners interview each other to help identify individual learning goals;
- take time for learners to talk together in small groups of shifting membership;
- use names and have constant name reinforcement;
- provide opportunities for individuals to share their personal learning goals for the course.

The facilitator will model the acceptability of making mistakes, self disclosure and self evaluation. A noted humanistic educator, Arthur Coombs (1975) has stated:

> *The humanist approaching educational accountability finds himself in a difficult spot. On the one hand he finds it necessary to resist the distortion produced by preoccupation with performance-based criteria as educational outcomes. Behavioural objectives have such apparent simplicity and straightforwardness and create such an illusion of business-like precision that the humanist finds himself regarded as soft, unscientific, fuzzy minded, and generally opposed to progress.*

Furthermore, Coombs continues, "the issue is one of overall goals. Methods of assessment have indirect as well as direct effects upon educational settings ... and such side effects cannot be ignored."

Evaluation of both the course and the students range through a continuum from objective to subjective, quantitative to qualitative, behavioural and humanistic. While objective criteria may call for papers and other evidence of learning, subjective evaluation is largely accomplished by student-referencing and self-evaluation of their accomplishments towards their own goals. Since evaluation is a guide to action, it is ongoing throughout the course and provides the feedback required to adapt the class sessions towards the attainment of identified goals.

In outlining some of the humanistic objectives for education Coombs stressed that problem-solving behaviour, creativity, values development and the discovery of personal meaning are all involved, and that accountability is concerned with the information aspects of learning. Humanistic objectives are "directed to the qualities that make us human – internal states like feelings, attitudes, beliefs, understandings".

Many of us, at least initially, may not experience the same success that Lesley has achieved in conducting her first course with adults. Yet by consciously improving our knowledge, skills and insights into how adults learn and helping to facilitate that process, we will begin to share Lesley's enthusiasm for teaching adults.

REFERENCES AND SUGGESTED READING

Argyris, C. and Schon, D. (1975) *Theory Into Practice: Professional Effectiveness.* San Francisco: Jossey-Bass.

Botwinick, J. (1973) *Cognitive Processes in Maturity and Old Age.* New York: Springer Publishing Company.

Brundage, D.H. and MacKeracher, D. (1980) *Adult Learning Principles and Their Application to Program Planning.* Toronto: OISE Press.

Coombs, A.W. (1975) "Sensitivity education: Problems and promises." In D. Read and S. Simon, (Eds.) *Humanistic Education Sourcebook.* Englewood Cliffs: Prentice Hall.

Fullan, M. (1982) *The Meaning of Educational Change.* Toronto: OISE Press.

Cross, K.P. (1981) *Adults as Learners.* San Francisco: Jossey-Bass.

Kidd, J.R. (1973) *How Adults Learn* (Revised). New York: Association Press.

Johnson, D. and Johnson, F. (1975) *Joining Together: Group Theory and Group Skills.* Toronto: Prentice-Hall.

Joyce, D. and Weil, M. (1972) *Models of Teaching.* Toronto: Prentice Hall.

Knowles, M. (1980) *The Modern Practice of Adult Education.* Chicago: Follett Publishing Co.

Knowles, M. (1984) *The Adult Educator: A Neglected Species* (3rd edition). Huston: Gulf Publishing Co.

McClusky, H.Y. (1970) "An approach of a differential psychology of the adult potential." In S.M. Grabowski (Ed.) *Adult Learning and Instruction.* Syracuse, N.Y.: ERIC Clearinghouse on Adult Education.

Chapter 8

Culture in the Classroom

Thelma Barer-Stein

Practitioner's Summary

Emphasizing that the topic of "culture in the classroom" is always present, the author explores meanings and relevance of both concepts of 'culture' and 'ethnicity' especially as they have significance for the learning situation. She notes that a sensitive awareness of cultural differences should be implicitly embedded within each course of study, program and attitude, and shared alike by teacher and student. That is to say that the tacit presence of cultural differences should be positively used as an enrichment to studies and to relationships.

The concept of culture itself may be defined in varying ways but is taken here as "the sum total of all aspects of the life patterns of daily living." While the concept of ethnicity is taken to mean the differentiation of a minority cultural group, the author points out that this could mean that every person may be considered as an 'ethnic' depending on their geographic location. When their cultural group is dominant, they are no longer 'ethnic'! The successful integration of peoples from differing cultural backgrounds develops most successfully when overt efforts are made in the host society to foster an ambience of security and comfort while encouraging an increasingly Canadian identity. This is supported by developing familiarity with new patterns of daily living. This can be important learning for adults, when the differences within the classroom can be seen as resources for possibilities, views, and ideas.

Implications for the part-time teacher of adults includes being aware that "the teacher is always teaching more than the content", and it is from this notion that the author draws several concrete suggestions:

1. offering students a choice in addressing you and doing the same for them,
2. learning to pronounce student's names;
3. being sensitive to current political situations;

4. being alert to cultural and racial slurs;
5. encouraging individual questions and contributions relating to cultural background and concerns;
6. being aware of differing language abilities;
7. being critical of class resource materials and persons;
8. being alert to the differing structure of the daily life of others;
9. permitting flexibility in the curriculum for the adult learner's needs, while enlightening him or her about mainstream Canadian ways;
10. replacing mere tolerance with serious and continuous efforts to understand cultural diversity.

Any factor that can help a teacher to be more effective is ultimately of value and worthy of effort. Especially for the part-time instructor of adults, attention to the matters listed above require no costly outlay, but can facilitate comfort and lessen the learners' anxiety. Learning is always enhanced when the learner feels at ease. Rather than considering cultural diversity a liability in the classroom, the adult educator needs to view such differences as the important resources for learning and interaction that they really represent.

Remember too that the instructor has a cultural heritage which will influence interaction with others. An understanding of one's own cultural heritage and assumptions is an imperative priority.

Chapter 8
Culture in the Classroom
Thelma Barer-Stein

Culture in the classroom is not a topic that you have the privilege of adding or deleting. Culture is always present in any human interaction.

Culture is what forms an integral part of each person's identity and behaviour. It exists and expresses itself whether or not we are overtly aware of it. Cultural differences are expressed in languages, appearances, beliefs, perceptions, lifestyles, attitudes and values. These find expression in behaviour.

It is in the interests of effective teaching, that each educator of adults has some understanding of the implications of culture on themselves as well as others, and how these may be applied to enhance communication and learning.

Implications of cultural understanding within a learning situation have been studied and discussed under many titles and labels. Here are a few:

- Ethnic Pluralism
- Immigrant Studies
- Development Education
- Multicultural Education
- Intercultural Education
- International or Comparative Studies

In order to appreciate and promote such human awareness and concern on a local or global basis, there must be knowledge and understanding first of one's own culture and ethnicity. Such study is neither esoteric nor egocentric. Such studies about others yield important information about ways of doing things in cultural contexts that differ from our own but which may have valuable implications for us. At other times, studies of processes of problem-solving and decision-making (for example) in other lands are helpful in business and marketing on both a local and international level. Just as any intercultural contact, whether on an individual, diplomatic, military or commercial level, benefits from awareness of personal behavioural characteristics, so too do the contacts between teacher and student.

In Canada, as in many other areas, diversity is a demographic reality. Canada is home to more than 100 differing ethno-cultural groups and it is this reality that motivated official government policy of Multiculturalism in 1971 to give explicit recognition of this fact. Since that time many programs have been developed and much effort has been expended to both encourage and promote multicultural awareness, and not without some criticism. Do such 'multicultural programs' encourage the status quo of minority groups and help to maintain the elitism of dominant groups? Instead of heritage programs and cultural celebrations, should we not be promoting 'Canadianism'? How, if at all, can teachers be educated for this 'multicultural reality' and would it matter if they weren't?

There are many questions and many questioners, and the debate will continue to rage even while the increasing presence of differing cultural heritages continues to express itself in differing ways. But if we accept that cultural heritage is an indelible part of each person's identity, then it follows that it must also be an advantage for the teacher of adults to find out more about culture.

> *This chapter will attempt to explore briefly some of the concepts of culture and what is meant by 'ethnicity'. Of special interest to teachers will be an overview of some approaches to dealing with culture that have been used with varying success in Canadian education.*

And finally, with some sensitivity to the subtlety of the issues involved, some suggestions for the teacher to enhance mutual learning that takes place in any learning situation.

Cultural awareness can make an important contribution to the learning in your classroom. Often when a teacher ignores the tacit responsibility of promoting an atmosphere of openness and respect with regard to cultural diversity, the unfortunate corollary may induce negative stereotypes, narrowing viewpoints and racial slurs, regardless of the subject-matter of the course.

> *This is to underline that teachers are always teaching both by the content of their work and also by the process of the teaching itself. This includes explicit words and terms as well as the whole realm of non-verbal communication in gestures, facial expressions, body postures and even seating arrangements.*

Therefore, the inter-relationships as well as the interplay between verbal and non-verbal communicative processes all contribute to the totality of what is happening in any learning situation, be it a classroom, laboratory, workshop, or a gathering under a tree. Mutual understanding based on knowledge and respect will enhance any such learning situation and must be the goal of any teacher.

What Is Culture?

Without at least a cursory examination of some concepts of culture as viewed by various scientists, it would be difficult to really comprehend the profound significance and implications of culture of each person's daily life. Just as Huxley said:

... the better you understand the significance of any question, the more difficult it becomes to answer it ...

so too, we will see that the more we uncover varying concepts of culture, the greater our difficulty to explain it simply.

Since anthropology is the study of humans, it's not surprising that most definitions come from this field of study. I have selected a few of these to present here to show that there are some commonalities even within the diversity.

John Walsh (1973) has stressed the importance of a world view and appreciation of cultures with his emphasis on the need for Intercultural Studies. He offers a succinct definition:

One's own culture is that life pattern within which one feels secure.

He also speaks of dynamism, evinced by the continuous changes represented by the traditionalists of any culture who seek to maintain the status quo and the progressives who strive for change. Walsh maintains that the people of a culture share:

- history and language
- theological or religious outlook
- common value system
- common political or juridicial system
- common educational system or/and literature
- similarities in physiological appearance

As early as 1944, Clyde Kluckhohn defined culture simply as "the total way of life of a people", but also included in his definition that this affects the individual's life and is perpetuated "so long as it meets the needs of the individual for orderly way of life and the satisfaction of biological needs." (Zborowski, 1962) In later writings Kluckhohn (1962) adds to his definition the whole realm of implicit and explicit behavioural patterns as well as ideas and artifacts integral to a particular cultural group.

Not satisfied with these, M.F. Ashley Montagu (1968) adds yet another vital characteristic of culture:

Man alone among the animated forms of nature...has moved into an adaptive zone that is entirely a learned one. *This is the zone of culture, the man-made, the learned part of the environment. (emphasis is mine)*

It was Alfred Kroeber, the first student of the famed American anthropologist Boas, who said that "the most significant accomplishment of anthropology in the first half of the 20th century has been the extension and clarification of the concept of culture". (cited in Kluckhohn, 1962)

Summarizing the main aspects of culture, we may arrive at a statement like this:

> *Culture seems to represent the total of all aspects of the patterns of daily life that are learned by an individual and that determinedly affects that person's behaviour, provides a sense of order, security and identity, and yet paradoxically is in a state of continuous change.*

Learning Culture

How does a person learn culture? When does this learning begin, and does it have an end point? Does an individual have any choice in this learning? Just how is behaviour affected? How is it possible for learned life patterns to offer one both security and identity and at the same time be in flux? Are there other reasons for retaining cultural membership? And is this stated culture of a societal group the only type of culture existing?

Cultural learning begins early

The differences so evident in cultural groups becomes even more apparent when we realize that learning begins (at least) in infancy. Even the briefest considerations of differing birthing beliefs and practices, child-rearing, parental responsibilities for example by a farming community in northern Quebec, a tribal group in Africa, and an aristocratic family in England are sufficient to bring to mind the disparity in values. Yet each family may believe that what they are doing for that child is "the best way'. Learning, whether directed by inner needs or outer forces of the society begins early and likely ends only with death. The flexibility of learning choices at any given period of one's development may well depend upon the mores of the total cultural group.

> *The most significant learnings, culturally speaking, may well be those accumulated through observation of others and through rote imitation and memorization. These are usually accumulated with scarcely conscious awareness.*

Consider for just a moment the huge package of behavioural responses, attitudes, communicative skills and so on that the small child brings to the first day of class in a school. Throughout the lifelong process of learning, approval of parents and family and later the approval of peers, teachers, fellow workers and managers as well as the cultural community as a whole, each play their part in shaping the daily life pattern for that person.

Culture is identity with rituals and traditions

Rituals and traditions are deeply embedded in cultural life patterns. Their routine practice and repetition provide security and reinforce the identity of each member. Yet choice and change do occur. If a choice of change enhances the life patterns and thereby the group survival, then it will be accepted. If suggested changes threaten the group's cohesion or survival, then the changes will be discarded by formal or informal consensus. Or the individual or group promoting change may be ostracized.

There are many reasons why an individual remains identified with a particular cultural group. These reasons may be voluntary or involuntary. Security also provides a sense of belonging and a sense of comfort with that which is familiar. Ways of doing things that can be done without conscious deliberation save a lot of time and energy. The well-worn rituals of daily life and the traditional routines in varying situations are all but taken for granted within one's own cultural setting and group. The merest gesture, the slightest intonation of speech, each are well-understood. Within such mutually understood rituals and traditions, it is not uncommon that a familial sense of care and concern as well as support, make group cohesion a daily advantage despite pressures for change. This may help to explain why cultural changes occur slowly.

Cultural Identity or Many Cultural Identities?

In the western world we take pride in the concept of individuality, yet without cultural identity, the individual would not get far. A great deal of what we claim as personal identity is actually composed of the myriad of involuntary attachments to customs, values, manners, beliefs and attitudes rooted in cultural soil and learned before we were aware that we were learning anything. But if personal identity is so closely linked to one's cultural identification, then how may we account for individual differentiation within each cultural group?

To shed light on this question, we must again examine our meaning of culture. Thus far, I have really only given consideration to the notion of culture in terms of familial and communal groups. What of other human groupings, not based on family? Other groups include corporations, institutions, colleges, schools, professions, occupations, socio-economic status groupings, age groupings, even male and female divisions of humanity. Different though they may be in direction and purpose, they retain identifiable characteristics and even rituals and traditions, that profoundly affect the daily life patterns of those individuals that are a part of them.

The complexity of culture increases on realizing that it is possible for one person to be a part of several 'cultural' groups at the same time.

For example, if we can separate out certain patterns as being intrinsic signifiers of particular cultures, then it's not difficult to see that an individual can at once be for example, Italian, Canadian, a member of the profession of medical practitioners within a specialization of psychiatry, and at the same time be a member of an upper-class socio-economic group as well as being elderly and female. It is as though each of these cultural memberships add extra layers to the individual's identity. Most importantly each of these layers was learned. Further, each addition heightens the uniqueness of that individual identity.

Cultural movement or adaptation

Wilma Longstreet (1978) writes at length of the problems that exist for example, between the culture of the home and the culture of the school.

> *When we speak of 'cultural adaptation' we may really be speaking of the awareness of a differing cultural setting that requires us to quickly learn those daily patterns (or accommodate to them in some acceptable way) that will grant us security in the new environment.*

Such adjustment or adaptation is crucial and although we are not usually aware of doing this, it is a process we assimilated early on.

Although Longstreet's work deals with children and adolescents, there are many factors which apply equally to adults and which profoundly affect ability to learn, learning styles, as well as attitudes to the learning itself. Adult's cultural patterns become more firmly fixed over time, but some important differences between children and adults in the adaptation from the home culture to the school culture (for example) rest mainly in the adult's greater degree of life experience in assuming new roles for differing situations, and in greater opportunities to exercise logic and reasoning to select from available choices in any situation. The adult may also have more control and/or power.

> *Adult learners have usually been able to exert some choice as to whether and what they will learn. Children more often may have learning imposed upon them.*

Culture shock

Movement from one cultural group to another whether permanent or temporary provides a shudder of shock to one's identity and sense of belonging. This seems true whether one considers movement from one country to another (as in immigration) or simply visiting another family or school. In some historic instances culture itself has been imposed upon others as in the historic Turkish occupation of Greece, the temporary disappearance of Poland from the map of Europe, and the Russification of the Ukraine. Yet while cultures may also be accepted voluntarily through learning (as in some intermarriages) ironically, it is often the forceful imposition of one culture upon another that does more to preserve the original culture, than does the peaceful coexistence of differing cultures. This phenomenon will be pursued in the next section. (See also Barer-Stein, 1988.)

What Is Meant By Ethnicity?

Just as the term culture conjures up varying interpretations, so too does the notion of ethnicity. Frequently one hears of the term with a distinct minority connotation to distinguish smaller cultural groups within a dominant one. At other times this term may connote reference to quaintness as in folk traditions of dance, song or foods. Within each of these usages, ethnic often carries a note of condescension by the speaker. This deserves closer scrutiny, particularly as we become aware of the many cultural groups in Canada's own multicultural society.

As in the varying concepts of culture, there are also many viewpoints of ethnicity. Two sources that view an ethnic group merely as a means of differentiation follow. Canadian sociologists Crysdale and Beattie create this definition:

> *Ethnic Group: Persons who share a common descent, a sense of collective identity and usually a common cultural heritage ... language and religion. The term is often incorrectly applied to only minority national groups but it can be used to refer to dominant groups such as the English or Scots. (Crysdale & Beattie, 1973) (emphasis is mine)*

The International Encyclopedia of the Social Sciences points out that ethnic group represents a "category of the larger population whose culture is usually different from its own".

> *But if one removes the sense of dominance from the definition, it becomes clear that the group characteristics are the same.*

Or put in another way, in the country of China the Han Chinese are the dominant cultural group and therefore within China are not usually termed as ethnics. Yet the Han Chinese living in other lands, whether first or fifth generation may according to some definition be called ethnics.

> *Therefore, any cultural group may at some time be considered to be ethnic in the minority sense of depending on their geographic location.*

Since any cultural group may at some time or place be considered to be ethnic, let us for the purpose of discussion proceed with the definition presented by Crysdale and Beattie (shared by many others) and assume that this is so. That is to say then, *that each person is an ethnic.* For those to whom no pejorative connation lies embedded within this term, there may be no affront. But for those to whom this concept implies "quaintness", "primitiveness" or "folk-customs", the reaction may be one of disbelief.

Pejoratives and disbelief aside, consideration of the meaning of ethnicity is important because of its widespread use in the western world (Isajiw, N.D.). Ethnicity conjures many questions. Some individuals and some groups do not accept that they are ethnic! How does one get to be ethnic? What is understood by the term ethnocentric? How can we gain some understanding of the interrelationships of ethnic groups that is sometimes referred to as assimilation, alienation, or conversely as acculturation and accommodation? Finally, if the notion of ethnicity is so troublesome, why does it endure, and why do people retain their ethnic identity?

It is difficult to separate out the qualities of ethnicity that actually differentiate from culture. There seems to be more uniqueness implied in a hyphenated Canadian derivation (such as Dutch-Canadian) than mere 'Canadian'.

> *Can it be that retention of ethnic (minority) identity is part of the personal need for identity and belonging, and in part a reason for the endurance of ethnicity? For this reason I offer the notion that ethnicity may also be understood as one's own personal slice of culture.*

Ethnocentrism is more widely spoken of than is 'cultural centrism'. Yet they mean essentially the same: the sense of superiority when a group feels that their way is the only way, superior to others and that therefore they have little or nothing to learn from others. As Fersh (1974) says:

> *The elders teach that the ways in which we do things are the natural ways, the proper ways, the moral ways. In other places, they are "barbarians" and "foreigners" and follow a strange way of life. Ours is the culture, and theirs is a culture.*

While this attitude may contribute to the survival and cohesion of the group, it can unfortunately lead to xenophobic tendencies where all who differ are denounced and hated for those differences. Listen carefully to news broadcasts of other areas of the world where populations are described variously as congested, trouble spots, underdeveloped and overpopulated, seething and so on. Is any area of Canada ever described in this way? Scan a report of a multicultural festival and note the terms of description such as colourful, folkways, quaint, different. Of course one group seldom considers its own areas as troublesome, or its traditions as quaint. But it is often those characteristics that may have enabled varying groups to survive and it is even possible that some inventions, ideas, and lifestyles could be adapted and prove helpful elsewhere.

Ethnocentrism taken to extreme may completely isolate the group from external contact and influence of both people and ideas. Such deliberate isolation may hold the seeds of racism and the sprouts of prejudice, discrimination and stereotyping. What is not known may be wrongly conjured.

Fortunately reality is like a continuum where ethnic groups varyingly open and close to others. Sometimes there may be cultural imposition, albeit with good intention. Such was the case of the many missionary groups many of whom truly believed that they had a better way. They used education, medicine and even food supplies to entice others to their 'better way'. The western world has 'shared' technology and aspects of materialism with parts of the world that neither needed it nor benefited from it. Only recently has there been a global reversal of such missionizing trends with more sensitive consideration of existing modes, conditions and even traditions of cooperative education, medicine, business and other fields. On a local level, deeper understanding of the cultures of others has provided people with fresh insights into their own backgrounds (for example Haley, 1976). The realization that most human values such as pride and shame, accomplishment and failure and the drive to survive in a world of peace - are universal, is making inroads past crusty barriers of ethno and cultural centricity.

Assimilation vs integration

This same sense of cultural superiority (over the ethnics) may have spawned the many stages in Canada's own history of attitudes towards immigrants. (Strange that both the English and the French as majority groups should so readily lose sight of their own positions at some point in history - as immigrants.) The early 1900s saw the period of assimilation where the WASP (White, Anglo-Saxon and Protestant) image was strongly and overtly presented in all forms of the media, and especially throughout the educational system with the express intent of producing homogeneous Canadians. Influx of more immigrants led to the popularity of the hyphenated Canadian, denoting pride of both past and present as in 'German-Canadian', 'Japanese-Canadian', etc. After World War II 'race' became a dirty word and 'assimilation' was too uncomfortable after the world had witnessed their dire meanings and expression by the Nazis.

> *Kovacs and Cropley (1972) describe assimilation as the process of groups becoming more similar to each other, in other words, as a diminishing of ethnic differentiation. Their description is one that incorporates varying degrees of adaptation.*

That is to say that assimilation is not an either-or, but a process that is individualized both in type and degree. For example in the work world many people readily adapt as far as clothing, routines, even jargon are concerned, yet maintain their ethnic language, foods, clothing and even manners upon returning home. Kovacs and Cropley point out that the opposite of assimilation is 'alienation' and although this is usually considered a negative term (one of loneliness, anxiety and estrangement), it may actually be that the assimilation of one factor or area of daily life may necessitate the alienation of another. It seems that one must leave something in order to add something else. Finally in their view, assimilation and alienation may depend on viewpoint. For example, the development process of the teenager may well be viewed by the parents as rebellious alienation from them, while the adolescent may see it as a movement toward independence and assimilating with peers.

> ***Similarly, the process of becoming more deeply identified with a cultural group could be seen as alienation from a former group.***

E.K. Francis (1976) considers the use of 'integrated' which seems to suggest a minimization of the problems of assimilation by 'better fit'.

> ***Francis notes that "ethnics may be said to have been integrated to the extent that they function properly within the social order of the host society." On the other hand, ethnics may consider themselves sufficiently integrated or assimilated when they feel secure or comfortable. (Barer-Stein, 1978)***

Culture or ethnic identity?

Now with some understanding of ethnicity, it seems to be clearer that whether one uses the term 'culture' or 'ethnic' to denote a particular societal group, *the identity accepted by the individual seems to be most important.* Movement between cultural groups, in the form of 'assimilation' seems to be a matter of degree rather than existence or non-existence. But this seems to open wider the question of ethnic endurance.

Despite pejorative connotations held by some people, many reasons could be advanced for the persistence of voluntary and involuntary ethnic identification. Such identification may occur not on the part of the individual or group so identified, but rather, from external sources. By this I mean the calling or labelling of someone or some group as belonging to a minority cultural group when they, themselves long ago considered themselves to be Canadian.

Persistent identification is often found where the group members are committed to varying but profound belief in the group. For example while Jews may speak many languages, bear physiological appearances similar to almost any world group, accept and adapt to varying political systems, and even vary in their religious beliefs from atheism to fundamentalist orthodoxy, all may claim to be Jews. And this even in the face of repeated historical discrimination, persecution and attempts at genocide. Books have been written in attempts at explanation.

Ethnicity has not only persisted, but for many groups there has been evidence of historical revivals and survivals, most recently in the "new ethnicity" (Novack, 1974). Isajiw (1977) offers some explanation. He pointed out that ethnic groups can be identified in two ways:

1. *as a group of people who share a distinct culture*
2. *people who identify themselves and/or are identified by others as belonging to the same group.*

That is to say some may actually share the culture while others may only share the feelings of identity.

Ethnicity and anonymity

Note how many times the term 'identity' has appeared in this chapter. Necessary in any personal search for identity are the qualities of pleasure and pride in that identification, a sense of belonging (acceptance), some link with past history, and some belief in self-worth. Isajiw discusses yet another factor. He feels that the fragmented and competitive society spawned by technology that marks the western world, has turned people towards ethnic identity because it is deeply associated with shared feelings related to human events and the seasons of nature. It seems that the greater the individual feelings of anonymity, the greater is the need for ethnic participation and identification.

From the preceding discussion, and even perhaps from personal experience, we can see that

> *Culture is an indelible facet of each person's identity and behaviour and since any form of education is linked with human communicating, it follows that cultural considerations must find an important place in that educational relationship.*

Approaches To Culture In Canadian Education

While it may seem obvious that recognition of multiculturalism may be the first step towards incorporating some global awareness into any program of studies, the means of doing this have varied. Some have been more successful than others. Ray (1980) has noted:

> *... all Canadian teachers share a responsibility in promoting an atmosphere of respect for cultural diversity, and teaching which ignores this function cannot be described as "good"...*

However, Ray is quick to note that there is also a lack of general agreement as to whether this is so. Vague expressions of dissension have been heard, and he lists some:

- *multiculturalism is a political issue,*
- *it is something for immigrants,*
- *emphasizing cultural diversity creates ghettos,*
- *multiculturalism will 'dilute' the curriculum.*

Cultural diversity in Canada is a demographic reality. Understanding of any reality, its shape and direction is urgent for human survival. Within Canada's policies and the resulting programs for multicultural understanding are many that are specifically directed to aid the immigrant newcomer in learning about his or her new home, job and language. But in the collaborative sharing of ideas and experiences, immigrant students, workers and professions are an enrichment to the entire society. With a policy of mutual encouragement and the participation of schools and communities in such learning activities, newcomers now feel more comfortable about participating in the general society rather than retreating to ghettos for security and comfort.

> *Such collaboration should never be in the stilted form of yet another course, but should be part of the sensitivity to cultural diversity that is projected through every program.*

1. Creating Cultural Uniformity

A brief review of some of the approaches and notions critically considered by T.R. Morrison (1980) in his historic review of teaching methodologies offers some insight. Up to the 1960s, these were all characterized by the goal of creating cultural uniformity. That is, the mission of all educational systems in Canada was to "absorb into itself those who differ from it", based on the old assimilationist theories. While this attitude has been officially dismissed, Morrison openly wonders how many teachers and programs across the country still favour (by their attitudes, programs and materials) the Anglo group?

2. Creating Cultural Appreciation

A condescending nod in the direction of the minority cultural groups after the 1960's brought a period in Canadian education of cultural appreciation. Indeed in Troper's (1976) view, it was really a period of confusion where "if educators related at all to the diversity of ethnic and cultural groups in Canadian society it was usually as a problem to be overcome rather than as a factor in Canadian society to be celebrated". Such appreciation seemed to include displays of foods, music and costumes as though cultural identity was an item that could be put on display and then dismissed. Morrison's belief was that such displays were only accepted passively and he questions the possible interpretation by audiences. The passivity of the presentations seem to have been reflected in the passivity of audiences.

3. Value Inculcation

The third approach to cultural education is described by Morrison as Value Inculcation. Here the general goal is to point out the role of values in developing cultural sensitivities. Hopefully, the learning of values would lead to "resocialization and value substitution" which is a euphemistic way to express that the open comparison of various cultural value systems would undoubtedly find Anglo values superior. But Morrison and others have noted that value systems are context-bound, depend upon interpretation, and may not be equally understood by adults and children. Finally, great responsibility rests with the person (teacher, parent etc.) defining, transmitting and interpreting such values, as well as with the recipient.

Realizing the pitfalls of the previous general teaching approach across Canada, the next approach was one of attempting a universal set of values and moral principles. But soon it became apparent that value conflicts exist not only between but also within individuals and societies. For example Canadians may as a whole view subjugation of women as a negative and yet it may be an integral aspect of some cultural traditions, thus leading to tensions and conflict.

Towards A Transcultural Reality

Morrison argues that all persons have both an individual as well as a collective identity "that is both rooted in the past and also moving toward different futures". He presses for "transcultural awareness" wherein a person's cultural commitments have transcended his or her own towards that of a universal identity.

> *What is unusual about the transcultural person is an abiding commitment to the essential similarities between people everywhere, while paradoxically maintaining an equally strong commitment to his or her own differences.*

The teacher sensitive to the cultural diversity of the learners within the classroom, must not only be aware of individual culture but also have knowledge and understanding of their similarities and differences. This implies an understanding of what this awareness should consist of, and how one may feel assured that sufficient awareness is being expressed. But how to evaluate something so elusive? So many approaches have been tried and found wanting, yet it seems that every effort should be made towards a transcultural reality.

An increasingly common view of the practical meaning of transcultural reality, recently expressed by Dixon (1992) suggests that appreciation of subcultures (or ethnic groups) should never take precedence either in policy or in action, over the national culture.

In other words, pride in one's own cultural group should always be seen in relationship to the success of the greater Canadian culture, and, I would add, its place in global society.

Implications For The Culture-Sensitive Teacher

Accepting the importance of cultural sensitivity may well prove to be the first important step to becoming transcultural. Since most of our own individual cultural knowledge is subconscious, a willful effort to take note of one's own cultural nuances may be the initiation to deeper personal knowledge as well as increased cultural respect generally. For example, the reader may have chosen to peruse this chapter just out of curiosity, but having read this far will already have a greater appreciation of ethnicity and culture than may have existed previously.

If nothing else at this point, the part-time teacher of adults will be aware that culture does have an impact on one's identity, behaviour, values and thus upon learning.

Regardless of the topic of the education, whether updating skills or extending cognitive knowledge, *the teacher is always teaching more than the content*, and the learners are not only learning, they are also inter-relating socially.

As educators of adults, we are continually making unobtrusive selections not only in the precise content of the courses being presented, in their pace and timing, but also in the type of resource persons and materials we are selecting. Even the timing of deadlines for projects and presentations which may be in conflict with special occasions need to be culturally considered. We express implicit or explicit implications politically, socially and economically in our own dress, manners of addressing and greeting and the handling of small unpredictable incidents within the learning situation. Have we always been aware of these?

Here are some concrete ways that the transcultural teacher can enhance ambience and thus contribute markedly to the comfort and learning of the adults, and incidentally gain credibility and personal respect. You will note that the following list includes cultural as well as sub-cultural differences. Overall, it seems that erring on the side of formality (at least) is better than informality which may be taken negatively.

1. Be aware that many peoples of the world are accustomed to offering and demonstrating great respect for teachers. Offerthem a choice in addressing you by first name or surname; accept each with aplomb. Do the same for them.
2. Make a point to learn and to pronounce the student's names correctly and as formally or informally as they indicate. They have pride in their names and identity even as you do. Recognize and respect this. Your effort will be appreciated.
3. Be sensitive to current political situations not only in the obvious arena of discussions, but also in groupings and seating arrangements and take care not to favour one culture over another.
4. Be alert to cultural slurs. Be open to incorporating several views of a discussion topic by making use of the differing views and backgrounds within the classroom to give a personal slant. Take the time for clarification and examples when there seeems to be evidence of prejudice, discrimination, stereotyping or just a misunderstanding.
5. Encourage individual questions and contributions relating to cultural background. For example, after an explanation of a skill or metaphor, encourage the offering of differing skills and differing metaphors from other cultural contexts.
6. Be aware of differing language abilities in English and take care to speak loud enough as well as distinctly. Use examples whenever possible and encourage

feedback to determine when further repetition or a better example may be required. Often simply speaking more slowly can be of great help.

7. Be critical of class resource materials and persons:
   - Do they represent varied points of view?
   - Do they appeal to varied senses and feelings?
   - Do they avoid offending minority groups?
   - Accuracy? Well-qualified? Current?
   - Are they stimulating and appropriate to the learner's development level?
8. Be alert to a different structuring of daily life. For example, in manners of greeting, inviting, praising and criticizing. "Yes" does not always mean that things are being understood; it may simply signify politeness. An invitation however casually expressed may be understood seriously. Laughter may indicate embarrassment rather than humour. There may be initial misunderstanding of punctuality and deadlines. It may be important not to insist on male-female mixed groups for projects or discussions: allow people to form their own groups, find their own seating. Respect those involved in differing holidays, eating restrictions, wearing unusual apparel or even stepping aside to perform prayers during class time.
9. Flexibility in the curriculum is important for all learners but especially for adults. Be alert to pick up personal concerns and current events or issues which can be related to literature, language or skills or whatever the content may be. Including the needs and experiences of the adult learners can be one of the most exciting aspects of an adult class. The teacher as the facilitator, is in a position to point out the similarities and differences in any situation and in this way increase the involvement of the people from differing cultures.
10. Replace mere tolerance with serious and continued efforts to understand and accept the reality of differing values and perceptions.

Why Should Culture Be An Issue For The Part-Time Teacher of Adults?

The need to increase awareness and understanding of a range of cultural differences is of importance in this global village of humans, if only for survival. But since the aim of most people transcends mere survival, then a mutuality of sincere caring is of crucial importance, but especially for teachers at any level.

> *Any factor that can help a teacher to teach more effectively is ultimately of value and worthy of sincere effort.*

Unrelenting efforts to develop awareness of ethno-cultural differences will help to expose previously overlooked areas of misunderstanding, intolerance, and disrespect both of teacher and student.

It is well-known that the atmosphere of a classroom can enhance or decrease the degree of learning. Cultural awareness and sensitivity and the development of a transcultural sense will help to make people more comfortable with one another, increasing both trust and respect. Even those who appear or speak in a way differing from the majority will soon come to see that it is their opinions, ideas and knowledge that are important. Even as they are aware of being regarded as individuals, so they will come to regard others similarly.

These factors are important whether the learners are children or adults. An atmosphere of understanding and respect (but not necessarily agreement) is an ideal worth striving towards. Especially important for the adult learner is to be recognized as having responsibilities, experiences and an identity of value and that these are valued through the teacher's encouragement to be active contributors within the learning situation.

The part-time teacher of adults is often teaching part-time adult learners, and the efficient use of available time is important. Feeling uncomfortable means time and energy removed from learning. Many of the previous list of implications and suggestions add not only to comfort, but also to the relevancy of the learning. Shared responsibility in contributing to the curriculum helps to make the learning a collaborative effort, and teachers and students become peers.

Making use of cultural identity as a resource material in itself can be accomplished readily in an adult group, and accepting differing behaviours, and sources can enhance literally any content. Classroom cultural differences are rarely considered as a viable and tangible resource, but they are there.

Culture As A Fundamental Ground Of Understanding

This chapter has explored something of the meaning and relevance of culture and ethnicity for the teacher of adults. This was seen as the necessary fundamental ground of understanding. Since cultural differences are indelibly a part of each individual, it follows that understanding and making positive use of this phenomenon will increase individual respect and responsivness and enhance the learning atmosphere.

> *The cultural diversity existing in any learning situation, but especially in a classroom of adults must be seen and utilized as the rich source of learning that it really is.*

REFERENCES

Barer-Stein, T. (1988)"Experiencing the unfamiliar: Culture adaptation and culture shock in aspects of a process of learning." *Canadian Ethnic Studies Association Journal.* Vol. 22, No.2.

Barer-Stein, T. (1978) "What is a Canadian?" (unpublished study and report of immigrant women in Canada) Toronto: Department of Adult Education, OISE.

Crysdale, S. and Beattie, C. (1973) *Sociology Canada.* Toronto: Butterworth and Co. (Canada Ltd.).

Dixon, D. (1992) *Future Schools: A Primer for Evolutionaries.* Toronto: ECW Press.

Fersh, S. (1974) *Learning About Peoples and Cultures.* Evanston: McDougal Littell & Co.

Francis, E.K. (1971) *Assimilation in Interethnic Relations (An essay in Sociological Theory).* New York: Elsevier Scientific Pub. Co..

Haley, A. (1976) *Roots.* New York: Doubleday.

Isajiw, W.W. (n.d.) *Definitions of Ethnicity.* Toronto: The Multicultural History Society of Ontario.

Isajiw, W.W. (1977) "Olga in Wonderland: Ethnicity in Technological Society" *Canadian Ethnic Studies Bulletin of Research.* Vol. 9 No. 1.

Kluckhohn, C. (1962) *Culture and Behavior.* New York: The Free Press.

Kovacs, M.L. and Cropley, A.J. (1972) Assimilation and Alienation in Ethnic Groups. *Canadian Ethnic Studies Bulletin of Research.* University of Calgary. Vol. 5, No. 1-2.

Longstreet, W. (1978) *Aspects of Ethnicity: Undertstanding Differences in Pluralistic Classrooms.* New York: Teacher's College Press.

Montagu, M.F.A. (1968) *Culture: Man's Adaptive Dimension.* New York: Oxford University Press.

Morrison, T.R. (1980) "Transcending Culture: Culture Selection and Multicultural Education" In K. McLeod (Ed.) *Intercultural Education and Community Development.* Toronto: Guidance Centre, Faculty of Education, University of Toronto.

Novak, M. (1974) "The New Ethnicity:, *The Center Magazine.* July/August.

Ray, D. (1980) "Multiculturalism in Teacher Education" In K. McLeod (Ed.) *Intercultural Education and Community Development.* Toronto: Guidance Centre, Faculty of Education, University of Toronto.

Troper, H. (1976) Multiculturalism in the Classroom: Pitfalls and Options. *History and Social Science Teacher.* Vol. 12.

Walsh, J.E.(1973) *Intercultural Education in the Community of Man.* Honolulu: University Press of Hawaii.

Zborowski, M. (1962) *People in Pain.* San Francisco: Jossey-Bass.

SUGGESTED READING

Banks, J.A. and Lynch, J. (1986) *Multicultural Education in Western Societies.* U.K.: Holt Rhinehart & Winston.

Barer-Stein, T. (1986)"Why can't they just all be Canadians?" *Multicultural Health Coalition Bulletin.* Vol.2, No. 4.

Barer-Stein, T. (1987) "The home economist as cultural educator. *Canadian Home Economics Journal,* Vol. 37, No. 1.

Barer-Stein, T. (1987) "Experiencing the Unfamiliar: Cultural Adaptation and Culture Shock as Aspects of Learning". Halifax: *Proceedings, Canadian Ethnic Studies Association Conference,* Halifax.

Barer-Stein, T. (1989) "Experiencing the Unfamiliar - Matrix for Learning". In B. Cassara (Ed.) *Adult Education in Multicultural America.* London: Routledge.

Cryderman, B.K. and O'Toole, C.N. (1986) *Police, Race and Ethnicity.* Toronto: Butterworth's.

Hall, E.T. (1976) *Beyond Culture.* N.Y.: Anchor Press.

Hall, E.T. (1983) *The Dance of Life.* N.Y.: Anchor Press.

Harris, M. (1974) *Cows, Pigs, Wars and Witches: The Riddles of Culture.* N.Y.: Vintage Books.

Harris, P.R. and Moran, R.T. (1987) *Managing Cultural Differences* (2nd edition). Houston: Gulf Publishing Co.

Landes, R. (1965) *Culture in American Education.* New York: Wiley and Sons.

McLeod, K. (Ed.) (1984) *Multicultural Education: A Partnership.* Toronto: Canadian Council for Multicultural and Intercultural Education.

Samovar, R.A. and Porter, R.E. (1976) *Intercultural Communication: A Reader* (2nd edition). California: Wadsworth Publishing.

Vorst, J. and others (Eds) (1989) *Race, Class, Gender: Bonds and Barriers.* Toronto: Between the Lines.

Chapter 9
Planning for Learning: A Model For Creative Decision Making

Reg Herman

Practitioner's Summary

In claiming "creative decision making", Herman underlines the explorative, evolving process that is integral to adult education. Indeed, when one considers planning needs of the learner and the experiences each brings to a learning situation, it seems that repetition, boredom and lack of relevancy would have a difficult time existing. Each situation differs markedly because of the contributions of the differing adult learners, and their concerns. Such variations have impact especially in the area of planning programs.

Citing the classic model format for planning programs as a sequence of steps such as: assessing needs, setting learning objectives, choosing resources and means, implementing and finally evaluating, Herman points out that the most important component, that of evaluating, is frequently neglected or completely overlooked because it occurs at the end of the process when "they are too tired!"

He cites Malcolm Knowles' model which includes the mutual planning of both student and instructor to set the climate, devise mutual planning, diagnose needs together, set objectives and plan methods and resources and then follow implementation with evaluation for re-planning. And he quotes in detail Ginny Griffin's model as being one of continuous evolvement with the inclusion of three extra ideas: that of the presence of "choice points" throughout the process and drawing of awareness to the possibilities; the explicit expression of philosophies: the instructor's, the student's and the institution's. And finally, the ongoing challenge for the teacher/planner, as exemplification of a model to continue to learn and to change.

Herman's own model for "Creative Decision Making" begins with what he calls "front-ending" all of the process with a clear statement of values and how they relate to the goals. Secondly he joins evaluative processes to both goals and objectives and suggests that a means should be found to evaluate every aspect of the program continuously, no matter how briefly. And thirdly, he adds the importance of the planners' search for alternatives to each aspect in an imaginative explosion of ideas and possibilities.

He defines and distinguishes many aspects of this process and in particular notes that goals refer to the "broader statements of purpose" while objectives may be used to distinguish the "more precise aims to achieve those goals". Examples of these are presented together with helpful suggestions to handle each aspect of this process. Perhaps most importantly, Herman notes that "there is never a guarantee that it is going to be the right decision" - hence the pressing need for continuous and ongoing evaluation to spotlight errors as well as successes.

Chapter 9
Planning for Learning: A Model for Creative Decision Making
Reg Herman

There is no neutral education
-Paulo Freire

Back in the free-spending, 99% male administration of the late seventies, a bright but inexperienced university graduate applied for and won the job as Director of Continuing and Professional Education at a Community College. The president drove him to a large building that the college had just bought and renovated into classrooms, and said, "Fill that building," got back in his car and drove off.

Rotten planning? Yes and no. It's entrepreneurial style at its vaguest, but it places confidence in the resourcefulness and responsibility of people, and there's much to say for that. What it lacks is just about everything else, especially any sense of adult education as a social force. The college president's planning style misses a whole range of issues. It is very likely that he doesn't even know how to make decisions, but he has lots of company in that failing. The trouble is that such a lack of planning decisions leads to a limiting, a shrinking of the educational potential for creativity and social change.

> *Every planning experience and each job, including teaching, can be dealt with in three ways: one, shrink it; two, do it efficiently and well; or three, expand it.*

Today, the job-shrinking college president would hand to the neophyte Director a computer program that neither of them understood, but which was supposed to decide for them the various kinds of training that were to go on in those classooms.

But because we come from a different value system, as adult educators we enjoy real freedom to be creative decision-makers in our planning: to clarify our values on social issues, to expand our goals and experiment with methods of evaluation, to invent learning methods that meet the learners' needs and go beyond these, to encourage the learners to become 'masters of their own destiny'. This is what I mean by a model for creative decision making, but I think the best way to understand and assess my approach is to compare it with other models of planning in adult education: the classic model, Malcolm Knowles' and Ginny

Griffin's. On the way, there are four main issues that the decision-making model raises.

1. This may surprise you, but the most frustrating issue for me is: where do you start? and wherever you start, how do you deal with the challenge of a non-neutral educational stance?
2. How to come up front with clear and precise program goals?
3. When and how to get evaluation into the act without breaking your back in requirements of time and energy?
4. What is creativity and how do you apply creative problem solving and decision making to planning in adult education?

Models for Decision Making

The classic model

In education, planners promote a myth that there is a 5-step sequence that goes like this:

1. Conduct Needs Assessment
2. Set Learning Objectives
3. Choose Methods and Resources
4. Implement
5. Evaluate

Sometimes this model is drawn as a horizontal continuum, sometimes a circle, but in effect the sequence always ends with evaluation and my theory is that's why no one ever does it. By the time they get to the end, they're too tired!

> *Planning for learning is not a linear sequence. Typically, it's a back and forth flow of problem solving and decision making.*

It is not unusual for planners to choose their techniques before deciding what it is they are going to do. Frequently, the length of the course is decided first (five days, 36 hours, three evenings), and then decisions are made to fill the time. Perhaps it doesn't matter where you begin in the classic model, but I suggest that you don't start by filling time. The first course I ever planned began just there, we filled a week.

Coming from a business background however, I was brash enough to evaluate every session and the total course with pre- and post-tests. The results were a disaster. The participants learned nothing and intended to change nothing.

> *But I learned. I learned two things: One, never start by filling time; and two, evaluate everything. However simply, however briefly, evaluate everything you do in the program.*

I would never have known the mistakes if I had not been so determined to evaluate every session. And another thing: keep your results. Over the years, these evaluations will be your best measure of how you're improving as a planner and a facilitator.

A good example of a self-paced learning program was Mel Rowe's course design team at Bell Canada. Planning begins with a needs assessment in the form of a job study, and continues with a series of information searches to determine objectives and methods. They go back and forth, writing and rewriting their objectives and methods, but they change the classic sequence in only one case: they bring the planning of evaluation up one step, ahead of implementation. Makes sense, but I would bring it up one more step still and join evaluation to my objectives.

Programmed instruction (PI) and computer-assisted instruction (CAI) and other self-paced designs offer many advantages: the learner enters when ready, mistakes are private and so do not lead to loss of self-esteem, and most importantly they provide early and continuous feedback and built in success. These two factors encourage self-confidence and should be included in all adult learning designs. However, PI and CAI have many shortcomings too. The teacher-programmer controls everything except the speed of learning (and even controls that to some extent) and the learner is given virtually no responsibility, freedom or opportunity to learn how to learn. PI and CAI tend to represent the empty heads theory of pedagogical teaching design. They are excellent for the straightforward transfer of information.

Malcolm Knowles' model

To the classic model, Knowles (1975) contributed two important additions, and in so doing, he changed the focus from pedagogy to andragogy. He defines andragogy as the art and science of helping adults (or even better, maturing human beings) learn. He equates pedagogy with teacher-directed learning and contrasts it with andragogy, self-directed learning.

Knowles comes to the planning function with a value system that esteems the knowledge and skills that adults acquire through life experience.

> *So he defines the adult educator as a colleague and co-learner with his or her students, a facilitator who works with the students to help them identify their learning needs, set their own objectives, choose methods appropriate to their learning styles and the ways that they wish to evaluate their progress.*

One of his goals as a planner follows directly: planning how to involve the learners in the planning. This was Knowles' first addition to the classic model, and it led to the need for the second.

> *For most adults, to be involved in planning their own learning in a classroom situation is a radical change. They have been conditioned to accept the teacher as the authority who tells the students what to do and think.*

As a good problem-solver, Knowles took a step back and recognized that the very first thing to plan is a learning environment that will help the participants to change in the direction of increased responsibilities. The learning climate should be informal, supportive, conducive to develop mutual respect and trust. This is the way his model looks:

- Set the Climate
- Devise Mutual Planning
- Diagnose Needs
- Set Objectives
- Plan Methods and Resources
- Implement
- Evaluate for re-planning

Virginia Griffin's model

In the best adult education style and consistent with her own prescriptions, Griffin's approach is continuously evolving and therefore difficult to render in abridged form. Nevertheless, she clearly adds three more ideas. First of all, Griffin draws attention to the great fact of decision problems:

> *All down the line of the planning process there are choice points.*

and it is the responsibility of the adult educator as planner to be aware of the consequences of each choice.

Secondly, she brings the planner's and the institution's

> *educational philosophies up front where they belong in problem solving and decision making,*

and after the process she raps the planner on the head and charges her or him: Be aware of what you believe about education and learning, and behave in your work-life planning in ways consistent with those beliefs. Finally, she challenges the planner to continue to learn and change.

What A Program Planner Should Know And Be Able To Do

Griffin's model is complex, but well worth studying:

1. Be aware of concepts of program planning, be able to use them in thinking and talking about job activities.
2. Be aware of the "principles" of program planning, know what evidence there is to support each of them, and have an informed opinion about the validity of each.
3. Recognize that program planning is a process.
4. Recognize that program planning is a process with choice points.
5. Be aware of alternative processes within each of the following areas of program planning, know when each is appropriate, and how to carry out each when necessary:
   i. developing and judging the initial idea for a program;
   ii. identifying the educational philosophy of the planners and the learners;
   iii. choosing a planning strategy and organizing for planning;
   iv. assessing the needs of the community and the learners;
   v. determining objectives and the priorities among them;
   vi. designing teaching-learning interactions;
   vii. planning program supports (resource people, A-V materials, program interpretation, registration, counselling, budget, etc.);
   viii. implementing the teaching-learning interactions and the supporting activities;
   ix. evaluating;
   x. using the results of evaluation.
6. Know when and how to involve students and other relevant people in the various parts of planning.
7. Be aware of personal beliefs about education and learning, and behave in work-life planning activities consistent with those beliefs.
8. Be a continuous learner in the area of programming and evaluating.

Herman: A model for creative decision making

This model proposes three additional strategies for planning in adult education. First, here we are again with where do you start? I think it's clear that all of us operate from a value base. The trouble is that, like the college president, we don't make our values explicit, so they don't help us in our decision making. Furthermore, Paulo Freire has shown us that there is no neutral education and the adult educator-planner must deal with this responsibility. So, in this model

> *we front-end all problem solving and decision making with the clearest possible public statement of our personal, educational and social values, and link them to our planning goals.*

Second, this model seeks to turn planning outside in,

> *to bring the planning of evaluation in from the cold and join it to the goals and objectives.*

This way, we increase the chances that the planner will actually conduct evaluations and, as you will see, we will also improve the clarity of the goals and therefore the likelihood of congruence between values and goals and methods.

Third, it is not enough for the planner merely to be aware of alternatives. In this model, the planner actively searches for all the information about known alternatives and then goes beyond even that,

> *to invent further alternatives still, especially alternative goals, but also alternative methods.*

Before I describe how to apply these ideas in actual planning, it will help to take a moment to identify the elements of decision making.

Five propositions of decision making

To three basic propositions of decision making, I have added two more.

1. The decision maker must recognize that he or she has a choice; to perceive at least one alternative.
2. Not to decide is also a decision. Slipping back into routine and sterile methods is an example of the decision not to decide.
3. Decision making always entails a search for information. In dealing with a decision problem, the decision maker should know how to use all resources, but must determine how much time, money and energy to spend in the information search.
4. All problem solving and decision making must be front-ended by values clarification. In the case of an organization, this may be called a statement of philosophy or of mission and purpose.
5. At every step, the decisionmaker has the opportunity to be creative, to surface and generate more alternatives, and this is most essential in the identification of goals – expanding the job.

Gordon Miller (1978) summarizes it this way: "The planner must deal with the crucial elements of all decisions: values, goals, alternatives and outcomes."

Front-Ending Decision Making With Values

'Neutral' adult education

All educational planning, including the planning of leisure courses, is a political act. To put it simply, education that does not seek to change conditions reinforces the existing system. Rural areas show this most clearly when much of their commerce is parachuted in by urban corporations and the local schools and colleges train the people for the company. In this way, the colleges help to turn the residents into dependents on foreign controlled economies, hardly a neutral education! What alternatives are there? Well, some of our colleges, like St. Frances Xavier University, have found ways to train people to set up their own industries.

Creative burnout

Even if we grant the adult educator-planner that the planning of a course in astronomy, say, is nonpolitical, the lack of values is still self-defeating. Planning that is not front-ended by a defined value system is trivialized.

William Gordon, inventor of the creative problem-solving strategy called Synectics, found that after a time, his best problem solving teams dried up. He thought their creativity had burned out. I think he's wrong and that his teams were simply not willing or able to go on spending enormous creative energies to invent new bottle tops and other gadgets for industry.

Similarly, decision analyst Peter Moore of London University finds that managers in large organizations are not willing to spend the time to conduct rigorous planning using probability decision trees even on vital decision problems. Like the creative problem solvers, decision analysts do not raise questions about the values implicated in their clients' decision making. Unaided by a clear statement of philosophy or purpose, these managers lack any rationale even to think about expanding their jobs. I suspect that the phenomenon of teacher burnout would reveal a similar gap.

> *People are turned on by creative challenges, but they need to feel that their efforts are contributing to significant values.*

Faced with problem solving and decision making that are not front-ended with explicit values, the planner will either fail to spend the time necessary for good planning or will burn out.

A Value base for self-directed learning

There is no one right way of teaching, but there are many strong arguments for planning self-directed elements in adult education programs (Knowles, 1975; Tough, 1979; Griffin, 1982). There is also a value base to this planning decision.

One of the reasons that so many people don't plan harks back to Proposition One of decision making: they don't believe or perceive that they have an alternative. These people disenfranchise themselves from life's options. It follows that a first concern – the mission and purpose – of adult education is to help people gain greater decision-making power over their lives and destinies, and this includes increased commitment to and control over their communities and society. Just think for a moment about the reasons why your students come to your course, and how they hope to gain opportunities for growth by acquiring new skills and knowledge. So:

> *As adult educators we construct the educational step toward these goals by planning programs that help participants gain control over their own learning, by designing strategies and methods that give them increasing responsibility for their learning within the educational program you design.*

The following scale oversimplifies our alternatives but it's useful in comparing teaching approaches. I'd like to invite you to do two things: first, add to this continuum other teaching methods or program designs, for example, Socratic teaching, experiential learning, and so on. Second, place your own planning and/or teaching style on the scale.

For the second edition of the handbook, *The Design of Self-Directed Learning*, I conducted a survey of the ratings of self-directed learning courses and learning contracts by students of OISE's Department of Adult Education. One finding was that students who developed learning contracts experienced the greatest sense of control over their learning. I'd be very interested in your additions to the scale, if you are willing to share them. Beneath the scale I have listed some examples.

Total Teacher Control	P.I. C.A.I.	Self-directed Learning in Schools	Total Learner Control
Lecture System	Bell Canada's self-paced learning	Learning Contracts individual learning	C-R and self-help groups projects

Values and Consciousness-Raising (C.R.)

Learning what to want

Sir Geoffry Vickers (1970) a British lawyer and Cabinet Member, wrote a kind of summing up of the twentieth century problems of democratic government in which he included this observation: "Learning what to want is the most radical, the most painful and the most creative art of life."

The common element of consciousness-raising programs is that the planners begin with values clarification in order to broach at once the problem of sex-role straight-jackets. In this way, they initiate a process of consciousness-raising that broadens with the generation of alternative goals (see the section in this chapter on Creativity in Decision Making). I interviewed several of these planners; and while they agreed that subsequent topics could vary in sequence according to the needs of the participants, consciousness-raising had to begin with values clarification.

Defining one's values isn't easy. In these workshops, the planners use Sidney Simon's (1974) very tough criteria to separate truly held values from pie-in-the-sky. The criteria for a full value are that it must be:

- chosen freely
- chosen from among alternatives
- chosen after due reflection
- prized and cherished
- publicly affirmed
- acted upon
- part of a pattern that is a repeated action

Still the best work on values, Simon's book is appropriately called *Meeting Yourself Halfway*.

Goals, Objectives And Evaluation

The distinction between goals and objectives

> *Most planners find it useful to distinguish goals as the broader statements of purpose and objectives as the more precise aims to achieve those goals.*

To use the Bell Canada example, one of the goals of the course design team was to protect and support the self-confidence of the learners by designing self-paced learning whenever feasible. The objectives included planning and designing a particular course to be installed by a specific date. That was one of the planners' objectives. Within the course design, there was be a sequence of learning objectives so precisely defined that they build in continuous feedback to the participants.

In the creative decision-making model, we use the same distinctions, but we always push for wider choices. Having taken a first shot at naming our values, (knowing that we're going to come back to them again and again), our next decision problem is to search for all the accepted alternative goals and objectives, then to try to generate alternatives beyond those. For example, if I were on the Bell course design team, I would say, "Look, let's brain-storm on a wider spectrum of goals to come up with some ideas about how to use the experience and the creativity of these participants. Maybe we'll end up with the same goals we started with, but I'll bet even then, that we'll open potentials in this course that we might not otherwise have seen."

> *Planning can become a series of adventures.*

These examples have barely touched the surface of the possibilities. They have been presented to stimulate the instructor of adults to think about innovative approaches to working with adults in assessing their own learning. The emphasis has been on devising challenging exercises that are seen as appropriate by the adult student and that provide clear, understandable feedback to both the student and the instructor.

Bringing evaluation in from the cold

In the early seventies, the Maryland Department of Education produced 24 video tapes for the training of Adult Basic Education teachers. When they were ready to implement the program they called in external evaluators. I'm sure you can guess the complaint in the evaluators' report: if they had been called in when the planning began, they could have helped the planners to conduct a more detailed and useful evaluation. On the other hand, they should have been grateful because precious few adult education programs conduct any evaluation.

One of the reasons why adult educators don't evaluate is that they don't want to hear the bad news, even though they know it's the only way they can hope to learn what to change and improve in their planning and teaching. Another reason is that evaluations can cost too much in money, time and energy. So there are two tricks that I'd like to recommend:

> *1. Write your statements of goals and objectives in behavioural terms and so specifically and precisely that evaluation is literally built into them. You'll make it or you won't, and you will know.*
> *2. Keep your evaluations short and simple and use a variety of strategies.*

Writing clear goals is a difficult skill that requires a lot of practice, but that's OK because in this model you're always changing and adding to your goals and objectives anyway. I use three resources for goal definitions. Two are by Robert Mager (1972): *Goal Analysis* and *Preparing Instructional Objectives.* A third brief, neat prescription is by John E. Jones (1972): *SPIRO, Annual Handbook for Group Facilitators. SPIRO stands for: Specificity, Performance, Involvement* (of the Planner), Realism and Observation. Jones titled these 'Criteria for Effective Goal Setting'. I would add, and for Evaluation.

Mager's books abound in wit and can be read in an hour. Even if you do not need to write a planning objective to his criteria, at the very least you will be able to distinguish between 'fuzzies' as Mager calls them, and assessable statements of goals and objectives.

Some proponents of self-directed learning, including Malcolm Knowles (1980), reject Mager for fear that lucid goals and precise objectives will limit the learner's freedom. Obviously, I don't agree. I find no contradiction between objectives and freedom if one of the objectives is freedom. For example, read the objectives of *McMaster Medical School* (Herman, 1982). And in Goal Analysis you will find objectives for creativity written by a music school. In any event, for creative decision making I commend the pleasure of cleaning the head of fuzzies.

But while I disgreee with Knowles, I also disagree with Mager's suggestion that if you give each learner a copy of your objectives, you may not have to do much else. It is a common planning mistake to think that having identified and defined the goals, subsequent decisions fall into place. That's just an invitation to both planner and learner to slip back into hackneyed and boring learning methods.

The experience of McMaster Medical School illustrates this problem. The School introduced an unorthodox group tutorial method of teaching problem solving. To provide a back-up for this anxiety-arousing experiment, the Education Planning Committee defined a large number of learning objectives – to Mager's criteria – within the problem areas. These were intended to be guidelines for self-evaluation. To the planners' dismay, the students took the objectives all right, and ran straight to the textbooks to memorize the 'answers', exactly as they do in conventional medical schools, thus totally defeating the learning of problem-solving skills. The objectives were withdrawn, but continued to be useful to the planners in formulating the problems for tutorials.

Like the medical planners, you will find that in a school setting, students are not oriented to thinking of alternative learning methods. Again like the medical planners, stick to your guns. You must challenge them to stretch and risk and join with you in the search for creative alternatives.

The second way to bring evaluation from the outside in, is to use a whole stream of simple, brief techniques. At the end of this chapter, you will find an easily adaptable instrument that I use in workshops and courses. I use it at the end of my first session and again at the end of the third. If there's no change, I slit my throat. These evaluations can prove that I'm a lot better planner and facilitator now than when I first used this instrument. (Keep your results.) Incidentally because it's brief, we do it at the end of class in one minute, and I always share the results.

An even more powerful method of evaluation is to train your participants how to conduct a group critique focused on what they learned, at the end of every session. Insist that the critique be planned into every session, that every learner participate, and allow about two minutes for each. This form of evaluation should help the participants to identify their learning needs and goals. It is the beginning of learning how to learn. For you, it is the opportunity to ask: Did we do anything creative today? Did we address any social issues? Are we congruent with our goals and values?

I know Lynn Davie will offer many useful suggestions in the chapter on evaluation and you will find good stuff in Peter Renner's (1988) *The Instructor's Survival Kit*, but I would like to offer four easy suggestions for end-of-course evaluations.

1. Allen Tough requires (!) that his students tell him three things that they liked and three they didn't about his courses, and he uses the results.
2. Ginny Griffin invites her students to be creative, to depict in some imaginative way, the learning journey that they experienced during her courses. In this way, she helps them to name their learning.
3. I have plagiarized Aidan Spiller's method of evaluating his Recreational Leadership Program at Fanshawe College. At the beginning of the course, I get two or three people to volunteer to design the end-of-course evaluation, giving them absolute freedom, but warning them to keep a weekly record of course sessions. The entire last session is turned over to implement the evaluation that they have designed. I can tell you this - they are never boring.
4. In one of my courses, I ask participants to define the learning objectives that they carry away with them. I couldn't ask for a better evaluation of what they learned.

For myself, the most effective evaluation technique of all is also the simplest. After every meeting, I set aside thirty minutes that day or the next, to record the salient things that happened and my observations of what succeeded and what failed and why, and what this means in terms of my goals and values, and so what I am going to change next time.

There are two other powerful techniques; they are learner-centred, and contribute not only to selfevaluation but to the whole spectrum of learning how to learn. You invite your learners to do two things: to keep a learning journal and show them how to do it (because they don't know) and to form learning partners, an innovative idea that has emerged slowly out of a whole chain of adult education programs and workshop strategies. The purpose of learning partners is not to plan together, although that's fine, too, but to share reflections on their learning in the program. These two methods are also probably the most reliable ways to help the participants to identify their learning needs.

> *To sum up on evaluation: decision making always involves risk. The planner clarifies values and goals, identifies and generates alternatives and revises the goals, conducts vigilant information searches and so seeks to make the best possible decision. But there is never a guarantee that it is going to be the right decision. In the absence of that guarantee, the planner must evaluate or go on making the same mistakes ad infinitum.*

Creativity In Decision Making

Definitions of creative problem solving

William Gordon (1972) has trained thousands of people in his Synectics methods. In recent years, he has switched from the group method, and now uses a more structured strategy that makes rich use of metaphors and analogies. One of the techniques is called compressed conflict. It helps the problem solver to step back from the problem to gain fresh insights. If I were seeking a solution to a problem in a self-directed design, examples of compressed conflict might be: caged flight, mute teacher, indecipherable resources, etc. The breakthrough or ultimate strategy is called algebraic analogy and might take a form like this: what serves the same function for an adult learner that a starter serves for a car? You would depict the equation like this:

$$\frac{\text{CAR}}{\text{STARTER}} = \frac{\text{ADULT LEARNER}}{?}$$

> *Gordon defines creative problem solving very simply as "making new connections."*

In his stimulating book *Conceptual Blockbusting*, James L. Adams (1979) puts it more elaborately: the combination of previously unrelated structures in such a way that you get more out of the emergent whole than you have put in. For creative decision making in planning, I find that Gordon's and Adams' definitions are valid but not sufficient. My experience leads me to add that the creative idea or act is one that is original and imaginative.

Applying creativity in the model

> *There are really two levels of creativity in the planning process. One is to make new connections, the other is to expand the frontiers, to invent new options. One is to surface the whole range of existing alternatives and marry them in new combinations, the second is to generate far-out inventions and risk testing them.*

If, as a planner, you conduct a search to identify alternative learning goals and methods, you may use imagination in seeking out information about goals and methods from colleagues, from similar programs in other institutions, from the journals - in other words, use your resources well. That is a vital function of good decision making as Janis (1977) calls it, the "vigilant information search." But that is not yet creative. It becomes a creative act when you synthesize ideas you have surfaced from different sources into new connections for your own planning.

But when you push still further to generate and invent alternative goals and methods, this brings together both originality and imagination in planning a creative leap. The clearest educational example I can point to is in the woman's movement. For example, in the book *How to Decide* (Scholz and others, 1975), a

Evaluation For Sample Improvement:
an easily adaptable instrument

HOW ARE WE DOING?

I. My understanding of the purpose and goals of this program is:

1	2	3	4	5	6	7
confused						clear

2. My understanding of the plan and methods of this program is:

1	2	3	4	5	6	7
clear						confused

3. The progress I made today in meeting my own goals is:

1	2	3	4	5	6	7
rewarding						discouraging

4. The climate of our meeting today was:

1	2	3	4	5	6	7
inhibiting						freeing

5. My feeling of openness and trust toward the members of this group are:

1	2	3	4	5	6	7
high						low

6. The contribution I made today was:

1	2	3	4	5	6	7
ignored						heard

7. In relation to the expressed Goals, I find the planning of this program to be:

1	2	3	4	5	6	7
observably connected & contingent on those goals						a total mystery

8. My motivation to read/practise some idea(s) before the next meeting is:

1	2	3	4	5	6	7
low						high

COMMENTS or SUGGESTIONS:

manual that emerged from the workshops referred to earlier for women entering the work force, reader-participants are shown how to clarify their values and extend their objectives by brainstorming alternatives that they never dreamed of.

Brainstorming is an enjoyable method of using small groups (3 to 12 people) to generate a great quantity of ideas. The rules are simple: no criticism of ideas is allowed and members are invited to build on each other's ideas. In a 15 minute brainstorming session it is not uncommon for a group to fill sheets of flipchart paper with 50 or 60 ideas. A group would then take a few minutes to organize the ideas into categories and set priorities for discussion and action.

Generating Alternative Learning Methods

Most of the emphasis in this article has been on developing alternative goals, but obviously the job can also be expanded through creative problem solving for new, more effective learning methods.

In creating problem solving, I have found Edward de Bono's (1973) *PO-1*-"the intermediate impossible", to be one of the most powerful techniques to break conceptual blocks and free new ideas. Think of a real problem, a decision problem, that you are facing at present. Write down all the ideas and solutions that would be impossible. These ideas are like signs on closed doors that appear where there were no doors before. And some, perhaps even all, of those doors can be opened. Try this. Try them.

The adventures in experiential education and self-directed learning have so enriched our choices of learning methods that a single example is a risky business. Briefly though, here's one: a teacher of secretarial science wanted to get away from drills. PO-1 produced something like this: in this situation, what is impossible would be to turn her classroom into a business office. So she did it by dividing her classes into two companies doing business with each other. Each group organized themselves exactly as a company must do and began to conduct business. I would guess that this creative idea is generalizable to a lot of other learning situations.

De Bono has also invented *PO-2*, random juxtaposition, which is similar in purpose to Gordon's compressed conflict, and *PO-3*, challenge for change. I hope you will go beyond even these to investigate and enjoy the many stimulating ideas of *The Universal Traveller* by Koberg and Bagnall (1972) and *Conceptual Blockbusting by* Adams (1979). Just browsing this arsenal of creativity from time to time will guarantee that you will enrich your problem-solving strategies.

One caveat: unlike education, creativity is neutral. In fact, very nasty people have found monstrous ways of being creative.

> *So there is nothing casual about the insistence that creative decision making be inextricably linked to a clear value system.*

A Planning Model For Creative Decision Making

1. Identify the Values and put them in writing.
2. Survey the full range of possible goals. Deliberately generate alternatives.
3. Use all your resources to conduct a vigilant information search for the objectives of the program that can serve as a reference base for your values and goals.
4. Decide on your program's goals and objectives and define them to some criteria: SPIRO, Mager, etc. Check: are they so clear that evaluation is built in, so clear that at the end of each session, the participants will be able to say, we made it - or - we didn't. Start planning your evaluation strategies.
5. Thoroughly canvass the spectrum of Alternative Learning Methods. Brainstorm new ones. Use creative problem-solving like Synectics' compressed conflict and analogies. Make new connections.
6. NAME YOUR DECISIONS - TO CHANGE, TO INVENT, TO ADVENTURE...

In conclusion, a personal note. This article began with a reminder that there is no neutral education. That's true, but it doesn't mean that planning can't be fun! I hope this model assists you, as it has me, to enjoy continuous challenges in your work. Finally, this model invites you to risk naming all your decisions. That's not only good planning, it's a great satisfaction.

REFERENCES

Adams, J. (1979) *Conceptual Blockbusting* (2nd edition). Toronto: George J. McLeod.

deBono, E. (1973) *PO: Beyond Yes and No.* New York: Penguin.

Gordon, W.J.J. and Poze, T. (1972) *The Basic Course in Synectics* (Direct inquiries to SES, 121 Brattle Street, Cambridge, Mass.02138).

Herman, R. (Ed.) (1982) *The Design of Self-Directed Learning* (2nd edition) Toronto: OISE. Press

Janis, I.L. and Mann, L. (1977) *Decision Making.* New York: The Free Press.

Knowles, M.S. (1975) *Self-Directed Learning.* New York: Association Press.

Knowles, M.S. (1980) *The Modern Practice of Adult Education* (2nd edition). New York: Association Press.

Koberg, D. and Bagnall, J. (1972) *The Universal Traveller.* Los Altos, CA: Wm. Kaufmann.

Mager, R.F. (1972) *Goal Analysis.* Belmont, CA: Fearon.

Mager, R.F. (1972) *Preparing Instructional Objectives.* Belmont, Fearon.

Maryland State Department of Education. (1977) *Teaching the Adult: A Teacher Education Series* (Maryland Video Tapes) Baltimore MD. Includes 30 videos and a guidebook.

Miller, G.P. (1978) *Life Choices.* New York: Thomas Y. CrowMoore, P.G. and

Thomas H. (1976) *The Anatomy of Decisions.* New York: Penguin.
Renner, P.F. (1983) *The Instructor's Survival Kit: A Handbook for Teachers of Adults* (2nd edition). Vancouver, B.C.: Training Associates.
Scholz, N.T., Prince, J.S. and Miller, G.P. (1975) *How to Decide: A Guide for Women.* New York: Avon.
Simon, S.B. (1974) *Meeting Yourself Halfway.* Niles, Ill: Argus Communications.
Tough, A. (1979) *The Adult's Learning Projects* (2nd edition). Toronto: OISE.

SUGGESTED READING

Argyris, C. and Schon, D. (1976) *Theory in Practice: Increasing Professional Effectiveness.* San Francisco: Jossey-Bass.
Freire, P. (1973) *Education for Critical Consciousness.* New York: Seabury.
Freire, P. (1970) *Pedagogy of the Oppressed.* New York: Herder.
Griffin, V.R. (1982) "Self Directed Adult Learners and Learning." In R. Herman (Ed.) *The Design of Self-Directed Learning* (2nd edition). Toronto: OISE.
Halpern, N. (1984) "Sociotechnical systems design: The Shell Sarnia Experience." In Cunningham, J.B. & White, T.H. (Ed) *Quality of Working Life: Contemporary Cases.* Ottawa: Labour Canada.
Herman, R. (1973) *Innovations for Learning.* Toronto: OISE. (colour film, 25 min. A comparative study of two innovative programs: McMaster Medical School and the University of Toronto Department of Architecture.)
Ingalls, J.D. (1973) *A Trainer's Guide to Andragogy: Concepts, Experience and Application.* Washington, D.C.: U.S. Dept. of Health, Education and Welfare.
Pfeiffer, J.W. (1993) *Developing Human Resources Annuals.* San Diego, CA: University Associates.
Pfeiffer, J.W., and Goodstein, L. (1986) *Developing Human Resources Annuals.* San Diego, CA.: University Associates.
Pfeiffer, J.W., and Jones, J.E. (1970) *SPIRO: Annual Handbook for Group Facilitators.* La Jolla, CA: University Associates.
Prince, G. (1970) *The Practice of Creativity.* New York: Harper & Row.
Rainer, T. (1978) *The New Diary.* Los Angeles: J.P. Tarcher.
Renner, P.F. (1988) *The Quick Instructional Planner* (A learn-as-you-go guide that takes you from rough idea to well-crafted course plan). Vancouver, B.C.: Training Associates.
Rogers, C.R. (1983) *Freedom to Learn for the 80's* (2nd edition). Columbus, Ohio: Charles E. Merrill.
Thomas, A.M., Beatty D., Herman, R. and Weyman, T. (1980) *Case Studies of Training in Industry: Bell Canada, CBC, Marks and Spencer and Wardair.* Toronto: OISE. (1977-1980).
Vickers, G. (1970) *Freedom in a Rocking Boat.* Middlesex, UK: Penguin. (Interesting quote on the cover: "If we can decide upon our priorities we can use our new machines rather than be used by them.")

Chapter 10
Program Evaluation for Instructors of Adults

Lynn E. Davie

Practitioner's Summary

Recognizing the importance of creating a context for any understanding about the evaluative processes, Davie escorts the part-time instructor of adults on a guided tour through a brief view of the complexities inherent in the topic. These include a growing awareness of the 'what', 'how', and 'by whom', and how each of these factors colours the results acquired by any evaluation means.

Since evaluation should always be exercised with a view to future actions and decisions, it is important to recognize just what it is that is being evaluated: the instructor, the program, the institution, or the learning – or even the program of advertising, and to what ends. That is, will the learner ultimately benefit from the actions and decisions arising from the evaluative methods?

Most importantly, for the part-time instructor, evaluation should serve the purpose of assessing the effectiveness of the instructor's part in facilitating the student's learning progress. This brings up a difficult question: "What constitutes evidence that the student has learned?" Evaluation of the student's learning by means of a student's own reports, test score results, or even by observation of skills performed, is a political task since some consensus "of the nature of the evidence which will be acceptable" must be understood by all engaged in a particular educative activity.

Evaluation in itself, must incorporate some means of comparison that includes the learner's previous level and in some cases, also a comparison with other learners. Ideally, the shared responsibility of evaluation between teacher and student has shown that "learning is enhanced if there is agreement concerning the goals", and how that may be reached. Such a mutuality of planning expresses a mutality in communicating as well. Do your students know what to expect? have they shared the possibilities of evaluative means with you?

To answer these questions, Davie explores two models of evaluation. One is based on the "learning contract" in which the learning "tends to be evolutionary" as the student explores and expands areas of interest, developing evidence of achievement as progress is made. The second model may be represented by a presentation of clearly worded, precise goals and objectives set out by the instructor but clearly understood and agreed to by the student. The former requires continual assessment, while the latter requires evaluative assessment only at predetermined points in the learning, although ongoing assessment is not precluded.

Based on the humanistic philosophy underlying most programs for the education of adults, mutuality in every aspect of the educative enterprise is valued and evaluation is no exception. Adults not only have a strong preference for learning what is relevant, but frequently insist on the mode of evaluation being relevant to the mode of learning as well.

This means that true-false and multiple-choice types of testing have less relevance for adults than do actual questions or problems that may be responded to in detail. Perhaps most importantly, the author notes the adult need for privacy in personal evaluation of achievement. This points to the preference for self-evaluation, or for evaluation to be a matter between the instructor and student only.

Chapter 10
Program Evaluation For Instructors of Adults
Lynn E. Davie

What is Program evaluation?

"Program evaluation is a process by which society learns about itself" (Cronbach, and others, 1980). This chapter examines the art, science and politics of the program evaluation of certain aspects of adult education. Specifically, we will examine program or course evaluation from the instructor's point of view. The collection and sharing of data concerning student learning will be examined as a means of providing feedback both to the student and the instructor to assist each in learning about themselves and in improving their performance. We look at program evaluation as an integral part of adult learning and attempt to make our evaluation activities support our facilitation of adult learning.

> *I see a program as an educational curriculum which assists a student or group of students to learn some particular knowledge or set of skills. The learning allows the student to do or know something which he or she could not do or did not know before the learning experience.*

An adult education program can vary in length and difficulty, such as a single course, a series of courses, a conference, a short course, or a coherent (to the student) set of educational experiences such as readings, consulting with experts, conferences, museum visits, or the taking of other courses. Allen Tough (1979) calls such coherent sets of educational experiences "learning projects", and you might look at his writings for another perspective on the question of planning and evaluation.

Differing evaluation perspectives.

> *One difficulty in program evaluation is that the set of learning activities may be defined differently by the student and the instructor.*

The instructor may be evaluating the outcomes of a course within a broader curricular framework, while the student has taken the course for purposes other than that intended by the instructor or the institution. Such differences in perspective may lead to quite different evaluations of the same events.

Another difficulty in talking about program evaluation is that evaluation itself may be undertaken for many different purposes.

> *Program evaluation may include evaluation of an instructor's effectiveness, evaluation of a student's learning, evaluation of a program's design, evaluation of a course's objectives, or even evaluation of the effectiveness of the advertising for a course or program.*

To deal with this variety of purposes, evaluation specialists have devised complex models of evaluation (Stake, 1967, 1975; Stufflebeam, 1984; Provus, 1971, and Eisner, 1985). These evaluation models generally apply to complex programs and most often were designed to use with programs designed for youth, although many have been applied to large scale learning programs for adults. A good overview of these and other models may be found in Worthen and Sanders (1987).

Purposes of Program Evaluation

How effectively did the program promote learning?

I think that it is most useful to begin a discussion of program evaluation by looking at the purposes of evaluation.

> *The general purpose of evaluation is to make value-based decisions about the worth of a program course or activity and to revise the program based on those decisions.*

The basic meaning of program evaluation is the determination of the value of a program's activities and outcomes. Because evaluation is based on the determination of value, some part of the evaluation process is always a subjective comparison of the program to a valued ideal expectation for that program. The reason we evaluate programs is to make decisions which might help us in our planning in the future.

We evaluate in order to decide if we should give the course or program the same way again, or whether we should modify the course before it is offered again. Within the course evaluation, we evaluate an instructor's effectiveness to see if the instructor should change his or her behaviour in order to assist student learning. Finally, we evaluate student learning in order to decide, among other things, whether the right students were selected for the course, whether the course has been effective in supporting student learning, and to provide information to students to allow them to make evaluative decisions for their own program planning.

Specifically we evaluate a course to see if the general design and activities have had the desired effect on the student's learning. The important concept is that evaluation is for decision making.

If we are to improve our instruction we must evaluate our effectiveness. Conversely, if there are no decisions to make about the future, then perhaps time and money spent on evaluation in the present are being wasted.

Important First Questions of Evaluation

Evaluating learning

One of the most important questions of evaluation is concerned with the nature of acceptable evidence.

Learning is, of course, the basic purpose of adult educational programs. However, learning is a private act and cannot be observed directly. What constitutes evidence for the instructor that the student has learned? Some individuals will accept a student's report that he or she has learned something. Others will accept scores on tests, while still others will accept only the observation of a student using the newly acquired knowledge or skill.

The question of acceptable evidence is political, because in order to evaluate a course, all of the individuals involved in the evaluation must agree on the nature of the evidence which will be acceptable.

There are several resources which might be examined concerning the collection of different kinds of evidence of learning. One of the best general books on useful adult education research is by Abbey-Livingston and Abbey (1981). It provides an attractive presentation of the basic research methods useful in adult education. Another book which is enjoyable to read and which clarifies some of the basic questions of research is *The Science Game* by Agnew and Pyke (1969). A third book which is interesting is *A Guide to Research for Educators and Trainers of Adults* by Merriam and Simpson (1984). Finally, you might like to look at a series of essays edited by Boud and Griffin (1987) called *Appreciating Adults Learning: From the Learner's Perspective.*

Evaluation Is A Comparison

Program evaluation always involves a comparison. This comparison is made between some concept of an ideal set of learnings and the perceived reality of the learning.

The ideal may be a statement of program goals and objectives, or it may be the experience of another program which was valued, or it may be a desirable increase in knowledge from some beginning point. For students, the ideal may also be an objective, an increase from some beginning point, or even a comparison with the progress of other students.

Identification Of Goals

One of the first steps in program evaluation is for the instructor and the students to identify the desirable set of learnings which are to be derived from the instruction. It is around this process that adult education varies most from youth education.

> *In adult education, most educators believe that the instructor and the student have a mutual responsibility for the identification of goals, and that learning is enhanced if there is agreement concerning the goals.*

Agreement may be reached by a variety of methods. A working agreement may be the result of the student accepting the instructor's goals, the instructor accepting the student's goals or perhaps best, a mutual negotiation of goals. It is useful if program goals and objectives are as explicit as possible, and that such goals be clearly related to an intended use by the adult student.

An important question is how can the students and the instructor arrive at a mutual set of goals? One of the most widely accepted models for arriving at a mutual set of goals is that of a learning contract. Although the origin of this idea is not clear, one of the most noted proponents is Malcolm Knowles (1980). His writings on this subject provide a clear guide to good practice in negotiating learning contracts with adults.

> *The general notion is that the instructor serves as a facilitator in helping the students consider their learning needs, and developing these expressions of need into attainable learning objectives .... planning tends to be evolutionary.*

In the process of setting the learning objectives, the evidence of achievement becomes clear. The evaluation of the student's achievements is then a fairly straightforward affair. Collection of data is an integral part of the learning process, and the meaning of the evidence is clear to both the student and the facilitator. Both may make judgments on the effectiveness of the learning activities. One characteristic of this kind of planning is that the planning tends to be evolutionary. Rather than operating from pre-set objectives only, the objectives tend to evolve as the student better understands the area in which he or she is studying. Thus, the kinds of evidence of learning to be collected must also evolve. It is the responsibility of both the facilitator and the student to attend to questions of constant evaluation throughout the learning process.

While the mutual planning of a learning contract is the preferable mode of goal identification for many situations, it does not seem applicable to all adult education settings. There are many instances in which the objectives for the learning process must be set before the students are even identified.

> *It is possible to arrive at a mutual set of goals by the student accepting the instructor's goals. In order to facilitate this kind of mutuality it is necessary that the advertising for the course be clear, specific, and comprehensive.*

If the advertising is clear enough, the potential student can make an informed choice as to whether he or she wishes to be involved in the learning experiuence. If the choice is informed, then the result is again a mutual agreement on the goals and objectives.

Even though we may have a mutual set of goals in programs with pre-set objectives, it is clear that the instructor or some external program planner is responsible for setting the original objectives. It follows that the instructor or external program planner is also responsible for the design of the evaluation. He or she is responsible for designing the collection of data for use in making evaluative judgements about both the student's progress and the efficacy of the course. A major user of the evaluative data is the instructor and any external program planner. However, the data must also be useful to the adult student for use in judging individual progress.

Even though this chapter focuses on collecting acceptable evidence of learning, it is important to recognize that the structure of the learning experiences is dependent on a knowledge of the psychology of adult learning. To be effective, the learning activities must be structured to take into account the principles of adult learning. An excellent book on adult learning principles has been written by Stephen Brookfield (1986) and I highly recommend it.

The models which follow outline the two basic evaluation relationships between instructor and student. One of the models pertains to the situation in which the goals are pre-set before the educational experience while the other presents the ideas in a situation in which the goals and objectives evolve during the learning process.

> *Therefore, there are two principle evaluation relationship (models) between student and instructor:*
> *1. evolving model requiring evaluation throughout the learning process; and*
> *2. pre-set model requiring evaluation at specific points only.*

Model of Instructor and Student
Evaluation for Preset Goals

Evaluation Function	Instructor	Student
Generation of Goals	Generates goals from needs analysis. -Expressed interest by potential students. -Problem analysis.	Generates goals from perception of personal needs. -General interest.
Setting Objectives	Derived logically from goals.	Derived from personal goals.
Mechanism for Attaining Mutuality	Informative advertising to attract students with compatible goals.	Accepts instructor's objectives for course. -May attempt to modify objectives. -Still maintains own goals.
Nature of Evaluative Evidence	Related to course goals. Evidence best when capable of being shared with students and other professionals.	Related to personal goals. Evidence best when personally useable. Evidence sometimes shared.
Decisions	Was course effective? What modifications should be made before course is offered again?	Was desired progress achieved? Should I take more courses from this institution or this instructor?

Model of Facitator and Student
Evaluation for Evolutionary Goals

Evaluation Function	Facilitator	Student
Generation of Goals	Generates goals in negotiation with student or group.	Generates goals in negotiation with instructor of group. Personal goals are generated from perception of personal needs.
Setting Objectives	Objectives are set by problem solving with student or group. Instructor goals are included as part of process.	Objectives are set by problem solving with instructor or group. Objectives must meet personal goals.
Mechanism for Attaining Mutuality	Negotiation	Negotiation
Nature of Evaluative Evidence	Evidence best when acceptable to student and group. Evidence best when capable of being shared with other professionals.	Evidence best when personally useable. Evidence best when related to personal goals.
Decisions	Have I been personally effective? Should process be altered?	Have I achieved desired progress? Should I take more courses from this institution or from this instructor?

Although it is not ideal, it is possible that learning activities will be conducted even though complete agreement may not be reached as to goals and objectives. An effective learning experience can be conducted if there is sufficient overlap of objectives among the members of the learning group and each is aware of the other's differing objectives.

Characteristics of Goals and Objectives

Let us now turn to the question of the characteristics of a good set of goals. I have been using the terms goals and objectives interchangeably. However, there is a difference between the two concepts.

> *A* Goal *refers to a general set of desirable learning outcomes which are intended for a specific purpose. This purpose may be to satisfy an intellectual curiosity, to answer a question, or to solve a specific problem.* Objectives *are specific goals which are attainable within a set period of time.*

Objectives often include specific learning outcomes and when several objectives are linked together their achievement may indicate progress toward a goal. It might be an individual's goal to learn to be a professional photographer. One of the objectives in that process would be to learn to develop a roll of black and white film to a specific set of professional standards.

What are the characteristics of good objectives? The first characteristic for an objective is that it should be clearly linked to something that the adult student wishes to know or to do. The utility of the learning should be obvious and fairly immediate. This characteristic is important not only to sustain motivation, but also to allow the student to test the adequacy of the learning in order to determine whether the original objective is being reached and is still valued.

Objectives Are Planning Devices

The more specific an objective is, the more direction it can give us as we design the learning experience, and conduct the evaluation.

> *The course planning is enhanced if the objective specifies the content areas which are to be included, the intended learning, and the level of achievement.*

At some point in the instructional process, the objective should include the specific evidence which we wish to collect to indicate that learning has taken place. This evidence may include behaviours which the student is able to perform, or it may include other forms of evidence of learning which we are seeking. Although most writings on objectives argue that specific behavioural objectives should be set before the learning activities take place, in adult education this advice is most appropriate to those instances in which the student is accepting the instructor's objectives.

In the case of objectives evolving as the student's learning progresses, it is clearly neither appropriate nor possible to specify all of the behavioural objectives before the learning takes place. Nevertheless, specificity is useful.

> *Consequently, during the evaluation of the learning process it is important for the student and the facilitator to make time to take stock of progress to date, and to set specific objectives for the next portion of study.*

Finally, in order to assist in mutual evaluation, the objectives are better when they are stated so that the students can assess their progress without the intervention of the facilitator.

> *Self-evaluation depends on the objectives being clear, and the evidence of progress being in an understandable form, to the student.*

Assessing Student Progress

In adult education, assessing student progress is a mutual responsibility of the student and the instructor. Knowledge of progress is often called feedback. In order to know whether certain activities are facilitating the desired learning, the amount and kind of learning which has occurred must be recognized by the student and must be comparable to some standard previously established through negotiation. This standard may be external to the student or it may be a comparison with some beginning point known by the student.

Testing

In general, testing is a desirable characteristic of adult instructional programs, for it provides both the instructor and the student with an independent assessment of student progress. However, most experienced instructors believe that adults do not like testing. I believe the resistance of adults to testing is based either on the format of the testing or on a public display of the results.

> *Adults seem to prefer that testing simulate the actual use of the learning rather than the use of multiple-choice or true-false formats. And that it be private.*

If the test approximates the use to which the learning will ultimately be put, and the results are available only to the adult and the instructor for use in assessing the student's progress, then the testing activity may be valued by both the adult student and the instructor.

While some adult student testing may gather data for use in certification, testing's most important function is to provide data to students for their assessment of progress. Thus testing also should follow the principles of good learning theory. Some important elements of the testing are that it be seen as

1. appropriate by the student,
2. motivating and
3. providing clear, understandable feedback to the student.

The testing should seem appropriate and be relatively frequent. The results should be easily interpreted by the student and not require an intervention by the instructor for understanding.

Evaluation Examples

The remainder of this chapter will present a number of examples of ways to collect data concerning adult learning, not meant to cover all adult learning settings, but rather to stimulate your interests and to suggest a variety of approaches.

> *It is ironic that as program planners we often direct our creative energy to constructing innovative learning programs, but fail to use the same creativity when designing the collection of evaluation data.*

Notice that each of the following examples yields information that can be used by all major stakeholders in the evaluation (facilitator, funder, and student). For the data collected to be useful, all of the stakeholders should be clear about the use to which the data will be put. Is the testing for feedback to the student only or will it also be used to assess the effectiveness of the course and the instructor?

Testing in programs with large audiences

Many adult programs involve large audiences. For example, we may have a large class or a lecture series, or a large plenary session at a conference. It is very difficult to collect evaluative data in such settings. The usual post-meeting reaction sheets are too seldom filled in by the audience, without excessive prompting. The following is an example of testing in a large audience which overcame these obstacles.

The setting was a lecture on nutrition to an audience of three hundred homemakers. We decided to test knowledge gain in three ways. First, we gave each participant four cards when they entered the auditorium. Two cards were white, one card was red, and one card was green. Much of the nutrition content was presented by using a set of slides to illustrate the lecture. At preselected times during the lecture, the lecturer asked the audience questions about the content just covered. In responding, the audience was asked to hold up the green card if the statement was true and the red card if the statement was false. The lecturer could tell immediately if the audience understood the concept or whether further review was necessary. More important, the audience, when informed of the right answer, could assess their own learning. The same cards could be used for a two choice multiple answer question. The audience participated enthusiastically.

To provide a more permanent record of the learning the two white cards were used. Before the lecture ten questions were selected as representing the content of the lecture. A deck of cards was prepared with one question printed on each of ten cards. Since we were expecting an audience of about 300 people, there were thirty cards with each question. The cards were shuffled and distributed randomly to people as they entered. The cards were each marked with an A. A second set of duplicate cards was prepared and distributed in the same way, except each card was marked with a B. At the beginning of the lecture, the audience was asked to answer the question on the card marked A and these were passed in. At the end of the lecture the audience was asked to answer the question on the card marked B and these were passed in. The audience again participated enthusiastically.

> *By calculating the increase in right answers on deck B over deck A, we could estimate the increase in nutrition knowledge during the lecture.*

After deck B was passed in, we gave the correct answers so all would know how they were doing.

While the form of the testing did not conform to the advice that testing simulate the actual use, the audience seemed to accept the test activities. I think the reasons are:

1. the testing was short;
2. feedback was immediate;
3. results of some activities (green and red cards) were immediately used by the instructor; and
4. other results (white cards) were not linked with individuals.

While some of the enthusiasm was clearly generated by the ability to judge one's own progress, some of the motivation to participate was due to the audience's interests in helping the instructor to improve. The results of the increase in knowledge were useful in preparing a report to the funders of the activity.

Finally, we wanted to know whether the audience enjoyed the lecture. As an alternate format, we set up a series of boxes at the back of the room. The boxes were marked Excellent, Good, Fair, Poor, and Not Worth my Time. We asked the audience to deposit their red cards in the box that represented their judgement as to the worth of the experience. Most of the audience voted in this way.

These activities helped establish a rapport with the audience. The activities helped the facilitator improve her lecture for its next presentation, helped the participants know how much of the lecture they were learning, and finally, allowed us to report to the funder.

Testing for skill

We can now turn to collecting evaluative data concerning learning in other kinds of educational experiences. Designing tests is in some ways easier in situations in which the objective is the acquisition of specific skills. In this, testing is a normal part of the learning experience. If one is learning to sail or to play tennis, the activity itself provides both the learner and the instructor with immediate feedback as to the present skill level of the learner. The problem here is to provide a form of record keeping that will allow the students to keep track of their own progress. This record keeping could be in the form of a personal log or it could be in the form of a chart. The chart would allow the student to record his or her progress for each session. In addition, the record system should provide the opportunity to compare individual performance with accepted standards. In sailing, for example, the Ontario Sailing Association has a variety of levels based on specific knowledge (knots, rules of the road) and skills (docking, gybing, etc.). These levels might be printed on the chart to help the student access his or her progress towards these goals.

Testing That Simulates Actual Use of Learning

There are four instructional activities that facilitate learning of higher level knowledge that also can provide feedback to the instructor and the student concerning the student's learning. While there are many variants of these techniques, they can be organized under four categories: case studies or problems, role plays, structured exercises, and simulations.

There are many sources of ideas about how to structure these techniques. Let us look at the techniques as a source of evaluative feedback. There seem to be four problems in the use of simulation for feedback purposes.

1. Simulations often involve a class or group of students. While this structure helps lend a sense of reality to the exercise, it often makes it difficult for a student to know how effective or accurate her or his individual contribution was.
2. Since the simulations are often complex it is difficult to capture and record data concerning individual achievement.
3. It is difficult to compare individual achievement to a standard or valued criterion.
4. It is difficult to provide accurate feedback to the individual student.

I believe that case studies or practice problems should be accompanied by model solutions. For a factual solution, these model solutions can provide the correct answer. Where there are multiple possible solutions, several examples might be provided.

The model solutions allow the student to see how a problem might be solved and more importantly, they provide organized feedback about individual learning and problem solving strategies.

The Anasynics Case Study approach

An example of an interactive case study approach which I have used was developed originally by Professor Robert Boyd at the University of Wisconsin and is called the Anasynics Case Study. The key components of the Anasynics Case Study approach include information gathering of the constituent components of the problem (analysis), and the provision of a creative solution through really understanding the nature of the problem (synthesis).

In real life, a proposal request is handled by first collecting general background information to use in designing a well-targeted proposal by calling to the program sponsor, the program manager and others involved. In class, the students are encouraged to write any of the people involved in the "program" requesting information such as perspectives, special interests and goals.

Working alone or in groups, students in my graduate course in program evaluation work as though they were members of a small consulting firm being asked to present a proposal for evaluation of a program.

After the information gathering phase, each group or individual prepares a proposal which is submitted to the instructor to provide feedback on strengths, questionable points, improvements.

Learning is enhanced by exposing several solutions to the same problem as well as considering aspects which none of the solutions may have contained.

REFERENCES

Abbey-Livingston, D. and Abbey, D.S. (1981) *Enjoying Research: A How To Book on Needs Assessment.* Toronto: Ontario Ministry of Culture and Recreation.

Agnew, N.M. and Pyke, S.W. (1969) *The Science Game: An Introduction to Research in the Behavioral Sciences.* Englewood Cliffs, N.J.: Prentice-Hall.

Boud, D. and Griffin, V. (1987) *Appreciating Adults Learning: From the Learners' Perspective.* London: Kogan Press.

Brookfield, S. (1986) *Understanding and Facilitating Adult Learning.* San Francisco: Jossey-Bass.

Cronbach, L.J. and others (1980) *Toward Reform of Program Evaluation: Aims, Methods and Institutional Arrangements.* San Francisco: Jossey-Bass.

Eisner, E.W. (1985) *The Art of Educational Evaluation: A Personal View.* London: The Falmer Press.

Knowles, M. (1980) *The Modern Practice of Adult Education: From Pedagogy to Andragogy* (2nd edition) New York: Cambridge Books.

Merriam, S.B. and Simpson, E.L. (1984) *A Guide to Research for Educators and Trainers of Adults.* Malabar, FL: Robert E. Krieger Publishing Co.

Provus, M. (1971) *Discrepancy Evaluation.* Berkley, CA: McCutchan.

Stake, R.E. (1967) "The countenance of educational evaluation." *Teachers College Record, Vol. 68.*

Stake, R.E. (1975) *Evaluating the Arts in Education: A Responsive Approach.* New York: C.E. Merrill.

Stufflebeam, D.L. (1984) *Systematic Evaluation.* Boston: Kluwer Nijhoff.

Tough, A. (1979) *The Adult's Learning Projects: A Fresh Approach to Theory Practice in Adult Learning* (2nd edition). Toronto: OISE Press.

Worthen, B.R. and Sanders, J.R. (1987) *Educational Evaluation: Alternative Approaches and Practical Guidelines.* Whiteplains, NY: Longman, Inc.

Chapter 11

Compared to What? Comparison Studies as an Added Dimension for Adult Learning

J. Roby Kidd

Editor's note: Professor Kidd died in 1982.
This chapter was written in 1981.

Practitioner's Summary

In his own sprightly manner, the author explains the meaning and the implications of comparisons and shows how such studies can add dimension to almost any research or field of study. Teachers are always on the lookout for something different. Kidd points out that making comparisons is commonplace, but crucial within anyone's development.

Using the development of a course in Comparative Studies at OISE as an example, the author offers some of the initial reflections in creating this program as a universal structure for inserting comparisons into almost any field of study. His method to do so is briefly outlined:

1. finding an example or specimen;
2. placing it beside another whose properties and functions are known;
3. drawing inferences through systematic comparisons of properties and uses;
4. replicating until sure of result.

Immediately several important points will be seen by the participants in such work: a re-examination of what they had taken for granted in their own culture, their own situation or study; a more careful look at what was known and assumed, to see if the newer knowledge may add importance or clarification; finally a deeper appreciation of differing ways and differing knowledge that may not have existed before.

The end result is "an acknowledgement that many disciplines, subjects, and kinds of experience may contribute to a better understanding of one's educational system, or one's own learning."

A listing of the reasons for making use of comparisons is offered by the author: to become better informed about other systems, other culture's ways of doing; historical roots, how other humans live and learn; differences within one's own country, community, relationships, in understanding oneself; and to help reveal cultural biases.

"For all of us, what seems to happen as we engage in comparative studies is a process of deepening reflection about ourselves, how we learn, grow, feel, appreciate, express ourselves."

In conclusion, the author's most valuable point may well be that "there is nothing foreign about comparative studies" and that these may be most important for the on-going development of the teachers themselves.

Chapter 11
Compared to What? Comparison Studies as an Added Dimension for Adult Learning
J. Roby Kidd

Everybody Does It

Everybody compares! Comparing is an activity that one does constantly, some people, excessively. The famous cartoonist of *The New Yorker*, James Thurber, was walking along Broadway one day when a friend approached, greeted him, and asked: "How is your wife?" The cautious comedian, who was very shortsighted, blinked, and asked a question in return: "Compared to what?"

It has been said that one way *Homo sapiens* differ from other animals is in the ability to compare, and thus, begin to build up experience and knowledge, socialize, develop standarads, emphasize, understand other people, and herself or himself. Actors are adept in this capacity of comparing, so are lawyers, and so are teachers. It is often said that an intelligent person is "well read". It might be said of good teaching that it is "well compared", it has been developed through a maturing process of seeing relationships between content and interest, between method and learning style.

> *A good teacher is not trained or instructed or molded by someone else, he or she becomes one. Among the process in this growth, constant comparing of other persons and other educational programs is paramount.*

In most fields of scholarship, there are branches given a title like comparative law, comparative psychology, comparative sociology, comparative education. Comparative psychology is primarily a study involving animals versus human beings, but comparative education is about the different ways that members of the human family respond educatively.

The Uses of Comparisons

One of the first decisions made when the Department of Adult Education was started at OISE was to begin systematic teaching and research in comparative studies of adult education. It was the first Department at OISE to offer comparative studies and OISE was the first institution in the world to offer graduate comparative adult education.

It is a very common phenomenon, happening many times everyday, that someone will make a statement, or a claim: a hockey player is undisciplined, a garment is gorgeous, an experience is wonderful, a learner is slow, a teacher is brilliant, etc., and the statement does not have much meaning until it can be seen in context, with the quality related to something else you do know. Compared to what?

Comparisons are often used to illustrate important differences between peoples or cultures. The philosopher, Albert North Whitehead, who had taught in both American and British Universities, used a comparison to state what he considered important attributes of the two peoples.

In England, if something goes wrong – say, if one finds a skunk in the garden - he writes the family solicitor, who proceeds to take the proper measures; whereas in America, you telephone the fire department. Each satisfies a characteristic need: in the English, love of order, and legalistic procedures; and here in America, what you like is something vivid, red, and swift.

I once remember Henry Marshall Tory, president of five different Canadian institutions of higher learning, claiming that you could derive the essence of three different nations from a simple formula:

ENGLAND:As it was in the beginning, is now, and evershall be, world without end, Amen.
UNITED STATES:As it was in the beginning is now, and By God, it's got to stop.
CANADA:As it was in the beginning, is now, and if there is to be a change, we will first appoint a Royal Commission.

Ways of Comparing and For What?

Comparative studies are not as simple as this elegant formula would suggest, but they are intended for the same purposes- to describe and analyze similarities and differences in order to understand meanings, essences, lessons from other cultures, institutions and peoples, and to better comprehend one's own society and oneself. All of the statistical tables, the computer printouts, the packed files of information, are so much pulp if the stage of understanding is not reached. Some comparativists want and claim much more than understanding. They aim for the ability to predict or claim a method that is valuable for decision-making and many other virtues are hoped for or expected. But the irreducible minimum is understanding and if that is richly achieved, it may be sufficient justification.

That is the purpose that prompted the application of comparing as an early and basic research method in the physical sciences. The method is a simple one.

> *You find a specimen; you examine it and place it in juxtaposition with another specimen whose properties and functions are already*

known, according to weight, hardness, colour, feel, taste, smell, etc., you draw inferences through systematic comparison of the properties of both specimens, inferences about origins, relationships, functions, uses, and so on, and then you replicate such a process again and again until you are reasonably certain of your result.

In the process, greater specificity becomes possible. An interesting example of this process is that the concept "warmer" eventually became the word temperature, and eventually led to specific statements of "warmness". This is something like what happens in comparative adult education, but the latter process is much more complex. Since it is a social and living experience, the data are more difficult to organize and control and are typically far from complete. There may be more unknowns than knowns.

From one point of view the whole "science" of statistical organization and expression is for the purposes of systematic comparing, and such measures as averages, means, medians, standard deviations, are primarily to provide a way to specify, with some accuracy, what are the relationships, similarities, dissonances. That use is so common that we don't think about it.

There is nothing esoteric about comparing. It is a traditional and much used process to achieve many kinds of learning. What is important about it is that it be systematic.

Research in education was rather slow to develop, and adult education was the last member of the educational family to organize systematic research. Over whole sections of adult education, the non-formal as well as self-initiated studies, statistics are almost unknown, and even formal adult education statistics are incompletely collected or reported.

Nevertheless, while the number of possible comparisons are almost infinite, only some are significant. At an international seminar on comparative adult education, held in Nordberg, Denmark in 1972, Professor George Bereday, who then held the only chair in Comparative Education, said: "You can make comparisons between any organisms – let us say between an elephant and a flea. You could say the elephant is a big breather, while the flea is a little breather. Of course, many kinds of comparisons are simply not worth making." Some comparisons, and there are a great many such, lack any significance, or importance, or relevance: they lack valence, to use a term of Benjamin Barber.

Comparing, to be meaningful, must be about significant relationships, and result from the ordering of data so that they can be rigorously compared. If this is not done, the result may be greater confusion or error.

For example, if casual relationships are interpreted as causal, it is possible to derive the most bizarre effects, all too commonly employed by politicians vying for office, who attribute the worst blunders to their opponents, and all of earth's blessings to themselves. I remember very well when I was at Columbia University how amused we were when we discovered, in examining some census data from the nearby city of Newark, that there was a one to one, a perfect correlation in that city between the increase in teachers' salaries, and the increase in the consumption of bourbon. Few politicians could have resisted the temptation to state that the one was caused by the other, but every educationist should examine faithfully the data on which such causal relationships are advanced.

A much more serious misapplication of comparing occurred during World War I when adults entering the American army were given a series of timed school tasks conducted under school conditions, based on school-like kinds of motivation, and called "intelligence tests". The performance of these men, many of whom had long left school, and had been compelled to take part, even though many of them had no interest in the project, was on the average, about the same as the performance of boys and girls in school of the age of twelve or thirteen. Such results should not have been surprising to anyone, but what was startingly, incredibly stupid, and resulted in damaging consequences, was that some psychologists concluded from such a comparison that the mental age of the average adult is about twelve or thirteen years. It has taken almost half a century to get over some of the consequences of that extraordinary blunder by some highly intelligent psychologists and newspapermen.

> *Comparing can be an excellent tool for understanding, but only, as is true of any good tool, when it is used well.*

Systematic comparing applied to education probably began at least three thousand years ago, perhaps in Egyptian times when hundreds of visitors came to the Nile Valley to learn about the educational and economic system of the Egyptians, or again in the first centuries A.D., in what is now India and Pakistan, when as many as ten thousand foreign students would enroll in universities, such as Nalanda and Taxilla, and again in the tenth century, when Arab universities in Baghdad and Cairo were world centres for art, music, poetry, medicine, chemistry, mathematics, and attracted thousands of visiting scholars. There is evidence that there was systematic analysis of the modes and outputs of these studies. Any of these periods might have been selected as the beginning of Comparative Education.

In Europe and North America, we still find it necessary to say that all progress began with us. Accordingly, we date the beginning of comparative education from the year 1817 when a distinguished French educationist, Marc-Antoine Julien, published his treatise, *Plan and Preliminary Views for a Work on Compara-*

tive Education, in which he proposed a method of collecting educational data from each country, using a carefully devised questionnaire, and went on to suggest that teaching methods should be standardized. Comparing, as he saw it, was primarily to assist each country to borrow the best practices of other countries.

For the next century, at least, the objective of cultural borrowing was primary for people like Egerton Ryerson of Canada, or Horace Mann of the United States, who themselves travelled widely to carry out comparative education. On the whole, it was also a period when other cultural forms, architectural, economic, fashions, were also borrowed without much discrimination, and when there was often misappreciation of the values of indigenous cultures.

Goals of Comparative Adult Education

What is, or what are, the goals of comparative adult education? Notice that we use the term comparative adult education to distinguish between comparative methods applied primarily to school systems for children and youth.

> *However, we prefer the term comparative studies because it is an acknowledgement that many disciplines, subjects, and kinds of experience may contribute to a better understanding of one's educational system, or one's own learning.*

Included are comparisons through history, literature, production, or art, religion and ideology, not just school statistics. Accepting such a term and concept prepares the ground for an acceptance of multi-purposes, not just the sole purpose of cultural borrowing. At various times, people in adult education have studied together what are the central goals, and the following list indicates some points of agreement:

- to become better informed about the educational system of other countries;
- to become better informed about the ways in which people in other cultures have carried out certain social functions by means of education;
- to become better informed about the historical roots of certain activities, and thus, to develop criteria for assessing contemporary developments and testing possible outcomes;
- to better understand the educational forms and systems operating in one's own country;
- to satisfy an interest in how other human beings live and learn;
- to better understand oneself;
- to reveal how one's own cultural biases and personal attributes affect one's judgment about possible ways of carrying on learning transactions.

Borrow or Resist; Comparison as Tool

In earlier times as we have noted, comparative education was fostered with the definite purpose of borrowing successful forms and activities from abroad to be attached to one's own system. The purpose was similar to the proverb from Ghana: "It is to blow dust from each other's eyes that one finds two antelopes always working together." In those early days, comparative educationalists were mainly reformers. Today, 'reformers", in this sense, have been replaced by educational planners, and comparative studies are as much a preparation for educational planning as are studies of economics or sociology. In more recent decades, comparative modes have been sought that might assist educationists in one country faced with difficult decisions about whether to welcome or resist cultural innovations from another. Comparative modes have been recommended as essential tools for educational planning, and for educational assessment.

> *One interesting objective for comparative adult education is to identify those characteristics or patterns of behaviour which are culture-bound, related to a given society, from those that have universal characteristics.*

Learning About Oneself Through Comparing

In other words, comparative studies may be part of vocational or career training for some people who will spend much of their careers in, or concerned with, other societies. For most of us, they satisfy curiosity and enlarge horizons, they are "liberal or humane" studies, and some writers, such as Wilfrid Cantwell Smith, who has written extensively on comparative religions, and was first Director of the Islamic Institute of McGill, believe that in the modern world, they are the richest, most effective, of the humanities, much more so in the contemporary world than Latin or Greek, and having as much emotional and aesthetic power. For still others, comparative studies can provide methods and techniques for research, or clues, or hypotheses, for both formative and summative evaluation.

> *For all of us, what seems to happen as we engage in comparative studies is a process of deepening reflection about ourselves, how we learn, grow, feel, appreciate, express ourselves.*

How often have you heard someone on shipboard, or on an airplane, state: "I never understood, or I never appreciated my country until I was away from it." To the extent that this process happens of valuing our country or ourselves, one need not search from other, or larger goals. This is justification enough.

However, personal development is not inconsistent or at odds with significant social purposes. Many people today have the responsibility for sharing in decisive choices about whether some cultural practice or method, or technique, or fashion, or product, ought to be accepted, adopted, or adapted, or should be resisted. We are now far more aware that millions of people and most, if not all, countries have accepted institutions and products that have been more harmful than helpful, and in many countries, the flowering of imagination, creativity, self-confidence, even human dignity, have been inhibited or stunted. Insights and knowledge from comparative studies can be utilized, either for thoughtful, careful borrowing, or for considered, but unyielding, resistance to borrowing.

Similarity and Difference

It is still true that most of the writing about adult learning is found in the English language, and has been derived from experiences primarily in North America and Western Europe. To a considerable extent, this has happened because the means of dissemination, such as printing presses, international press services, and broadcasting channels are owned and controlled primarily by a few dominant countries. It is also well established by now that western institutions and styles of educational organization have often been found to be unsuitable, sometimes seriously harmful, when adopted or applied in other countries.

Perhaps this is also true about learning styles and learning skills: may these also be culture-bound? Recently, Malcolm Knowles and I were discussing our experiences in offering seminars in other countries. While we did not seriously disagree, Knowles stressed similarity, and I stressed difference, both of us drawing on our individual experience. But the matter is too important to be left to personal and independent observation. Careful, sustained, replicating research, particularly studies that are not locked into methods and mind sets of western social scientists, are needed before very much application is made of ideas, concepts, strategies, methods, techniques, and organizational plans devised in the west.

The Need For Diversity In Study and Research

The attention that has been given to qualitative methods of research (phenomenological enquiries, grounded theory, etc.), and to participatory research modes, are indications that a greater array of research modes are needed in our own country, that certain assumptions about the objectivity of science need to be questioned, and that the use of research to control the lives of others, needs to be checked.

There are many examples today of processes and institutions that have been effective in one part of the world, from which others might learn, if sufficient care is used when any such transfer is contemplated.

The success of the British Open University and of certain forms of non-traditional studies in the United States and Canada have attracted the interest of educational policymakers from many countries. It is known that to be productive, open access learning depends on (a) strong motivation (b) at least occasional human encounters with tutors and fellow students, and (c) an infrastructure of media. But what proportion and what mix of these factors will make possible the effective application of non-traditional methods in other countries? Who should make these judgments, using what kinds of analysis?

> *A strong case can be made for the importance of research in adult education using comparative methods, for guiding those who make the important decisions in education, how much they might borrow from other cultures, how much they should reject, how many indigenous foundations and influences should be supported and developed.*

Questions like these should be answered as rationally as possible, based on need and result, not through believing that something is better because it is imported, or rejection that it is worse because it is imported. On the whole, people in education are less likely to jump to the conclusion without some evidence that other ways are better than their own. At the same time, there are some examples of careful and judicious borrowing and adapting of ideas, and concepts. It is to be hoped that it may not be always necessary to invent the wheel again and again,19that some educational principles and practices will be effective for all members of the human family.

> *This is one reason why it is so important to discriminate between what may be human and universal, and what is culture-bound, limited to a particular group.*

For a field that is comparatively so "young", adult education provides many examples of cultural borrowing that seem to have been beneficial. For example, the Canadian program, National Farm Radio Forum, has attracted attention in many countries, and there have been some adaptations of it in countries such as Jamaica, Colombia, Ghana, and India. Those who tried it out in the new setting made many changes in design, format, and organization. In Colombia, the differences were so far-reaching that one might not recognize the original. It is precisely this effort to carry out a similar function that was served in Canada by Farm Forum in a markedly different manner, suited to conditions in Columbia, which seems to have been19so successful. In turn, the Colombian program has been a kind of model for other viable programs throughout the Spanish-speaking Caribbean. However, had the Colombians simply adopted the methods and techniques of Canadian Farm Radio Forum, without making it their own, it might have languished and died long ago. But this is speculation. These are questions that should be studied systematically because the answers are so important.

There's Nothing Foreign About Comparative Studies

A field of study that has been developed with so much effort should not be applied only to trivial problems and projects, but for the central purposes of learning as a strategy for economic, social, political, and spiritual, development of people everywhere, particularly, the comparatively least advantaged. Many of these are close to home, there is nothing necessarily foreign about comparative studies.

In most Canadian cities, there are significant numbers of people from more than 100 countries and cultures, people who are learning to live in a new culture, perhaps with a new language, and different economic, social, and political realities, yet all maintaining their own identity, and their own heritage. Examples of cultural differences, cultural borrowing, cultural rejection, are all around us. There is no better laboratory for comparative studies than life in our communities, if we keep alert.

Or observe the fascinating similarities and differences that join and separate us from our francophone friends, residing in substantial large numbers in at least six of our provinces, not just Quebec. What more could one want for comparative studies than the observation of two systems of colleges, the CEGEPS of Quebec, and the CAATS of Ontario, initiated about the same time, comparable in function and size, and markedly different in philosophy, methods, outcomes?

Comparing can be done over time. Teachers may wish to study and present the changes that have occurred in Canadian secondary schools, or politics, or the teaching of mathematics, or changes in our theatre and literature, in the past fifty years. And how will that understanding help us cope with life in the balance of the century?

> *Teachers have so much to compare — the many learning styles chosen by themselves, or by their students, successful teaching modes of other teachers, how some teachers manage also to be good counsellors, the meaning and usefulness of a concept like "animateur", or "consciencizing".*

Instead of always sheltering under a conventional assessment mode such as multi-choice tests, a teacher might study the amounts of participation evoked as a response to various kinds of evaluation procedures.

At home or abroad, the questions are enriching.

The problems and decisions should not just be relatively simple ones, such as what proportion of the educational budget should go to elementary schools, secondary education, higher education, and adult education. Research results might guide such practical decisions, not just traditions of practice or educational business-as-usual attitudes. But comparative education can also help with a different order of questions. For example:

- Why and how do people in some countries work more effectively and willingly than others?
- How do countries prepare people for political or economic participation?
- Why and how, in such a fascinating world, do many adults become bored, apathetic, isolated, alienated, the prey to restlessness, alcoholism, violence?

Many other questions might be considered, questions which are rarely asked in any sustained way, but they are at the heart of the educational enterprise.

In the international conference on adult education for development held in Dar es Salaam in 1976, President Julius Nyerere said:

> *Development has a purpose; that purpose is the liberation of Man. But Man can only liberate himself or develop himself. He cannot be liberated or developed by another. For Man makes himself. It is his ability to act deliberately, for a self-determined purpose, which distinguishes him from the other animals. The expansion of his own consciousness, and therefore, of his power over himself, his environment, and his society, must, therefore, ultimately be what we mean by development.*
>
> *So development is for Man, by Man, and of Man. The same is true of education. Its purpose is the liberation of people from the restraints and limitations of ignorance and dependency. Education has to increase men's physical and mental freedom - to increase their control over themselves, their own lives, and the environment in which they live. The ideas imparted by education, or released in the mind through education, should, therefore, be liberating ideas. The skills acquired by education should be liberating skills.*

It is for personal development so conceived that instruction and research in comparative adult education has much to offer.

REFERENCES AND SUGGESTED READING

Bennett, C., Kidd, J.R. & Kulich, J. (1975) *Comparative Studies in Adult Education: An Anthology.* Syracuse: Syracuse University.

Blakely, R. (Ed) (1972) *Report of Nordberg Seminar on Comparative Adult Education* Syracuse: Syracuse University.

Canadian and International Education. Journal of the Comparative and International Education Society of Canada. (General resource.)

Charters, A. (1981) *Comparing Adult Education Worldwide.* San Francisco: Jossey-Bass Inc.

Comparative Education Review. Journal of the Comparative and International Education Society of the United States, Quarterly. (General resource.)

Convergence. Journal of the International Council for Adult Education, Toronto, Canada. (General resource.)

Harris, W.J.A. (1980) *Comparative Adult Education: Practice, Purpose and Theory.* London and New York: Longman.

Jones, P.E. (1971) *Comparative Education: Purpose and Method.* St. Lucia, Queensland: University of Queensland Press.

Kidd, J.R. *Comparative Studies in Adult Education.* (Reports of International Seminars held at OISE in 1968, 1969, 1971 and 1973). Toronto: Department of Adult Education, OISE.

Kulich, J. (1972) *World Survey of Research in Comparative Adult Education: A Directory.* Vancouver: Centre for Continuing Education, University of British Columbia.

Lowe, J. (1975) *The Education of Adults: A world Perspective.* Paris and Toronto: UNESCO and OISE Press. (Second Edition: 1982)

Peers, R. (1958) *Adult Education: A Comparative Study.* London: Routledge & Kegan Paul. Also New York: Humanities Press.

Titmus, C.J. (1981) *Strategies for Adult Education: Practices in Western Europe.* Chicago: Follett.

Ulich, M.E. (1965) *Patterns of Adult Education: A Comparative Study.* New York: Pageant Press Inc.

Chapter 12
Adult Distance Learning: Challenges for Contemporary Practice

Elizabeth J. Burge

Practitioner's Summary

Beginning by listing the three challenges of balancing the science and craft aspects of teaching, balancing all the elements in the learning context, and thinking holistically, Elizabeth Burge then provides a background to the burgeoning field of distance education by outlining some astonishing statistics.

To those who wonder why it is necessary to even think about distance education (aside from the increasing participation figures she quotes) Burge explains that distance education provides access for those who may be physically challenged, for those who have difficulty getting time off, for those with an unsupportive home context, for those who cannot get training at their workplace, and for all those for whom this mode of learning provides flexibility of place, time and privacy.

It is important to recognize the broadest possible meaning of "distance" and Burge defines this as "those logistical, economic, and cultural separations between providers and potential students, as well as geographic ones, that make it difficult for people to access training and education."

For others, distance education may be an exciting means to enhance their daily lives, to continue learning and developing new skills and knowledge, no matter where they may be living.

She notes too that "distance and face-to-face modes (of education) are finally beginning to merge in the recognition that educators have to work together if they are to attract adult students and give them greater flexibility in programs and modes of delivery."

In returning to the challenges of distance education, she describes balancing both the science and the craft. She describes the science as being for those who believe in prescriptions and treatments from scientific theories, and the craft as being for those who regard the key source of knowledge as their own reflections and their skills in adapting to the demands/needs of the students.

Her second challenge is not to permit any single element, for example, technology, to dominate. Teachers have to recognize that their roles will have to change from a transmission mode to a facilitation mode, but that this does not mean a change in skill or status. To do so, requires a familiarity with a range of productive teaching and learning strategies and the appropriate use of technology, both for delivery of information and for dialogue and critical analysis. She suggests a list of key questions to critically appraise the role of technology in any program.

In citing Clark, Miller and Griffin, Burge points to the final challenge of developing holistic approaches in distance education, and defines this as "wholeness rather than completeness, unity rather than conformity and diversity, not just differences." Her lengthy list of strategies to help promote holistic approaches is well worth remembering.

She even provides a discussion of four concepts: relationships, responsibilities, individuality and organization as her own "chunks" of information to aid recall and application. Her discussion ends on a note of the importance of feelings, one's own and that of others, and sometimes just to "let go" without "feeling silly or that time has been wasted."

Chapter 12
Adult Distance Learning: Challenges for Contemporary Practice

Elizabeth J. Burge

"Keep it direct, keep it relevant, but explore a little," Thelma said, with some conviction, persuading me to dig into my experience as a distance educator and talk about what is important to me in helping adults learn in distance mode programs.

I have decided to identify three challenges for my work as an adult educator who lives in visual classrooms (the traditional type) and the new classrooms of distance education. I will also discuss four ways of organizing the key information that helps me deal with those challenges. This chapter is not an exhaustive treatment of course design or of how to tutor in distance education. Nor is it a comprehensive and detailed explanation of adult teaching and learning strategies. It does, however, give some background about distance education as a context for exploring challenges. Further information is found in the Suggested Reading.

The challenges are
- *Balancing the science and craft aspects of teaching,*
- *Balancing all the elements in the learning context,*
- *Thinking holistically.*

Distance Education Expansion

With a history of innovation, partnerships and professional risk taking, distance education is expanding as never before.

Thirty-eight universities across Canada listed approximately 2,500 credit courses available in distance modes for the 1992/93 academic year. The 36 discipline areas are diverse in content, ranging through the arts, humanities, social and applied sciences (CAUCE/AEPUC, 1992). For Ontario, the estimate for the 1992/93 year of distance university courses is 780-800. The community college sector is developing interests in distance education as they seek to attract new clients and better serve existing ones. At the high school level, the Ontario Ministry of Education, through its Independent Learning Centre, is helping approximately 96,000 students, most of whom are adults, complete their high school diploma.

Continuing professional education is another area where distance education has already established itself and is attracting new client bases. For example, medical and para-medical professionals have their own extensive network (now called Telemedicine Canada) to deliver a large variety of short courses by audio conferencing and slow-scan video to thousands of practitioners (Roberts, 1984). In 1992/93 addictions workers in police, social work and allied fields successfully used a four-province link-up (Ontario and the Atlantic Provinces) by telephone for the delivery of five continuing education workshops (Burge, Smythe, Roberts & Keough, in press). Newfoundland and Labrador, as our most eastern province, has had a distinguished record since 1977 for its wide range of innovative adult education programs using a variety of distance methods. Other provinces can record similar success, but with a proportionately larger resource base.

The Canadian Association for Distance Education/Association canadienne de'education a distance (CADE/ACED) celebrates in 1993 ten years of vigorous work. (Rogers, 1993). CADE/ACED has run many workshops and conferences in face-to-face, phone and video formats. Its refereed journal, *Journal of Distance Education*, is one of the four international distance education English language journals. The others are *Open Learning* (UK), *The American Journal of Distance Education*, and *Distance Education* (Australia).

A growing body of books, monographs, and conference proceedings attest to the current expansion in practice. Overseas, the success of The Open University (UK) since 1970 has led to its imitation in nearly 20 countries. Estimates of numbers of distance education students world-wide are difficult to provide, especially since the size of some of the specialist (that is, distance mode only) universities have 90,000 students and more. The majority of the world's distance education students are women.

Modes of program delivery are variable and several modes may be integrated into a single course. For example, in addition to using well-designed attractive print materials and completing regular assignments for grading, a student may use the telephone for tutor advice, attend a residential school, discuss course content at local tutorials or in groups by audioconference, or communicate with peers and the tutor with computer conference software. In Western countries, distance education attracts proportionately more urban students than rural ones. Distance educators refer to the statistic that approximately 60-64% of their students live in towns and cities. While this fact may be a surprise to many adult educators, it is understandable if we look at why people use distance modes of delivery.

Why Distance Education?

The answers relate to barriers, outreach and how distance is defined.

> *Distance educators define distance as those logistical, economic, geographic and cultural separations between providers and poten-*

tial students. Barriers include whatever makes it difficult for people to access the education and training they want.

Sometimes structural barriers are inherent in the systems of education and could include timing of courses and location of classes, inadequate daycare facilities, employers who do not allow time off for studies, inability to transfer credits across educator's jurisdictions and many other reasons. Those who are physically challenged or who are uncertain about their ability to study successfully, or who travel a lot in their jobs, whose home context is unsupportive, or who simply prefer to learn on their own, enrol in distance mode programs so that they gain place and time flexibility and privacy if needed.

Another answer lies in the general societal demands for people to learn their living, to gain basic skills or to upgrade them.

Workers who cannot get training at their workplace may (if arrangements are in place) take distance mode courses and then 'top up' at a local institution if necessary.

Distance courses may help people enhance their living. Retirees for example, who want to achieve long-delayed ambitions to learn a new subject, skill or language. These students prove to be highly motivated.

Two further reasons for the increasing popularity of distance education lie in changing economics. Educational institutions need more students but cannot accommodate them physically, so they go searching for students who can stay in their local site. The quality preparation of many distance courses has convinced some skeptics that indeed there can be quality in distance courses. That level of quality is usually dependent upon a team-skill approach to course design and production, with learning designer, graphic design expert, and media producers working with the content expert. Librarians now provide sophisticated client services such as computer-based catalogue and CD-ROM data base searching, with fast delivery of documents.

Given all this activity, contemporary distance education is giving learners more choices of courses and greater flexibility in how they take these courses.

It is also challenging the dominance and alleged superiority of the walled classroom with its fixed time and place features:

> *The shift from school to home as the locus for the delivery of education appears at first sight to be a relatively simple change of location, but it is much more*

complex, not least because it causes us to rethink what we take for granted about education in institutional settings. We too readily assume that the organizational features of schools — classroom teaching, institutional timetables, simultaneous instruction — taken together constitute what counts as education, when they are essentially means not ends. (Walker, 1993)

Three Challenges for Teaching Adults by Distance

The first challenge: Balancing the science and craft aspects of teaching

Despite the evidence of growth and quality, there remain challenges for the science and craft of teaching adults by distance. The three that I discuss here are also relevant for educators working in walled classrooms, not only because adults are adults in any educational context, but also because

> *distance and face-to-face modes are finally beginning to merge in recognition that educators have to work together if they are to attract adult students and give them greater flexibility in programs and modes of delivery.*

The three challenges are inter-related in effect but are distinguishable in definition and substance.

> *The first challenge is to balance the science and craft involved in helping adults learn.*

This apparent dichotomy has been recognized by distance educators in our great 1990 debate in Caracas between the "Neats" and the "Scruffies."(Research in Distance Education, 1991)

The "Neats" are the applied scientists who insist that practice is driven by the prescriptions and treatments from scientific theories. The "Scruffies" are the reflective practitioners who regard such prescriptions and treatments as merely one source of knowledge; their key source of knowledge is their reflection in and on action, and their skills in 'flexing' to the demands of the context.

The Science Aspect ...

The Neats for distance education live mostly in the worlds of cognitive psychology, social psychology, and instructional technology. They use theories and research results to guide their prescriptions for action (for example, Gagne, Briggs & Wager, 1988). The cognitive psychologists have developed taxonomies of learning strategies (for example, Tessmer & Jonassen, 1988) to help us understand how people process, store and recall information. The researchers and the teachers who follow a strictly cognitive approach to learning, believe that we use particular strategies in order to actively make our own meaning out of the information that we select to process. Such construction is also an internal process (West, Farmer & Wolff, 1991). You cannot see it, but you can assess the results. The educational technologists use models to ensure that teachers follow sequential and analytical procedures to plan courses.

Having these bundles of scientific knowledge helps us pay attention to learning processes and the generic procedures most likely to promote those processes. The existence of this knowledge also helps us figure out how to apply those processes and procedures for adult learning settings. But is that all there is? Are the models adequate?

... and the Craft Aspect

Here the knowledge is tacit, the kind that skilled practitioners apply. (Schon, 1987) It is made up of values, past experience, internalized knowledge networks, and sophisticated problem-solving procedures. These components help make up the Scruffy style and philosophy. Scruffies show the craft aspects of teaching because their strategies are not standardized nor directed solely by theory, nor tightly prescriptive, nor carried out with cool, conscious rationality. The results are never exactly the same in form, the goals relate to individual contexts, and the thinking is often intuitive and divergent. The decisions and actions taken by Scruffies require personal integrity and authenticity if they are to be consistent and accepted. As craftspeople are not always sheltered and regulated by the blanket of established knowledge and traditional procedures, neither are the Scruffies. Especially vulnerable are Scruffies when they count the costs of reflecting-in-practice:

> *...we must give up the rewards of unquestioned authority, the freedom to practice without challenge to our competence, the comfort of relative vulnerability, the gratification of deference (Schon, 1987)*

When I reflect on my own practice, or quietly focus on how classroom dynamics are playing out (as distinct from how the class is studying the content), I invariably gain insights into the importance of the interpersonal dynamics in educational settings. I also recognize that I cannot fully control the impact of my interventions in people's ways of making their own meanings and that is quite humbling. (Burge & Haughey, 1993)

The second challenge: Balancing all the elements in the learning context

> *No single element in an adult learning context (for example, a technology) should dominate that context.*

Balance and integration are important because they support the conditions necessary for all the elements and their dynamics to flourish, and thereby create a rich, lively and coherent environment for learning. In such environments learners can 'grow their minds' and enjoy affirmation and challenge from peers and the teacher.

In confronting distance teaching for the first time, some teachers fear that because they are not actually standing or sitting in front of the students, they will not be able to function with authority or sensitivity. Others think that they should use their habitual style of lecturing for 50 minutes. After all, how else in traditional educational settings does one transmit information authoritatively.

> *The challenge is to explain that their roles have to change from a transmission mode to a facilitation mode, and that this change is not a reduction in skill or status.*

Teachers still have to think about providing adequate information, but now the emphasis is on planning and managing interactive activities that help learners to talk about their learning and to be exposed to the different perspectives of their peers.

After "traditional" teachers have experienced the distance education team process of planning the content structure and the sets of individual and group structured activities, it is not uncommon for some of them to happily admit to gaining ideas for better management of their visual classroom work.

But for a range of productive learning and teaching strategies to be used, we have to insist that any technology be used appropriately. Audio conferencing, for example, is designed for fast, two-way talk. That is how people use telephones. In a three hour credit course class, therefore, I guide the novice teacher to use a variety of on-air and off-air activities, with and without the teacher "present", to ensure that two-way talk actually happens and that the teacher does not dominate or control in dysfunctional ways.

> *Small learning groups are therefore organized to go off-air and complete structured tasks that directly relate to the specified learning objectives.*

When the whole class reconvenes, the students report back and critically respond to each other. Hopefully this is across the teacher so that the students sustain their discussion momentum, keep it multi-directional, and free it from any dysfunctional, continual "traffic management" by the instructor (however well-intentioned). When directly encouraged to assume half the responsibility for the class productivity, students will often rally and do lots of interesting things! In computer conferenced classes, students have to assume some responsibility and "response-ability" to ensure that two-way communications are sustained, and that people are not kept waiting too long for replies to messages.

I organize communication technologies in two ways: ones designed primarily for the delivery of information, and ones for dialogue and critical analysis of that information.

Delivery technologies most in use now are print materials, video and audio cassettes and library materials. Some of the dialogue technologies such as audio, video and computer conferencing, have been applied in education only since the late 1970's. Other forms, such as face-to-face tutoring, residential schools and weekend workshops have longer histories of successful use.

All the formats, however, present three key challenges to adult educators: how not to be driven by their "glitz and glitter"; how to ensure that they fit the general context in an ecological sense (their functions integrate with other contextual technologies and their use maximizes their unique features); and how to sustain the dynamics of group learning.

The double burden of distance educators

So distance educators have a double burden. We have to command the same repertoire of skills as a visual classroom teacher in order to promote learning alone and learning together. But we also must be critical and careful in our use of the technologies.

Technology can create two levels of impact: the first is the efficiency level where people see the technology as helping them do the same things faster, better, etc. This effect is called amplification. The second level effect is transformative where the technology actually produces qualitatively different and permanent changes in how we do things. (Kiesler, 1992)

Estimating impact through a critical approach

A critical approach to technology is described by the set of key questions I use to guide my own thinking or my response to eager educators who are (apparently) seduced by the glamour of "high tech":

- *Is the technology really necessary? Could another medium do it better?*
- *How exactly will it help the use of cognitive strategies?*
- *How exactly will it help the affective elements in learning?*
- *To whom will it deny access to education?*
- *How much on-going technical support is needed?*
- *Will it conquer the tyranny of distance, only to create new tyrannies of information overload, pace of class events, or mismanagement of agendas?*

These problems have emerged in some students' perceptions of learning in computer conferencing. (Burge, 1993; Harasim, 1987) With 24-hour access over seven days a week to write and send messages to classmates, prudent students will log on frequently to keep up with the discussion topics. Large numbers of mail messages go into all the subconferences of the course. The class discussions in a three month credit course, for example, could be divided into 12 - 15 subconferences, each having its own topic. If students are being graded on their participation, then the total amount of messages can add up quite quickly. The teacher or moderator, therefore needs many skills to manage the flow of information. (Davie, 1989)

The Third Challenge: Developing Holistic Approaches

The promotion of a holistic approach to my practice is the third challenge. It is the biggest in scope and impact. It has not been discussed widely in adult education (Maxfield, 1990: Griffin, 1988), and is almost absent from the distance education literature.

> *I understand it to focus on wholeness rather than completeness, on unity rather than conformity, and on diversity not just differences.*

Clark (1991) elaborates:holistic thinking is supported by the three principles of
- unity (the interconnectedness of everything in an environment),
- diversity (the mix of environmental qualities, functions and species necessary for the stable operation of that environment), and
- interdependence (the complex set of communication, organizational and other processes necessary for environmental viability).

Jack Miller (1988) focuses on interconnections and relationships:

> *...between linear thinking and intuition, the relationship between mind and body, the relationship between various domains of knowledge, the relationship between the individual and community and the relationship between self and Self.*

Virginia Griffin emphasizes the intrapersonal connections, and she describes her perceptions elsewhere in this book.

Strategies specifically related to adult holistic learning are gaining increasing attention. These strategies focus on developing an alert, open, flexible mind in a physically relaxed body, accessing information that was stored unconsciously, getting new ideas from old information, seeing the familiar as unfamiliar, and engaging in creative and divergent thinking. In working with adult learners, educators have to confront such issues as the potentially inhibiting effects of reduced self-concept and self-esteem that are experienced during the uncertainties of growth or change, especially in cases when significantly new cognitive frameworks are built.

One well-known example here of transformed knowledge is the adoption of feminist frameworks to analyze their world by women who have just gained insights about gender socialization and who have decided to do something about the negative effects of societal patriarchy to strengthen their presence in the world.

Another example could be the change by some western-world adults from their years of rational, analytical, logical ways of thinking and talking about their worlds to seeing that holistic and non-rational strategies are equally as valid. Professionals working in multicultural settings, for example, learn to accept that people of different cultures think differently about their worlds.

Strategies to promote holistic approaches

The following strategies are appropriate for most adult learners, and course designers can apply them in distance mode courses as well as in face-to-face modes. Griffin's chapter details others.

- Use intuitive and creating thinking, as well as analytical thinking.
- Generate metaphors, analogies and images to help understand concepts.
- Be aware of messages from the body (such as tiredness or fear) that may inhibit learning.
- Apply thematic and interdisciplinary treatments to the structuring of course content: look for ways to link different contents.
- Use multiple sources of information including autobiographical, artistic and dramatic expression.
- Look for patterns in information that may be more interconnected and complex than first thought.
- Legitimize the positive and negative feelings associated with learning.
- Have learners work in small peer groups without your omniscient presence, but ensure clear directions and realistic goals, and use learning partnerships to help learners reflect on their activity and progress and difficulties.
- Design assignments to have learners explore library collections and enjoy a serendipitous approach.
- Be in touch with your own cultural heritage and respect the heritage of others (no country is 'the greatest in the world').
- Legitimize and use relaxed silences in groups.
- Have learners use first-person language to help them claim ownership of personal values, experience and insights.
- Help learners experience unfamiliar ideas or see familiar ideas in unusual contexts.

How does a Busy Practitioner Remember All this Information?

It is one thing to be familiar with good ideas in books, but I have to cope with my own information overload problem! The solution is to follow one of the principles in processing information: chunk it for easier recall and application. My own chunking process has resulted in the emergence of four key concepts, each having a cluster of key issues and ideas that need my attention. Once I focus in on each issue or idea, I find it easier to think of relevant strategies.

> *The four concepts are:*
> - *Relationships*
> - *Responsibilities*
> - *Individuality*
> - *Organization*

Relationships

Clustering in the big oak tree of Relationships are different kinds of relationships, human ones and cognitive ones. The human ones are grouped into intrapersonal and interpersonal issues.

The *intrapersonal* ones focus on what we know about ourselves (self-concept), and feel about ourselves (self esteem), and how we link our past experience and present learning needs. They also include the existing knowledge frameworks in our heads and how these are being added to or changed by incoming information.

Another set of relationships lies in the cognitive learning objectives of the course or workshop. Taken as a group, are the objectives related in such a way that higher order thinking or performance skills are required? In other words, do the objectives require the learner to analyze and critique, or do they keep the learner at the lowest levels of understanding?

The *interpersonal* category of relationships has several branches. One branch shows the connections between the individual learner and everyone else - teacher, guest experts, class peers, library staff, etc. Another branch refers to the relationships that develop (or don't develop) in the context of small group activities and cooperative learning. Some groups experience the stages of being initiated as a new group (Forming), setting rules for conduct (Norming) and going through adjustments and conflicts (Storming) before they settle down to get things done (Performing). The quality of thinking in small groups will depend to some extent on how the group task and social elements are balanced.

As an educator, I have to think about the best conditions for supporting the different kinds of relationships, and helping the learner to develop the skills for sustaining the relationships that are most useful.

Responsibilities

The hedges of Responsibilities show the divisions between the obligations of learner and educator.

> *My responsibility as a distance learning designer is quite clear. It is to provide a structure of content and process choices to ensure that learners process relevant information in productive and enjoyable ways, and that teachers can promote effective peer learning and teaching.*

For example, I have to provide activities that help people organize new information into manageable chunks, analyze and explore the information, re-integrate it into new wholes, and then add it to existing knowledge frameworks. I also have to plan for small group tasks and whole class discussions that promote open-mindedness and exposure to new perspectives and information.

When I teach, my responsibilities are somewhat different. I group them into a list of 6 C's because they are easy to recall (chunking again ...):

- construct the climate for learning;
- connect learners to resources;
- confirm learners' insights and evidence of new learning;
- correct misunderstandings;
- change the agenda as needed;
- challenge learners to more sophisticated thinking.

Individuality

The thicket of Individuality needs careful negotiation! I cannot presume to understand the idiosyncratic ways in which people learn, nor how their cultural and life experiences influence their learning. I can draw learners' attention to the different ways in which we learn and that no two people learn in exactly the same way (we each have a 'cognition-print', like a fingerprint). People as a collective therefore may provide rich resources for learning that are available if the whole class uses its skills for pre-structured and experiential learning.

I also legitimize the pains of learning and the need sometimes to pause, or, as one of my students once called it, "taking a tactical advance to the rear." Giving learners time to pause, reflect and jot down notes in journals is one way; others are to prevent a breakneck speed of moving through course content, or not imposing on learners an overwhelming quality of information to be processed.

Organization

The obstacle course of Organization contains the minutiae as well as The Big Questions of logistics, materials preparation, local site preparation, checking of technical equipment, etc. Anything to thwart Murphy and his relatives from making things go wrong ...

Adult students in my experience, do not object to a sense of organization and structure if it helps them use time efficiently and exercise choices. They do, however, object to logistical and conceptual confusions, especially at the beginning of a course.

And finally, on feelings ...

I suspect, if my own experience is any guide, that many busy adults who are actively and deliberately learning, may need some encouragement to consciously take time out for themselves so that mind, body, and feeling can let go, are allowed to play and create, without feeling silly or that time is being wasted.

Writing this chapter has helped me take a "tactical advance to the rear" for a short time, to gain some perspective, and to think holistically in order to weave a new piece of fabric from a mass of threads. I hope that you too may connect some ideas and feelings and identify some key challenges to guide your practice.

REFERENCES

Barer-Stein, T. (1987) "Learning as a process of experiencing the unfamiliar." *Studies in the Education of Adults* (UK) Vol. 19, No. 2.

Burge, E.J. (1993) Students' Perceptions of Learning in Computer Conferencing: A Qualitative Analysis. University of Toronto. Unpublished doctoral dissertation.

Burge, E.J., Smythe, C.L., Roberts, J.M., and Keough, E.M. (in press) "The audioconference: Delivering continuing education for addictions workers in Canada." *Journal of Alcohol and Drug Education.*

Burge, E.J. and Haughey, M. (1993) "Transformative learning in reflective practice." In T. Evans & D. Nation (Eds.) *Reforming Open and Distance Education.* London: Kogan Page.

CAUCE/AEPUC: Canadian Association for University Continuing Education/ Association pour l'education permanente dans les universites du Canada. *Canadian University Distance Education Directory/Repertoire de l'enseignement a distance dans les universites canadiennes.* (1992/93) Ottawa: CAUCE/AEPUC.

Clark, E.T. (1991) "Holism: Implications of the new paradigm." Response to Purpel, Miller and Gelb. *Holistic Education Review.* Vol. 4, No. 2.

Collett, D.J. (1990) "Learning-to-learn needs for adult basic education." In R.M. Smith and Associates (Eds.) *Learning to Learn Across the Lifespan.* San Francisco: Jossey-Bass.

Davie, L.E. (1989) "Facilitation techniques for the online tutor." In R. Mason and A. Kaye (Eds.) *Mindweave: Communication, Computers and Distance Education.* Oxford: Pergamon Press.

Gagne, R.M., Briggs, L.J. and Wager, W.W. (1988) *Principles of Instructional Design.* (3rd edition). Fort Worth: Holt, Reinhart & Winston.

Harasim, L.M. (1987) "Teaching and learning online: Issues in computer-mediated graduate courses." *Canadian Journal of Educational Communication*. Vol. 16, No. 2.

Kiesler, S. (1992) "Talking, teaching, and learning in network groups: Lessons from research." In A.R. Kaye (Ed.) *Collaborative Learning Through Computer Conferencing*. Berlin: Springer-Verlag.

Kolb, D.A. (1984) *Experiential Learning: Experience as the Source of Learning and Development*. Englewood Cliffs, NJ: Prentice-Hall.

Maxfield, D. (1990) "Learning with the whole mind." In R.M. Smith & Associates (Eds.) *Learning to Learn Across the Lifespan*. San Francisco: Jossey-Bass.

Melamed, L. (1987) "The role of play in adult learning." In D. Boud and V.R. Griffin (Eds.) *Appreciating Adults Learning: From the Learners' Perspective*. London: Kogan Page.

Miller, J.P. (1988) *The Holistic Curriculum*. Toronto: OISE Press.

Research in Distance Education. (1991) "Neats versus scruffies" (Applied scientist versus reflective practitioners). Vol. 3, No. 1.No author given.

Roberts, J.M. (1984) "The use of teleconferencing in continuing medical education in Canada." *Annals of the Royal College of Physicians and Surgeons of Canada, RCPS*(C), Vol. 17, No. 1.

Rogers, K. (in press) *Innovation, Risk-taking and Collaboration*. A Celebration and History of CADE/ACED and Distance Education in Canada.

Schon, D.A. (1987) *Educating the Reflective Practitioner*. San Francisco: Jossey-Bass.

Tessmer, M., & Jonassen, D. (1988) "Learning strategies: A new instructional technology." *World Yearbook of Education*. London: Kogan Page.

Walker, R. (1993) "Open learning and the media: Transformation of education in times of change." In T. Evans & D. Nation (Eds.) *Reforming Open and Distance Education: Critical Reflections from Practice*. London: Kogan Page.

SUGGESTED READING

Adult Learning and Teaching

Anderson, J.R. (1990) *Cognitive Psychology and its Implications* (3rd edition) New York: W.H. Freeman.

Cranton, P. (1989) Planning Instruction for Adult Learners. Toronto: Wall & Thompson.

Davidson, N. & Worsham, T. (Eds.) (1992) *Enhancing Thinking Through Cooperative Learning*. New York: Teachers College Press.

Galbraith, M.W. (Ed.) (1991) *Facilitating Adult Learning: A Transactional Process*. Malabar, FL: Krieger.

Gronlund, N.E. (1991) *Stating Objectives for Classroom Instruction*. (4th edition) New York: Macmillan.

Distance Education

Burge, E.J. (in press) "Thinking holistically" A new perspective on distance learning." To be published in the *Proceedings of The Second American Symposium on Research in Distance Education May 22-24, 1991*. College Park, PA: Penn State University, The American Center for the Study of Distance Education.

Burge, E.J., J.M. Roberts and their Associates (1993) *Telecommunications for Learning: A Practical Introduction for Educators.* Toronto: OISE Press.

Burge, E.J. and Snow, J.E. (1990) "Interactive audio classrooms: Key principles for effective practice." *Education for Information.* Vol. 8.

Eastmond, D.E. (1992) "Effective facilitation of computer conferences." *Continuing Higher Education Review.* Vol. 56, No. 1 and 2.

Department of the Secretary of State of Canada, Canadian Studies Directorate (1993) Open learning and distance education in Canada (2nd edition).Ottawa.

Faith, K. (Ed.) (1990) *Toward New Horizons for Women in Distance Education: International Perspectives.* London: Routledge.

Harasim, L. (Ed.) (1990) *Online education: Perspectives on a New Environment.* New York: Praeger.

Hiltz, S.R. (1992) "Constructing and evaluating a virtual classroom." In M. Lea (Ed.) *Contexts of Computer-Mediated Communication.* New York: Harvester/Wheatsheaf.

Moore, M.G., Thompson, M.M. and others (1990) *The Effects of Distance Learning: A Summary of Literature* (ACSDE Research Monograph, No. 2). College Park, PA: Penn State University, The American Center for the Study of Distance Education.

Race, P. (1989) *The Open Learning Handbook: Selecting, Designing and Supporting Open Learning Materials.* London: Kogan Page.

Chapter 13

The Future of Adult Learning

Allen Tough

Practitioner's Summary

Allen Tough notes that although adult learning is probably as old as human civilization, it has been changing over the years. Changes are noted in the purposes and the curriculum as adult educators realize the effect of education on the community as well as on the individual adult learners. New technologies, roles, functions and services are also changing the face of adult education.

People need to learn more in order to travel, improve their personal relationships, engage in their own projects, and maintain a livelihood with the increasing job complexity. The primary purpose of adult education is to foster these practical sorts of learning, and adults are more willing to pay for learning that is practical. Liberal arts education has declined in recent years.

Adult educators are becoming increasingly involved in social mission issues, that is, in the wide range of social, global and national issues that increasingly affect us all. Futurists agree that educators of adults will be playing increasingly important roles in fostering individual changes in attitudes, understanding and behaviour. Affective aspects such as feelings, intuition and empowerment will also have to be understood.

Demand for facilitating adult learning will be continually increasing in at least four populations: those who need basic literacy and numeracy skills, upgrading for employment, professional upgrading of skills and knowledge, and retired adults eager to learn.

Technology will become increasingly interactive, and these will enhance the already burgeoning percentages of adults engaged in self-planned learning.

Tough concludes with a practical list for adult educators who want to "do something":

- Consider your own sense of social mission.
- Clarify your own personal meaning of life.
- Incorporate local and global issues into all teaching.
- Expand your own learning and your own learning about the future.
- Learn more about the potential future for adult learning.

Chapter 13
The Future of Adult Learning
Allen Tough

The activity of adult learning is as old as human civilization. It changes over the years, though. Major changes are now occurring in its purposes and curriculum: more and more adult educators realize that they can affect the future of their community or nation as well as the lives of individual learners. Major changes are also occurring in the populations served by adult education and in its new technologies. And some new roles, functions, and services are being added.

Changing Purposes

> *Most knowledge and skill is learned because the adult expects to use it in some practical way.*

As jobs generally become more complex, they require more learning. As people travel more, try to improve their relationships, take on more do-it-yourself projects, and begin new recreational activities, they must *learn* more in order to do these things successfully.

The primary purpose of many adult education institutions is to foster these practical sorts of learning. Adults are generally more willing to pay for learning that they will put to practical use than for learning that satisfies their curiosity, puzzlement and general learning interests. Learning that seems clearly practical and useful, is increasingly emphasized by institutions under pressure to market adult education effectively and to be financially self-sufficient or profitable. Non-credit liberal arts education and education about world issues, that were popular with the general public well past the middle of the century, have unfortunately declined in popularity in recent years.

Although many adult educators are not yet heeding this,

> *a significant number of adult educators are calling for a renewed sense of social mission, with major or even radical social changes as the central purpose.*

Virtually all adults are interested in at least one issue. This is partly because many of the issues affect us significantly or will someday affect our children and their children. Even if they have not experienced the issue firsthand or through conversations and mass media, almost every adult has heard about poverty, hunger, violence, crime, war, injustice, human rights, environmental issues, feminist issues, racism, and inner-city problems. As a result of familiarity with such issues, and maybe also with being puzzled, upset or eager for change, many adults want to learn more through courses, workshops, discussion groups, self-planned learning, media, or reading.

> *There are several pockets within adult education that are particularly committed to teaching about social, community and global issues.*

Within peace and environmental education for adults, for instance, and within many grassroots movements, a high commitment to fundamental social change is still central. Within the adult education department at OISE (Ontario Institute for Studies in Education) faculty and students in the Critical Global and Community Issues focus are exploring effective ways of fostering learning about the wide range of social, national, and global issues. More and more adult educators are realizing that they can make a difference to the future of their community and nation as well as to the lives of individual men and women.

Most futurists (people who study various potential futures) agree that

> *any successful path to a positive future will require huge changes in the attitudes, understanding, and behaviour of adults and youth.*

Clearly, educators of adults will play a key role in fostering these individual changes. Our vision of our vocation of teaching adults can include our impact on society. Politicians, business leaders, and writers will affect the future of course, but so will we!

As more and more people teach others about various issues, we realize that we have to deal with the heart as well as the head, with feelings and intuition and empowerment as well as information, reason and logic. Most issues arouse strong fear, sadness, horror, anger, or even paralysis — the feeling that "things just feel too overwhelming for me to make any difference." Anyone teaching about global issues or social problems needs to help the learners express and deal with their emotions in order to move from paralysis to empowerment and commitment. People also want help in sorting out the implications for their own lives: "What should I do about these problems? What part can I play in achieving a happier, more humane world?"

Who Will Learn?

> *Almost every adult already learns intentionally, and the amount of learning may well increase in the future as our rapidly changing world becomes even more complex.*

Demand for knowledge and skill will continue to be very high. In any given year, 90% of adults already engage in at least one major learning effort. In fact, they conduct an average of five of these highly intentional learning efforts, and spend an average of loo hours at each one. These findings seem to apply to much of the world: confirming results come from Australia, Canada, France, Ghana, Holland, Jamaica, New Zealand, United Kingdom, United States, and Zaire.

> *Demand for institutional programs to facilitate adult learning shows no sign of diminishing. Demand is likely to increase for serving at least four target populations:*
> *l. people who need basic skills in reading, communicating, speaking English as a second language, arithmetic, and applying for a job;*
> *2. employed people who need to upgrade their job skills or prepare for new responsibility as technology and the work world rapidly change;*
> *3. professionals and experts who need to keep up with new knowledge and techniques in their field;*
> *4. retired adults, who are becoming more numerous and more eager to learn.*

A wide variety of educational enterprises will provide education or training for each of these target groups, sometimes with the cooperation of governments and employers. Adult education is a vast and expanding enterprise, already much larger than elementary education or secondary education.

Educational Technologies

Computers have assisted instruction for more than twenty years. Using computers to communicate with other students and the instructor is increasingly common in distance education. No matter how far apart they are, computers can send messages to other computers instantly; the receiving computer then stores the message until the user requests it at a convenient time. Despite the lack of face-to-face interaction, early experience indicates that this communication may feel even more social and personal than the typical classroom.

> *Adult learners are already using teleconferencing, electronic mail, computer bulletin boards, radio and television broadcasts, video cassettes, laser videodiscs, and CD-ROM reference publications.*

Access to data and to educational programs, as well as communication among learners, will presumably become faster and easier as technology and media develop further. There is also a trend toward integrating various functions in just one or two user-friendly machines. Voice recognition may even eliminate the need for a keyboard. In addition, artificial intelligence may enable computers to function as sophisticated mentors to the learner, making the instruction much more individualized.

New Roles, Functions, and Services

Several new roles, functions, and services are likely to develop within adult learning during the next few decades.

> *These new roles will arise as teachers of adults pay more attention to* self-planned *learning, also called self directed learning.*

Although we usually don't think much about it, self-planned learning efforts are in fact a very normal natural part of our work and our life. Close to 100 surveys of various groups in 10 countries have confirmed that about 90% of all women and men conduct at least one highly intentional learning project in any given year. Even more impressive, as I mentioned earlier, the typical (median) adult learner spends about 500 hours a year at these various learning efforts — about 10 hours each week! About 70% of these learning projects are planned by the learner himself or herself. Clearly then, self-planned adult learning is a natural and normal activity, at least in the 10 countries that have been studied.

Educators of adults are paying more and more attention to self-planned or self-directed learning. Instead of ignoring it, they are finding ways to foster and facilitate it. This leads them to experiment with new roles in adult learning - new functions and services that they can provide —far beyond the role of simply transmitting information to a class.

For instance, new types of counselling services and workshops are helping adults choose their broad learning goals and broad strategy, and improve their individual competence in guiding their own learning. Information services provide plentiful information about the wide array of available opportunities and resources. Libraries and other sorts of self-directed learning centres are interested in fostering the planning, learning, and assessment tasks faced by adults during their self-planned learning. Life-planning centres help people cope with a rapidly changing world beset with major problems, and decide how to make their optimum contribution toward a positive future for humanity.

What Can We Do?

What can we suggest to the individual teacher of adults who wants to do something about all this? Several possible suggestions come to mind:

- Think about your own sense of social mission, your own hopes about making a difference to the world.
- Clarify your own personal meaning in life, your own motivations for teaching adults, and your highest values.

- Try to bring local and global issues into everything you teach, no matter what the subject matter. And bring in the potential futures for your subject matter: what might be happening in your field 20 years from now?
- Remember that you yourself are a learner as well as a teacher. Learn as much as you can about global issues and the amazing range of potential futures for humanity. Browse through the recent library issues of *Future Survey* or some other thoughtful writing about the future. My own book, *Crucial Questions About the Future,* is written as an introduction to the "big questions" about our future.
- Learn more about the potential future for adult learning.

SUGGESTED READING

Brockett, Ralph, (Ed.) (1987) Continuing education in the year 2000. In *New Directions in Continuing Education, no. 36.* San Francisco: Jossey-Bass.

Lewis, H. (1989) New educational technologies for the future. In S. Merriam and Cunningham P. (Eds.) *Handbook of Adult and Continuing Education.* San Francisco: Jossey-Bass.

Tough, A. (1987) "Potential futures: Implications for adult educators." *Lifelong Learning.* Vol. 2, No. l.

Tough, A. (1991) *Crucial Questions About the Future.* Lanham, Maryland: University Press of America.

Chapter 14
Advice and Empathy: Teachers Talking With Teachers

James A. Draper

Practitioner's Summary

Part-time teachers of adults have sometimes been referred to as "the neglected species", but here in this discussion of the findings of a four-year study of part-time teachers of adults in continuing education departments of school boards, colleges and universities, Draper offers a framework of familiarity - others who have trod the same path – together with sensitive and significantly practical insights. The previously "neglected" are highlighted.

How they feel about themselves as both teachers and learners; how teaching adults has affected their own lives as well as their other teaching; the advice gently offered and the empathy expressed in handling common problems are all here in plain language.

The 'teacher as a learner in the classroom' is shown to be more manifest when the students are the same age or older, with life experiences going far beyond the classroom, and when the emotion attached to learning is openly evident. Two basic principles of teaching loom more strongly than ever before:

1. beginning the teaching process from where the students are.
2. how capacity for learning begins with self-perception.

Recognizing what you yourself as a teacher need and want to learn, may be the first step to understanding your students as adults and as learners. Many teachers expressed a general enhancement of their other work and their daily life as a result of a deepening sensitivity for the needs and abilities of others. Many spoke also of a deepening ability to reflect on their own teaching and derive a more profound meaning. Much of what they learned in teaching adults such as: taking time to include more discussion, more planning and evaluation, and more input of daily life, led them to teach in this way with younger students as well, and with increased satisfaction.

"Reflection is the first step to giving advice and experience is the basis for empathy" may well become the adult teacher's bywords. Taking the time to give consideration to the individuals in the classroom and drawing on your own as well as their experiences enriches the content, the process and even the outcome of the educative process. Planning and preparation is always important, but so is flexibility and spontaneity and the readiness to relinquish all-knowing and authoritative stances. "Being human" stood out as an important attribute.

Much of the excitement of learning is in the evolving, unpredictable and unanticipated learning that inevitably occurs. Being open to this was something that many teachers had to learn for themselves. Persistently sticking to prepared lesson plans resulted in a stilted class. Realizing that "the richest resource in the classroom are the members present" helped teachers to relax and enjoy themselves too. Such congruence between belief and practice enhanced all.

Chapter 14
Advice and Empathy: Teachers Talking with Teachers

James A. Draper

Part-time teachers of adults have sometimes been referred to as a 'neglected species', meaning that they are sometimes neglected by the schools, colleges, or other institutions that employ them.

Traditionally, but less so today, these teachers have been marginal to the system, like phantoms of the night that rush in weekly to share the gems of their knowledge or skills, only to disappear again into those activities of work and personal life that occupy the centres of their daily living. This image is rapidly changing. Increasingly, it is realized that the effectiveness of these teachers is determined by the extent to which they are integrated into the system that employs them.

Are part-time instructors integrated into the system? Are they adequately supported, as teachers and as learners, by their part-time employer? Even today, little is known about this rapidly growing cadre of educators of adults.

- What motivates these teachers to continue to teach adults, part-time?
- How do they feel about themselves as teachers and as learners?
- Does the experience of teaching adults influence their personal or full-time working lives?
- What did these instructors need to learn in order to work with adults?
- By what means did they achieve this learning?
- What sustains their interest in working with adults, and what proportion of them would like to make a greater commitment of time to teaching adults?

A four year longitudinal study of such instructors (Draper, 1987) has attempted to answer these, and many other questions, to understand more fully the interests, characteristics, and commitment of the part-time teacher. The illustrations and quotes within this chapter come from the teachers who participated in this study.

In this chapter, attempts are made to present the teachers themselves as learners, to discuss the broader goals of teaching, as well as to show some of the factors that inhibit and enhance both teaching and learning. After presenting a framework for teacher reflections, this chapter records the advice which part-time teachers give to newcomer teachers of adults and concludes by identifying some of the factors that characterize the craft of teaching adults. Even though references are made to the part-time teacher of adults, the basic ideas and practices apply to all aspects of teaching, whatever the goal or setting.

Central to the act of teaching is sharing, reflection and introspection. Teaching and learning are inseparable acts.

Teachers As Learners

It is not always stated that the teacher is as much of a learner in a classroom setting as the adults who enroll in the course.

This comes as no revelation. The teacher must continue to keep abreast of the subject matter or skill being taught, but the teacher learns much more. The context of teaching is an environment for learning and so the teacher learns how to relate to others, to communicate more effectively with others, and to organize materials more efficiently. We have to acknowledge as well the emotional learning which arises from the physical and social setting within which the teaching takes place. More and more it is realized that the roles of teacher and student, of giver and receiver, are interchangeable. Each adult person in a student role has years of experience that need to be taken seriously. To live is to learn, to change and to grow. Each adult has some experience with the content or skill that is being taught. It becomes obvious that there is a wealth of resources within the classroom that needs to be tapped and creatively shared. When asked what they have learned from their part-time teaching, teachers refer to the exciting challenge of orchestrating the resources and experiences within the learning environment. Special skills are required to do this.

To categorize the various responses from part-time teachers, we would have to include their learning about adults as learners; about themselves as teachers and learners; about the process of teaching; and the process of relating to others. Teachers have said that they have learned that adults can be highly directional and demanding; that most adults have a strong motivational drive to learn; that adults desire to cooperate; that there is a greater appreciation of the wisdom that comes from normal life experiences; that adults are often forgiving, and will overlook minor errors; and that adults have natural insecurities about themselves as learners and in aspects of their daily lives. The part-time teachers also expressed a great respect for adults returning to school.

What They Had to Overcome

When asked what they felt they had to overcome to improve as instructors, they commented that they needed to become more understanding, patient and supportive of the adult learners. They said that they also needed to re-examine the pace in which they organize and present content; to be flexible in developing a schedule in order to allow for student goals and interests to become more integrated into the teaching; and to learn to speak and explain things more slowly and clearly. They spoke of having to overcome their own insecurities, of having to face their age peers, or even adult learners that were older than themselves. "When I began teaching adults, I was younger than my students, and so I first had to grow up". They gradually became more sensitive to what their adult students were thinking about the teacher and the presentation. The importance of sharing information, the stimulation which comes from posing and solving problems, and a greater appreciation for the rate at which learners learn, (which is not just a matter of age differences) are also some of the things that teachers learn from teaching adults. Acknowledging the counselling in which they often become involved, the teachers realized that by being less judgemental they were able to gain insight into the personal problems faced by adult students.

> *Teachers quickly become aware that the concerns of students go beyond the world of the classroom.*

Because of this, it is important for teachers to be less structured and rigid in the classroom. Adults are evolving and complex. The roles of worker, parent, spouse, friend, and the concerns and emotions of living are not left behind as the adult enters the clasroom. This applies to adult teachers as well as to the adult students. Teachers continue to learn about the many factors which influence commitment - such factors as a sick child, an aging parent, the death of a friend, the break-up of one's marriage, financial problems, job insecurities. All these and more will influence the attention that one gives to learning. Teachers realize too that blaming someone for not being motivated can be as obscure or as inappropriate as blaming someone for being sick. Blaming others for lacking enthusiasm for learning, can often be an excuse for the inadequacies of the teacher or the mismanagement of learning. As one part-time instructor commented:

> *Success is not always dependent on me, the instructor. Adult students have a responsibility, as I have, to make things work and to facilitate their own learning and the learning of others. This helps to explain why I have differing feelings of success, from class to class.*

What is to be learned within the classroom is not limited to the subject matter or skills to be taught. All subject matter has an emotion associated with it.

Two Basic Teaching Principles

> *Two basic principles of teaching are paramount. The first is that one should begin the teaching process from where the students are.*

Second, that the openness and capacity for learning is critically determined by the learner's self-perception.

Teachers also said that they have more sensitivity about themselves and others and had developed a greater willingness to share, as well as a greater feeling of confidence in themselves. Being more self-reflecting is another achievement that was valued by teachers. "Recently, I have become a student myself, in a non-credit course, and this has made me more aware of my practice as a teacher of adults".

Sensitive teachers quickly realize that the content to be taught must often take second place to dealing with the student's self-concept. If adults have internalized mythologies that they are not able to learn, then the first step in the teaching-learning process is to change this self-concept. It may be helpful to examine the labels that have been internalized, such as stupid, lazy or retarded. Labelling within the educational system has been one of the greatest deterrents to learning.

Asking teachers what they want to learn is one way of describing the breadth of the tasks and skills which encompass their craft.

Asking teachers what they do and do not do well in class is another way of assessing the instructor's perception of teaching, recognizing what has been satisfactorily acquired and what is still to be learned and practiced. Teachers in the study had much to say about their own learning, covering aspects such as:

1. wanting to learn more about alternative methods for assessing learning,
2. how to build on the trust of others,
3. how to more fully exploit the strong learning drives of adults,
4. the handling of interpersonal relationships.

Balancing The Equation Between Teaching and Learning

What is learned is not limited in its application.

Teaching adults affects all teaching

Part-time teachers of adults were asked if their experiences from working with adults had any influence, directly or indirectly, on their personal or professional life. Many of those that were professional full-time teachers of children and youths, felt that their teaching of adults had helped to make them better teachers. Many found that they were more tolerant of others as learners and more confident of themselves. Teaching adults has "influenced me to upgrade my qualifications", and "has helped me to more effectively keep up with my subject matter". Many felt that they were more explicit in giving instructions and in communicating. Some instructors commented that they felt that they had developed better working habits. Another remarked that: "Because of having a better understanding of adults, I feel that my counselling of high school students has improved". Having a greater awareness of the teacher-student relationship and having a different perspective of the educational process and the sequencing of learning, building on what people have learned as a way of facilitating further learning, were additional ways that teachers improved professionally as an outcome of their working with adults.

Teaching adults affects personal life

The experience of teaching adults was also said to influence the personal lives of many of these part-time teachers. Some expressed the feeling that they were more consciously attempting to apply, for others and themselves, their content areas to daily living. Others commented on their improved skills in listening, delegating and managing of time. Other experiences that influenced their lives beyond that of teaching included: feeling that the quality of their personal interaction with others had increased; having a greater understanding of the learning problems of others; being more sympathetic and empathetic of others and feeling more relaxed and confident with others; working more cooperatively and effectively in committees and groups; having a greater understanding of how people 'tick'; and an improvement in their own ability to handle concepts.

Other expressions of learning transfer are exemplified by such comments as:

- *As a result of my teaching adults, I feel that my life is fuller and happier.*
- *I now have a greater appreciation of my own ongoing learning and experiences.*
- *Working with others, as a teacher, has helped to mirror myself.*
- *Working with adults has greatly broadened my outlook.*
- *I now have a greater respect for and appreciation of the contribution from others.*
- *I feel that I now have a better understanding of human nature and the variations among people, including why some people seem to try harder than others.*

A person who taught photography to adults symbolically remarked: "Working with adults has helped me to 'see' better."

> *Being involved with teaching should encourage one to reflect on the act and the meaning of teaching.*

Many of the part-time teachers said that, as a result of working with adults, they had re-examined their role as teacher, not just as one who imparts knowledge, but also as one who facilitates the learning of others. Some even raised the question: Does it make sense to compartmentalize teaching by age groups? One teacher comments: "Teaching adults is no different than teaching anyone else."

In a 1978 (Draper) study, the deans of education in the province of Ontario were asked: What is the purpose of your Faculty of Education? Most responded: "The purpose of this Faculty is to produce teachers to work with children or youth, in order to find employment primarily within the public school system."

It is interesting that the response should link the preparation of teachers to working with specific age groups (younger people) for the purposes of finding employment with specific publicly-supported institutions.

One dean responded differently, "The purpose of this Faculty is to produce effective and qualified teachers." He made no reference to any specific age group or to a specific employer. In fact, within this particular Faculty of Education, the teachers-in-training were allowed to do their training practicum with any age group. Some teachers-in-training were working with adults in business, industry, and in prisons.

Some of the teachers in this study expressed a greater understanding of the learning process as a result of their part-time teaching:

> *I don't feel that I need to rush through the course that I teach. There is more to my course than the content that I am attempting to teach.*

Here we can make a distinction between the process and the product of teaching and learning. For all learning, the outcome (product) is to acquire some mastery and appreciation of the subject matter or skills being taught. The intended outcome of training teachers, medical doctors, electricians, carpenters, or any other profession or trade, is to produce a qualified person in that field. Frequently this is linked to a particular method or 'process' of training. However, the journey of learning is the process. Slowing down to absorb from this journey, to experience it to its fullest, to value the input of experiences from others as well as the individual and collective reflection and sharing of these experiences, are, in themselves, worthy goals for learning.

> *The process should be enjoyed as well as the destined goal.*

Generic goals in teaching/learning

Learning is not a one-time experience but occurs throughout our life span. Undue attention is often given to mastering a specific subject matter or skill. Much more occurs and is intended to occur in the teaching-learning process. Many generic goals for teaching transcend the imparting of knowledge. Some of these are: improving one's self-concept as a learner and developing the skills of learning how to learn; increasing the independency or interdependency of learners; increasing one's sensitivity and skills for facilitating the learning of others. The quality of living and learning is enhanced through sensitive interaction with others.

> *Developing our competencies to assess our own learning, understanding our own learning style and internalizing the value of learning as a lifelong process are other examples of generic goals. 'Learning To Be' is the goal of all education. (Faure, 1972)*

Frameworks for Reflections

Reflection helps to make sense of experiences giving greater direction and meaning to learning. Reflecting can focus on relationships with others, extending our meaning of achievement, helping to grasp meaning and significance, or understanding the structure of a problem.

Some Factors That Facilitated or Inhibited Teacher's Work

Political/organizational factors

These areas of concern relate to planning and conceptualizing and includes issues relating to certification and professionalism. These determine who will teach, administer or counsel within educational programs. The bureaucratization of adult education programs can be especially distracting and disturbing especially if the system's organization is in philosophical contradiction to that practiced within the program or within the classroom.

For instance, if the intended classroom teaching environment is that of trust, self-direction, learner-centred and informal, then the administrative structure needs to reflect this. This in turn is influenced or governed by policy and legislation at various levels which govern the way power is perceived and applied. What is the degree of flexibility and tolerance within the larger system? This cluster of concerns relates to the way in which decisions are made, the way in which programs are administered and various issues relating to the legitimacy of adult education programs within institutions.

Social/psychological factors

This category encompasses one's view of human nature and includes the governing principles of teaching and learning, and especially focuses on the affective aspects of learning. If individual adult learners do not have a positive, growing self-concept of themselves, and for education and learning; a sense of trust for themselves, their instructors, administrators, counsellors and for the system, then effective learning is not likely to occur. A lack of positive feelings affects the initial and sustaining motivation for learning and therefore can inhibit intended learning.

Resources/management factors

This category of concerns includes the allocation and effective management of resources of all kinds — money, materials and human resources and encompasses the planning and implementation of programs including: the advertising of programs; the recruitment and selection of participants/learners, instructors/teachers, administrators and counsellors; the procurement and use of physical facilities and materials; and the way in which the media and audiovisual materials and equipment are used.

> ***Having resources alone does not automatically produce good educational programs, but the availability and effective management of resources are crucial to good programs.***

Evaluation/accountability concerns

Each participant in an educational program should be accountable for its success. Each individual knows what constitutes 'success' and 'effectiveness' since these are personal perceptions. Reflection on one's participation in a program is usually based on initial goals and values which in turn will largely influence the criteria or stated indicators for assessment. Accountability can be both objective and subjective, and include the quantitative and qualitative aspects of one's observations, feelings, and experiences. Evaluating educational programs needs to be flexible enough to allow for the unintended outcomes of learning as well as individual creativity and curiosity. A lack of flexibility, vision, and clarity on educational goals can become inhibiting factors to learning.

It is obvious that there is much overlapping of the components of these four categories. The degree and seriousness of specific inhibiting factors, few of which would exist in isolation, will depend on the perceptions and character of the personalities involved. Training, research, coordination, continuity, culture, psychology and management transcend all of the categories. Expressions of opinion and feelings from teachers are varied and complex. *What is not said is sometimes as important as what is said.* It was to emphasize this that the four categories have been presented, as a way of accounting, not only for what was said, but also for what was not expressed by the teachers.

Advice with Empathy

> *Reflection is the first step to giving advice; experience is the basis for empathy.*

You want my advice? Dare I give it? This section summarizes the advice that part-time teachers offer to new teachers of adults. The reflections and resultant advice were offered with the feelings of humility, excitement and encouragement. All of the responses implied an enthusiasm for teaching adults, encouraging the newcomer to "allow yourself to become involved".

Individual teachers have said: "Here is what I have learned. Here is what I tried." Advice included comments about the adult student, what constitutes a good teacher, communication, methods of teaching, and the underlying beliefs that give meaning to working with adults.

As obvious as it seems, many of the teachers commented on the necessity of knowing the subject matter thoroughly, being well organized, and to logically sequence any presentation from simple to complex. Selecting and using handouts in class makes it essential to know how and when these will be used in class.

> *"Plan good and interesting lessons, but at the same time, be realistic and practical. Good planning allows for spontaneous interaction." "Don't panic", "Be yourself", and "Take the attitude that you will enjoy the experience."*

The need to communicate

Comments along this line included advice about allowing time in class for discussion and for the sharing of experiences, the importance of the teacher to also share and interact, the importance of injecting fun and enjoyment into the instruction to set a favourable climate for learning, enhancing communication. Further examples included:

- *Share your teaching interests and don't apologize for being enthusiastic about what you are doing.*
- *Understand why adults drop out from your class. It's not necessarily because of you. Don't feel that you need to take this personally.*
- *Use class input when you are planning your class sessions.*
- *At the beginning of each class session, have a weekly overview, possibly having adult students taking turns to do this.*
- *Take time to explain and make every effort to avoid misunderstandings.*
- *Give clear and simple explanations and demonstrations.*
- *Remember that listening is an essential part of communicating.*
- *Do not patronize adult students or underestimate their intelligence.*
- *Don't assume you know everything.*
- *Be caring and take the questions asked in class seriously.*

Learning styles

Each adult has a preferred style for learning and a teacher can usually assume that styles will be varied within a given class. As a long-term investment in learning, teachers might begin their course by discussing the various styles and the assumptions people have about learning. (Kolb, 1976) Such discussions can help to explain the different ways of perceiving the value of process, of group interaction and the place and value of sharing experiences. Teachers and students can benefit from knowing their own learning styles, especially if the generic goals for teaching and learning values "learning how to learn".

Alternative approaches to teaching

Being familiar with alternative approaches to teaching and learning applies as much to teachers as to students. One teacher made the point that:

> *Many of the adults came to my class expecting the same structure which they remembered from their past experience. They wanted a strict, Socratic lesson based on readings, homework assignments, and tests, even though that might not have been the best process of learning for them. It appeared that they had this*

stereotype of education and had convinced themselves that there was security in doing things the old way.

Teachers and students all have stereotypes and expectations of education, including stereotypes of the role of a teacher or a student. Each has expectations of how these roles are performed and the relationship between them.

> *Beginning where people are is acceptable, but striving toward seeking alternative ways of involvement can become an exciting experience for those committed to learning. Teachers quickly realize that the richest resource in the class are the members present.*

The challenge of this statement is how to make constructive use of these resources, so that people will want to share what they know and will want to participate and learn from others. What often distinguishes the experienced from the inexperienced teacher is the ability to use appropriate methods for a given situation. The experienced teacher, adult educator, is aware of alternative methods. The purpose of what is being taught, the experience of the learner and the time available, will all determine the method that is most appropriate. Part of the excitement of teaching is to share the orchestration of learning.

Practicing the principles

Experienced teachers also spoke of "practicing what you are preaching." Teachers should exemplify lifelong learning, being self-directing and sustaining a curiosity for learning. Whether stated or not, the teacher is a model to others. One teacher illustrated this point by commenting on the way in which she handles questions:

> *In class, I am not ashamed to say that I do not know the answer to every question. I want the students to see that I am human and I don't expect myself or others to 'know it all'. What is important is that we collectively know how to go about finding the answer. This approach develops skills and attitudes that transcend the specific course that I am teaching.*

Appropriate evaluation

Many teachers said that following an honest approach not only increased their own self-confidence, but also involved them more closely with the adult students in the process of learning. There are many ways to sustain the dynamics of teaching.

Re-examining the generic goals for learning is a continuous task: "What am I really trying to achieve? Am I teaching more than a subject matter or a skill?" If our philosophy of learning is learner-centred, then self-evaluation will be valued and practiced. Teachers can assume with some certainty that adult students have had some prior experience with the subject matter being taught.

This point may not always be recognized by the teacher or by the adult student, whether the content is chemistry, music, painting, accounting, psychology, or whatever.

> *Evaluation is not always based exclusively on pre-stated objectives. To do so would overlook the unanticipated learning that occurs.*

Reference has already been made to emotions. There is a place for quantitative evaluation in education but the qualitative components of learning, such as feelings and attitudes, are equally, if not more, important. The purpose of learning is to bring about change. This may not always be visible and certainly not always measurable. One teacher said what many others have experienced.

One of the most exciting moments in my career, teaching adults, occurred just last semester. I started teaching a subject that I had never taught before - Creative Dramatics. I was teaching to a varied group. When we discovered together that the study of creative drama could influence and enhance all areas of life and human interaction, we all headed into the course with anticipation and excitement. During the course of the semester, the students occasionally asked: "Do you think this activity is appropriate?" And I was truthfully able to say: "If you can make the connection, I will accept it", because I really felt that anything waspossible. When evaluating this course in the middle and at the end of the semester, students said they had gained more self-confidence than they ever thought they could have and when I saw the shyest, most introverted student presenting herself both verbally and physically the last night of class, I knew that this had been one of the most successful courses I had taught.

Setting the climate for learning

A number of part-time teachers had comments and experiences to share about setting the climate for learning. If the social, psychological, and physical climate is not conducive to learning, then little if any learning will occur. The teacher's excitement can be an important first step for setting and promoting a climate for exchange. They also noted:

- *Try to have several social occasions so the students get to know each other. An informal atmosphere helps them to relax and learn better.*
- *Call on others to share their experiences in order to enrich the process and the content and don't be afraid to share your own experiences.*
- *Don't be afraid to dive in and get your feet wet. Once you get going and get some time under your belt, you'll begin to enjoy yourself and so will your students, at any age.*
- *Be pleasant, show interest, and remember little things about your students from lesson to lesson. This will help to make them relax and have more confidence in you and in what they are about to learn.*

• *Give of yourself as a teacher and as a friend.*
• *Proceed slowly at first. Give lots of encouragement. Many adults are intimidated at first by this experience.*
• *Make the students feel welcome, comfortable and relaxed and let them know they have made a wise decision.*
• *Remember how important it is to have a sense of humour.*
• *Relax. Enjoy yourself. These students are here because they want to be. Half the teaching battle is already won.*
• *As a mother, it was important for me to be home with my family. At the same time, it was important for me to fulfill myself. Teaching adults part-time provided me with the opportunities to accomplish both.*
• *I find that I am able to relate better and with greater quality with family and friends, as a result, partially at least, from my working with adults. Some of the principles of learning and teaching I find apply well to these relationships.*
• *I find it important to take advice from other instructors. It is also important to find out what kind of students are in your class and what are their expectations, before you get too far into the course and find out, too late, that you are not teaching them what they want to learn. There are many ways to learn what the students expect from the class.*
• *And then there are unexpected outcomes from the adult courses that I teach. How are you to know what influence learning can have?*

Comments from the students, such as: "I hope there's not too much work to do in this course, since I have a family and a part-time job"; and "I hope you don't expect us to be perfect; it's been quite a few years since I've been in school", reflect some of the realities and insecurities that many adult students feel when they enter a classroom.

Houle's Categories of Learners

In any educational setting, it becomes clear that students and teachers alike live a life beyond the classroom.

This fact influences why and what people learn. A number of teachers talked about student motivation and why they felt students came to class. There is a natural tendency for teachers to assume that students are present because they are interested in the subject matter or the skills that are to be taught. A word of caution might be struck here through a study that was conducted by Cyril Houle (1961). He asked a number of adults enrolled in non-credit courses, what had brought them to the course. From their responses, he identified three categories of learners:

Learner-oriented

Adults in this category are excited because they are involved in a process of learning. The content of the course is less important than the act of being involved. Learning was exciting and fun for these persons and had an intrinsic value.

Goal-oriented

Adults in this category had a specific goal they wanted to achieve. Completing a course was part of achieving that goal. They were there to learn the content or the skills that were advertised as the object of the course.

Activity-oriented

Initially at least, these adults were not necessarily in class to learn what was being taught. Their responses included: "Because my friend is taking the course, and I'd like to be with my friend. It is our night out"; or "Because this evening was the only night I could find a babysitter"; or "Because my husband and I decided that this evening should be my night out". For some teachers such responses may be personally deflating. "I'm excited about my subject matter. Why aren't they?" or "If they aren't interested in what the class is supposed to teach, then why are they here"?

Some factors that inhibit learning

The part-time teachers expressed an awareness of the many factors that inhibit learning. Turning up in class is in itself, a great achievement for many adults. To do so, they have had to overcome financial barriers; negative feelings about themselves; past experiences that have created feelings of inadequacy or feelings of failure; discouragement from spouse or from friends; barriers from one's job, such as working night shift; or apprehensions about entering a school and a classroom after so many years. The list can be greatly extended. Teachers of adults are encouraged to reflect on other factors that make it difficult for adults to attend and remain in the courses. The question of participation also relates to broader social issues. The challenge of the teacher is to give people reasons to stay.

> *It is important* not *to think of non-participants as non-learners. "Non-learner" is a contradiction to being human.*

About communicating crossculturally

As a result of their teaching, many part-time teachers became more aware of cultural differences: "I have a better understanding of ethnic and cultural differences"; "I have more understanding of non-English-speaking immigrants"; "I am better able to understand foreign accents"; and "I have more sensitivity in teaching immigrants". The influence of culture on learning is not to be under-estimated. Values and traditions provide much of the meaning of what is learned as well as the expectations that individuals and groups have of the roles of teacher and student. Working with persons from other cultures can help to re-emphasize one's own culture which is so often taken for granted. It is frequently through the acknowledgement of differences that a person learns to value one's own heritage and customs.

> *Overall, these teachers have a great deal of faith and confidence in the adult students that they are working with. They are able to offer advice humbly, because they live and understand the empathy they have for others. As learners, teachers themselves are in transition.*

Teachers have much to share with each other. Because of this, every effort needs to be made to encourage teachers to interact. For instance, through professional development activities and other means, teachers of children, who are also teaching adults part-time, might be encouraged to share and discuss their experiences. Do administrators and coordinators encourage this to happen? Do they attempt to decrease the institutional marginality of part-time teachers?

The Congruence Between Belief and Practice

> *The words we use to describe what we do also express what we believe.*

Similarly, the principles which teachers expound are to be lived and practiced. If the principles are really believed, then their application is not limited to the classroom. The teaching-learning transaction and the principles that guide the transaction are well documented and are not discussed in this section.(Brundage and MacKeracher,1980). It is well known that learning is a consequence of experience, that learning is a process of self-discovery, that the process of learning is emotional, as well as intellectual, and that many factors influence learning. Each of these are values to be internalized. Effective educators learn these principles through experience and they are often intuitively practiced. Further understanding comes from being familiar with the vast literature in adult education. It is important to understand not only what one does but why. There needs to be a congruence between what teachers believe and what they practice.

Distinguishing pedagogy and andragogy

To illustrate congruence between belief and practice, let's look at the meanings of pedagogy and andragogy.(Ingalls,1973; Knowles,1970; Nottingham Group,1986). Traditionally, pedagogy has referred to the art of teaching children and andragogy to that of teaching adults. The two terms have been compared, using a number of variables, for instance:

- *the concept of the learner within the pedagogical framework is that of a dependent learner, whereas in the andragogical framework, the learner is increasingly self-directed and independent;*
- *pedagogically, motivation is based on external rewards as compared with internal incentives and curiosity within andragogy;*
- *the climate for learning is characterized, for pedagogy, by one of formal authority, competitiveness and judgment, as compared with an informal climate in andragogy, which is mutually respectful, consensual, collaborative, and supportive.*
- *planning is primarily done by the pedagogue as compared with andragogy where participation in decision-making prevails;*
- *in pedagogy, the diagnosis of needs is done primarily by the teacher as compared with mutual assessment in andragogy;*
- *learning activities are either transmittal techniques and assigned readings as compared with inquiry projects, independent study and experimental techniques within andragogy;*
- *in pedagogy, evaluation is primarily external to the student and done by the authority teacher, as compared with self-assessment which characterizes the andragogical approach.*

> *The differences between the terms "andragogy" and "pedagogy", described above, are traditionally described according to age groups. However, the differences between the two have nothing to do with age, but rather represent different philosophical orientations or approaches to teaching and learning.*

Both approaches can be appropriate to working with any age group, even though andragogy is a term that is often used synonymously with adult self-directed learning and the humanist tradition.

If the adult learner has experienced only the pedagogical orientation to teaching and learning, then this experience must be acknowledged and that is where the educational program begins. The adult educator needs to gently lead the student from what is known and experienced toward the humanist orientation which values the responsibility, independency and judgment of the learner. It seems entirely appropriate for a teacher to begin with structure and direction, while at the same time, being open to discussing and explaining another orientation to be valued.

> *Andragogical and pedagogical orientations really describe the ways in which people relate to each other.*

The andragogical learner-centred orientation is primarily a humanistic one (Elias and Merriam, 1980), which applies to persons of any age. The question then is not whether one is teaching children or adults, but what philosophical stance is being taken in a teaching-learning situation? This relates as well to the assumptions made about human nature and the ability of people to learn. One set of assumptions is that people need to be threatened and coerced into learning. A more humanistic orientation assumes that people are willing and able to take responsibility for their own learning, if only given the freedom and support to do so. How much thought have teachers given to this?

> *Regardless of what content or skills are being taught, a discussion on learning and teaching can greatly enhance the outcome of personal growth.*

Teaching adults needs to be more than an act of doing. What is practiced needs to be conceptually and philosophically understood as well.

The relationship between the values held and the methods used may be different than risking something new and perhaps more appropriate. It is like the difference between talking and doing. If the classroom becomes an atmosphere of sharing and participation, then the risk is shared by teacher and student. "Together, let us try something new". Another way to perceive the relationship between student and teacher is in terms of the dynamics of power. Does the teacher continue to use the lecture method, perhaps inappropriately, because of a lack of awareness of other methods, or because lecturing is a way of retaining control, and therefore, power? Teachers seldom speak in these terms. Should they? Do those who call themselves 'master teacher' understand the complexity of teaching? Do they and others clearly understand the philosophy and the essence of learning and education? The challenge is to be consistent between the beliefs and the practices of teaching.

The Craft of Teaching Adults

Practitioners we are, but what is our craft? If 'craft' refers to the skills required in planning, implementing and evaluating educational programs, then the 'craftsperson' is expected to perform these skills with ease and competence.

> *The 'craftsperson teacher' is one who is aware of the uniqueness of what is being practiced, and has the ability to view content, as a prism, from different angles and with different illumination.*

Such a person can see the personal and social processes which bring about modification and change. The craft of teaching adults is based on particular assumptions about people. With both pride and satisfaction, those who have acquired the craft of teaching adults have developed the skills of working with adults, but at the same time have the knowledge and understanding of the literature in adult education, so that they are able to understand the 'why' of one's practice. The 'how' and the 'why' are the equations of the craft.

Time, experience and reflection are variables in practicing a craft.

> *Our awareness of what has been experienced and therefore what has been learned will depend on the depth of our reflection.*

Reflection is essential to the craft of teaching and the recognition of quality is the basis for the ethics of what one does. Skills follow from attitudes which in turn affects behaviour and practices.

Teachers are not just enthusiastic guides. Helping to design learning experiences for others and for ourselves requires a knowledge about how adults learn. Part of that knowledge is to understand the relationship between the methodology of teaching and learning effectiveness. Learning and teaching then are highly individualized. The craftsperson teacher is one who has a commitment to social justice, helping others to achieve degrees of self-determination. The core concepts of the craft of teaching will include those of tolerance, honesty, shared responsibility, critical thinking, discovery, adaptability, enthusiasm and the confidence to take risks.

> *Teachers are responsible for their own learning but are also responsible for the image of the teaching profession.*

Teachers of adults or adult educators?

An interesting distinction can be made between 'teachers of adults' and 'adult educators'. The latter might be referred to as those who have integrated skills of teaching with a knowledge of the vast body of knowledge which makes up the 'discipline' of adult education. These educators identify with the field of adult education and are committed to its development. Almost all who took part in the study of part-time teachers were unaware of the literature in adult education and were unfamiliar with the professional adult education associations. These educators of adults, although 'successful doers', were not fully aware of the reasons or the theory which explains the 'why' of what they are doing. The craftsperson is one who makes use of more than just knowledge.

A recent policy guideline, *For Adults Only* (Ministry of Colleges and Universities,1986), perceives lifelong learning as permeating all levels of education, from primary to post-secondary. A society that expounds on the values of lifelong learning also acknowledges the barriers that prevent people from fully participating in a lifelong process of learning. As more people become involved in part-time education, more part-time teachers will be required. The part-time teacher has an important role to perform in achieving individual and societal goals.

There has been a fairly recent shift from a focus on education to a focus on learning. Learning is lifelong, it is natural to daily living, and it may occur anytime and in any place. Education is more sporadic and is intentional or planned learning. Learning is the larger and more encompassing process. The ideal goals of education are to "liberalize" individuals, refining the quality of living.

As educators and as those possessing a refined craft, we must not only look to the future, but also help to shape the future as well.

> *We underestimate the value of teaching if we limit its description to the classroom.*

Learning is a much larger process of growth and development that is both fluid in its presence and tangible in its influence and outcome. The teacher of adults is an important part of a larger process of individual and social change.

> *Advice with empathy is offered by teachers as learners themselves, for they know the worth of what they do.*

REFERENCES

Brundage, D. and MacKeracher, D. (1980) *Adult Learning Principles and Their Application to Program Planning.* Toronto: OISE Press and the Ministry of Education.

Canadian Association for Adult Education (1964) *A White Paper on the Education of Adults in Canada: A Canadian Policy for Continuing Education.* Toronto: Canadian Association for Adult Education.

Canadian Commission for UNESCO (1983) *Learning in Society: Towards a New Paradigm.* Ottawa: Canadian Commission for Unesco.

Devereaux, M.S. (1985) *One in Every Five; A Survey of Adult Education in Canada.* Ottawa: Statistics Canada and the Department of the Secretary of State.

Draper, J.A. (1987) *Understanding the Part-Time Instructors of Adults.* Toronto: Department of Adult Education and OISE Press.

Draper, J.A. and Keating, D. (1978) *Instructors of Adults.* Toronto: Commission on Declining School Enrolments in Ontario (CODE) and OISE Press.

Elias, J.L. and Merriam, S. (1980) *Philosophical Foundations of Adult Education.* Huntington, New York: Robert E. Krieger Publishing Co.

Faure, E. and others. (1972) *Learning To Be: The World of Education Today and Tomorrow.* Paris: UNESCO.

Houle, C. (1961) *The Inquiring Mind.* Madison: The University of Wisconsin Press.

Ingalls, J.D. (1973) *A Trainer's Guide to Andragogy.* Washington: United States Department of Health, Education and Welfare.

Knowles, M.S. (1970) *The Modern Practice of Adult Education.* New York: Association Press.

Kolb, D. (1976) *Learning Style Inventory Technical Manual.* Boston: McBer and Company.

Ministry of Colleges and Universities (1986) *For Adults Only* (Continuing Education Review Project). Toronto: Government of Ontario.

The Nottingham Andragogy Group (1986) *Towards a Developmental Theory of Andragogy.* Nottingham: Department of Adult Education. (U.K.)

SUGGESTED READING

Clarke, R.J., and Brundage, D.H. (1982) "Adult education opportunities in Canada". In *Adult Education Training in Industrialized Countries.* Toronto: Department of Adult Education, OISE Press.

Conti, G.J. and Fellenz, R.A. (Eds.) (1985) *Dialogue on Issues of Lifelong Learning in a Democratic Society.* Texas: A & M University.

Draper, J.A. and Barer-Stein, T. (1980) "Plain Talk for Administrators and Teachers of Adults". In A.B. Knox, (Ed.) *New Directions for Continuing Education: Teaching Adults Effectively.* San Francisco: Jossey-Bass Inc.

Davenport, J. (1985) "Andragogical-Pedagogical orientations of adult learners: Research results and practice recommendations." *Lifelong Learning.* Vol. 9, No. 1.

Draves, W.A. (1984) *How to Teach Adults.* Manhattan, Kansas: Learning Resources Network.

Gross, R. (Ed.) (1982) *Invitation to Lifelong Learning.* Chicago: Follett Publishing Co.

Ironside, D. (1985) "Adult education: concepts and definitions." In *International Encyclopedia of Education: Research and Studies.*

Lenz, E. (1982) *The Art of Teaching Adults.* New York: CBS College Publishing; Holt, Rinehart & Winston.

Menson, B. (1982) *Building on Experiences in Adult Development. New Directions for Experiential Learning.* No. 16. San Francisco, CA: Jossey-Bass.

Merriam, S. (Ed.) (1986) *Being Responsive to Adult Learners.* Washington, D.C.: AAACE Adult Education Series/Scott Foresman & Co.

Mezirow, J. (1981) "A Critical theory of adult learning and education". *Adult Education.* Vol. 32, No. l.

Novak, J.D. and Gowin, D.B. (1984) *Learning How to Learn.* Cambridge: Cambridge University Press.

Rogers, A. (1986) *Teaching Adults.* Philadelphia: Open University Press.

Selman, G. and Dampier, P. (1991) *The Foundations of Adult Education in Canada.* Toronto: Thompson Educational Publishing, Inc.

Sheehy, G. (1976) *Passages: Predictable Crisis in Adult Life.* New York: E.P. Dutton & Company Inc.

Yonge, G.D. (1985) "Andragogy and pedagogy: Two ways of accompaniment." *Adult Education Quarterly.* Vol. 35, No. 2.

The Vast Network of Adult Education

James A. Draper

One way for practitioners to identify with and understand the field and practice of adult education is to familiarize themselves with and become members of the networks and associations in adult education.

At the end of this section is a listing of the names and addresses of selected international associations in adult education. The founding dates are also given, emphasizing the history and increasing commitment to this specialized field. The establishment of an adult education department within UNESCO (United Nations Educational, Scientific and Cultural Organization) contributed greatly to international sharing and cooperation in adult education and especially in examining and dealing with Third World issues, such as illiteracy. Since its first internationald world conference on adult education, held in 1949 in Denmark, UNESCO has organized similar conferences in 1960 in Montreal, 1972 in Tokyo, and 1985 in Paris. Out of the latter came "The Right to Learn" Declaration which highlighted the role of learning and education in dealing with basic world problems and viewed learning as a human right.

Non-government organizations (NGOs) are among the greatest providers of non-formal adult education programs based on local needs in most parts of the world. The expansion of such local agencies has paralleled the development of national as well as international NGOs as well. Notably among the international is the International Council for Adult Education which was formed in 1973 by J. Roby Kidd. Its membership includes national and regional adult education associations. The ICAE has organized four world assemblies of adult education: in Dar es Salaam in 1976, Paris in 1982, Buenos Aires in 1985, and Bangkok in 1990. These and other events organized by the Council and promoted through its international journal *Convergence*, have added a new dimension to cross-national collaboration, to acknowledging current issues, to extending the availability of resources for education and to acting as a catalyst for social action.

The political, social, economic, cultural, and historical context influences what, where and why people learn. It was these influences and the resultant learning that occurred that focused the attention of both the practice and study of adult education. International conferences and other events focused attention on adult education as did the support of UNESCO and other international agencies such as the International Labour Organization (ILO), the Food and Agricultural Organization (FAO), The World Health Organization (WHO), UNICEF, the Council of Europe and the Organization for Economic Cooperation and Development. One can also mention the International Cooperative Alliance. It became evident to these and many other agencies that to accomplish their tasks, learning had to occur. To varying degrees, all became advocates of adult education.

The various regional offices of UNESCO including the Institute of Education in Hamburg and the International Institute for Educational Planning in Paris have further helped to decentralize and yet focus the work of this international organization. These organizations have published materials and organized conferences on a wide variety of topics, including distance learning, non-formal adult education and literacy, as well as producing research materials and a glossary of terms in several languages.

Soon after the UNESCO World Conference on Adult Education in 1960, in Montreal, a group of adult educators from 14 countries met at Syracuse University (U.S.A.) and organized the International Congress of University Adult Education. The Congress has sponsored several international meetings of university adult educators, promoting the study of comparative adult education and publishing a journal and occasional papers.

At present, there are upwards of 90 national adult education associations and six regional adult education associations in the world, all member organizations of the International Council for Adult Education. The regional associations are the Arab Literacy and Adult Education Organization; the Asian and South Pacific Bureau of Adult Education; the Caribbean Regional Council for Adult Education; the European Bureau of Adult Education; the Regional Centre for Adult Education and Functional Literacy in Latin America; the African Association for Literacy and Adult Education; and the North American "regional" member of the ICAE is at the stage of advanced discussions. Most of these associations produce journals and other materials and while their primary purpose is to facilitate interaction and support for their members, they also serve as rich resources for international and comparative studies and exchanges.

In some ways, adult education has been recognized internationally for its expressions of social conscience. Adult education can also be seen as a social movement, concerned with the social issues confronting humankind, such as class inequality, environmental concerns, peace, racism and sexism. The desire for social justice is a dynamic force, encouraging all those involved in adult education to work with the poor, the oppressed and politically powerless in bringing about social, political, economic and cultural changes, as well as promoting cross-cultural communication and understanding.

The most recent international adult education association is the Commonwealth Association for the Education and Training of Adults, (CAETA) founded at a conference in India in March, 1987. The Association is especially interested in strengthening the linkage with practitioners. It is divided into five regions, encompassing all of the member countries of the Commonwealth. Canada is in The Americas region, with the Caribbean. Since most of these countries are new and Third World nations, most of the issues which it deals with arise from the concerns of these countries.

The above overview illustrates the philosophy and extent of commitment of adult education internationally. International studies in adult education are dependent on a multitude of structures that support it, notably the ICAE, others NGOs, UNESCO, national and international associations and universities. Collectively they provide the energy and the resources for international and comparative studies in adult education.

The traditions and events which have helped to support the development of adult education have been attributed to professional associations of adult educators, as well as to the host of other agencies which are involved in some way, in stimulating and guiding the learning of adults. The field of adult education, frequently through national and international conferences and special events has made a contribution to the diffusion of concepts and thereby the changing of practices in adult education. Creating a learning society, the transforming knowledge, dealing with health and environmental issues, the meaning and influence of culture, the relevance of lifelong education, and the democratization of research and knowledge have now become international values. A predominantly humanistic philosophy, centring on the development and growth of people, has become closely identified with the field of adult education.

Selected International Adult Education Organizations

CAETA: Commonwealth Association for the Education and Training of Adults (1987)
c/o Department of Adult Education,
University of Zimbabwe
P.O. Box MP 167
Mount Pleasant
Harare, Zimbabwe

ICAE: International Council for Adult Education (1973)
720 Bathurst Street
Toronto, Ontario, Canada, M5S 2R4

ICUAE: International Congress of University Adult Education, (1961)
c/o Department of Extension and Summer Session
The University of New Brunswick
P.O. Box 4400
Fredericton, New Brunswick Canada, E3B 5A3

Note: The author wishes to thank Budd Hall and Alan Thomas, faculty members at OISE, for their suggestions in up-dating this section.

Introduction to the Selected Canadian Bibliography

This bibliography is intended to be more than the listing of selected Canadian writings on adult education. It portrays as well the rich historical heritage of this ever-expanding field of practice and study. Throughout the ages adults have always been learners but may not have been recognized as such. Intended and organized learning (which we call 'education') has always been an important part of such history, especially today when the opportunities for education have never been greater. As the demand for adult education increases, adults find themselves in interchangeable roles of both student and teacher.

Understanding our historical roots helps to reveal our own cultural stance and biases, and the richness of our own identity. The history of the profession of adult education is closely linked to international events and issues. Understanding our heritage helps us to understand the roots of present-day institutions, values and practices. A historical perspective sensitizes us to the present, and the various forces and factors which influenced, why, where and what people learned. Economic, political and social events such as wars, agrarian reforms, industrialization, and the Depression of the 1930s would be historical examples of these forces. The application of new technologies, re-entering the workforce, learning a second language, and continuing professional training are present day examples of such forces.

Canada has had a long history of innovation in adult education. Present day institutions such as the Banff School of Fine Arts, the co-operative movement, university extension programs, and the Worker's Education Association grew out of the efforts of adult educators.

The outcomes of learning have seldom been singular. Learning has transcended the home, the workplace and the community. Adult Educational programs have helped to build regional and national identity, citizenship and leadership. A wide array of institutions have been involved, in order to meet the special needs of individuals and groups. Finally, there has been the tradition of the voluntary associations and the recognition of the value of the volunteer worker. Adult education has become synonymous with identifying and overcoming new frontiers of challenge.

From this bibliography one can sense the way in which adult education has attempted to deal with societal issues such as illiteracy, unemployment, socio-economic development, environmental concerns and workplace learning. At all times, the learning that occurred went beyond mere content or skills, because at the same time, people were also learning attitudes, values and behaviours about learning itself which in turn influenced their concepts as learner, worker, parent or friend.

The field of adult education has been instrumental in integrating these life-long learnings into a philosophical premise of learning and education as human rights.

Some of the writings that follow are based on personal reflection, and some on systematic research. Some tell the personal story of a struggle, others depict beliefs such as "learning a living" or "learning for life". Coady's book *Masters of Their Own Destiny*, expresses a profound faith that learning brings empowerment, increasing the control that people have and feel over their lives. Each publication in its own way has a message for the teacher, planner and administrator in adult education.

The bibliography is listed alphabetically, and you will notice many overlapping themes. The criteria for selecting the publications was that the material had to be written by a Canadian and/or published in Canada. The focus has been on books and major reports rather than journal articles or chapters in books. One source of literature in the field of adult education not to be overlooked, however, is the masters and doctoral theses that have been completed at Canadian universities. A listing of these represents some of the most current research and is given in reports by Dobson and by Draper. It is acknowledged that many more publications could have been included and the editors apologize for any serious omission.

James A. Draper

Compiled by James A. Draper and Thelma Barer-Stein with the assistance of Retta Alemayehu, Lynn Kirkwood and Professor Diana Ironside. Joylaxmi Saikia assisted in the updating of the bibliography. Kathleen Sparacino typed and helped to organize new sections in the bibliography. Their time and effort is gratefully acknowledged.

Selected Canadian Bibliography

Adams, R.J., Draper, P.M. and Ducharme, C. (1979) *Education and Working Canadians: Reports of the Commission of Inquiry in Educational Leave and Productivity.* Ottawa: Labour Canada.

Anderson, E. (Ed.) (1978) *Annotated Adult Basic Education (A.B.E.) Bibliography.* Toronto: Movement for Canadian Literacy.

Armstrong, A.K. (1977) *Masters of their own destiny: A comparison of the thought of Coady and Freire.*(Occasional Paper No. 13.)Vancouver: Centre for Continuing Education, University of British Columbia.

Baker, H. (1972) *Education and Socioeconomic Development: Four Monographs on Social Indicators.* Toronto: New Press.

Baker, H.R. (Ed.) (1977) *The Teaching of Adults Series for Beginning and Part-Time Instructors and Program Planners.* Saskatoon: University of Saskatchewan Extension Division.

Baker, H.R., Draper, J.A. and Fairbairn, B.T. (Ed) (1991) *Dignity and Growth: Citizen Participation in Social Change.* Calgary: Detselig Enterprises Ltd.

Barer-Stein,T. and Draper, J.A. (Eds.)(1993) *The Craft of Teaching Adults.* (2nd edition) Toronto: Culture Concepts Inc.

Bartram, P.E. (Ed.) (1984) *Proceedings of the 3rd Annual Conference. Canadian Association for the Study of Adult Education.* Toronto: OISE Press.

Bartsch, W. (1984) *Practical Visionaries: Innovators in Learning and Change.* Atikokan, Ontario.

Boshier, R. (1980) *Towards a Learning Society: New Zealand Adult Education in Transition.* Vancouver: Learningpress Ltd.

Boud, D. and Griffin V. (Eds.) (1987) *Appreciating Adults Learning: From the Learner's Perspective.* London: Kogan Page.

Bradwin, E. (1972) *The Bunkhouse Man: A Study of Work and Pay in the Camps of Canada 1903-1914.* Toronto: University of Toronto Press.

Brundage, D.E. and MacKeracher, D.M. (1980) *Adult Learning Principles and Their Application to Program Planning.* Toronto: Ministry of Education.

Burge, E.J., Howard, J.E. and Ironside, D. (1991) *Mediation in Distance Learning: An Investigation of the Role of Tutoring.* Toronto: OISE Press.

Burge,E.J., Roberts,J.M. and associates.(1993) *Telecommunications for Learning: A Practical Introduction for Educators.* Toronto: OISE Press.

Campbell, D. (1977) *Adult Education as a Field of Study and Practice: Strategies for Development.* Vancouver: Centre for Continuing Education, University of British Columbia and the International Council for Adult Education.

Campbell, G. (1977) *The Community Colleges in Canada.* Toronto: McGraw-Hill.

Canadian Association for Adult Education (1982) *From the Adult's Point of View.* Toronto: Canadian Association for Adult Education (CAAE).

Canadian Association for Adult Education (1975) *External Examiner's Report: Educational Policy in Canada,* 1976 (from OECD Draft Review of National Policies for Education: Canada). Toronto: Canadian Association for Adult Education (CAAE).

Canadian Association for Adult Education (1964) *A White Paper on the Education of Adults in Canada: A Canadian Policy for Continuing Education.* Toronto: Canadian Association for Adult Education (CAAE).

Canadian Association for Adult Education and Institut Canadien d'education des adultes (1976) *Manpower Training at the Crossroads* (Conference). Toronto: Canadian Association for Adult Education (CAAE).

Canada, Government of (1983) *Learning a living in Canada: Background and Perspectives;* and *Policy Options for the Nation.* Ottawa: Minister of Supply and Services (Cat. No. MP43-134-1983E). Vol. 1 and 2.

Canada, Government of (1984) *Learning for life: Overcoming the Separation of Work and Learning.* Ottawa-Hull: Public Affairs Division, Canada Employment and Immigration Commission. (Cat.No. LU 2-87/1984E)

Cantor, J.A. (1992) *Delivering Instruction to Adult Learners.* Toronto: Wall and Emerson Inc.

Cassidy, F. (Ed.)(1984) *Creating Citizens: Reflections on the Recent History of Continuing Education in British Columbia.* Vancouver: Pacific Association for Continuing Education.

Cassidy, F. and Faris, R. (Ed.) (1987) *Choosing Our Future* (Adult Education and Public Policy in Canada). Toronto: OISE.

Centre for Continuing Education, The University of British Columbia (1981) *Introduction to Teaching Adults.* Vancouver.

Clark, R.J. and Brundage, D.H. (1982) "Adult education opportunities in Canada". In R.E. Peterson and others (Eds.) *Adult Education Opportunities in Nine Industrialized Countries.* New York: Praeger.

Coady, M. (1939) *Masters of Their Own Destiny.* New York: Harper & Bros. Publishers.

Commission d'etude sur la formation des adultes (1982) *Learning: A voluntary and Responsible Action* (Statement of a comprehensive survey on adult education). Quebec: Gouvernement du Quebec.

Commission on Educational Planning (Worth Commission) (1972) *A Choice of Futures.* Edmonton: Queen's Printer.

Commission on Post-Secondary Education (1972) *The Learning Society.* Toronto: Ministry of Government Services.

Corbett, E.A. (1954) *Henry Marshall Tory.* Toronto: The Ryerson Press.

Corbett, E.A. (1957) *We Have with Us Tonight.* Toronto: Ryerson Press.

Cranton, P. (1992) *Working With Adult Learners.* Toronto: Wall and Emerson Inc.

Cranton, P. (1989) *Planning Instruction for Adult Learners.* Toronto: Wall and Thompson.

Crux, S.C. (1991) *Learning Strategies for Adults.* Toronto: Wall and Emerson Inc.

Davie, L., Davie, S., MacKeracher, D. and Ironside, D. (1978) *Educational Needs and Learning Conditions of Adult Learners.* Toronto: Department of Adult Education, OISE.

DeCoito, P.A. (1984) *Women and Adult Basic Education in Canada: An Exploratory Study.* Toronto: Canadian Congress for Learning Opportunities for Women.

Deveraux, M.S. (1985) *One in Every Five: A Survey of Adult Education in Canada.* Ottawa: Statistics Canada and Education Support Sector, Department of Secretary of State.

Dickinson, G. (1973) *Teaching Adults: A Handbook for Instruction.* Toronto: New Press.

Dobson, J. (1984) *The Study of People, Programs, Places and Processes: Canadian Adult Education Literature, 1977-1984.* Antigonish, N.S.: St. Francis Xavier University.

Dobson, J. (1986) *Adult Education Theses in Canada, 1980-1986.* Antigonish, N.S.: St. Frances Xavier University.

Draper, J.A. (Ed.) (1971) *Citizen Participation in Canada.* Toronto: New Press.

Draper, J.A. (1981) *Adult Education Theses: Canada.* Toronto: OISE Press.

Draper, J.A. (1984) *National and Regional Adult Education Associations (A World Survey).* Toronto: International Council for Adult Education.

Draper, J.A. (1985) "Adult Education". *The Canadian Encyclopedia.* Edmonton: Hurtig Publishers.Vol. 1.

Draper, J.A. and Alden, H. (1978) *The Continuing Education of Employees: A Review of Selected Policies in Ontario.* Toronto: OISE Press.

Draper, J.A. and Clark, R.J. (1980) *Adult Basic and Literacy Education Teaching and Support Programs within Selected Colleges and Universities in Canada.* Toronto: Department of Adult Education, OISE.

Draper, J.A. and Keating, D. (1978) *Instructors of Adults.* Toronto: Department of Adult Education, OISE.

Draper, J.A. and Taylor, M.C. (Eds.) (1992) *Voices from the Literacy Field.* Toronto: Culture Concepts Inc.

England, R. (1980) *Learning, Living and Remembering.* Vancouver: Centre for Continuing Education, The University of British Columbia.

Fales, A.W. and Burge, E.J. (1984) *Freedom With Structure: The Integration of Adult Learning and Distance Principles.* Toronto: OISE Press.

Faris, R. (1975) *The Passionate Educators.* Toronto: Peter Martin Associates.

Fitzpatrick, A. (1923) *The University in Overalls.* Toronto: The Frontier College Press.

Fournier, R.M.E. (1982) *Educational brokering: The women's resource centre experience.* (Occasional Papers in Continuing Education). Vancouver: Centre for Continuing Education, The University of British Columbia.

Gaskell, J., McLaren, A. and Novogrodsky, M. (1989) *Claiming an Education (Feminism and Canadian Schools).* Ontario: Our Schools/Our Selves Education Foundation.

Gaskell, J. and McLaren, A. (1987) *Women and Education: A Canadian Perspective.* (2nd. edition. 1991). Calgary, Alberta: Detselig Enterprises Ltd.

Hall, B.L. and Kidd, J.R. (1978) *Adult Learning: A Design for Action.* London: Pergamon Press.

Harrison, J.F.C. (1961) *Living and Learning, 1790-1960.* Toronto: University of Toronto Press.

Harvey, R.E.E. (1973) *Middle Range Education in Canada.* Toronto: Gage Educational Publishing.

Herman, R. (1984) *The Design of Self-Directed Learning: A Handbook for Teachers and Administrators.* Toronto: Department of Adult Education, OISE.

Herman, R.A. (1984) *A Social Service Model of Adult Basic Education.* Toronto: Department of Adult Education,OISE.

Herman, R.A., & Draper, J.A. (1982) *Towards a model of adult basic education for Ontario's school boards: A summary of the report.* Toronto: Department of Adult Education, OISE.

Hofmann-Nemiroff, G.(Ed.)(1987) *Women and Men: Interdisciplinary Readings on Gender.* Canada: Fitzhenry & Whiteside.

International Council for Adult Education (1990) *The Moon Also has Her Own Light.* (The Struggle to Build a Women's Consciousness among Nicaraguan Farmworkers). Toronto:ICAE.

International Council for Adult Education (1990) *Literacy, Popular Education and Democracy: Building the Movement.* Proceedings of the 4th World Assembly of Adult Education, 8-18 January 1990, Bangkok, Thailand. Toronto: ICAE.

Ironside, D.J. (1985) "Adult Education: Concepts and Definitions" *International Encyclopedia of Education.* London:Pergamon Press.Vol. l.

Ironside, D. and Jacobs, D.E. (1977) *Trends in counselling and information services for the adult learner.*(Occasional Papers 17) Toronto:OISE Press.

Jameson, S.S. (1979) *Chautauqua in Canada.* Calgary: Glenbow-Alberta Institute.

Keating, D. (1975) *The Power to Make it Happen.* Toronto: Green Tree Publishing Co.

Kidd, J.R. (1950) *Adult Education in Canada.* Toronto: Canadian Association for Adult Education.

Kidd, J.R. (1956) *Adult Education in the Canadian University.* Toronto: Canadian Association for Adult Education.

Kidd, J.R. (Ed.)(1963)_*Learning and Society.* Toronto: Canadian Association for Adult Education.

Kidd, J.R. (1966) *The Implications of Continuous Learning.* Toronto: Gage.

Kidd, J.R. (1974) *A Tale of Three Cities: Elsinore, Montreal, Tokyo.* Syracuse: Syracuse University Publications in Continuing Education.

Kidd, J.R. (1976) *How Adults Learn.* New York: Association Press.

Kidd, R. (1979) *Some preliminary notes concerning an enquiry into the heritage of Canadian adult education.* (Occasional Papers in Continuing Education) Vancouver: Centre for Continuing Education, The University of British Columbia.

Kidd, J.R. and Selman, G. (Eds.) (1978) *Coming of Age: Canadian Adult Education in the 1960s.* Toronto: Canadian Association for Adult Education.

Kidd, J.R. and C.J. Titmus (1985) "Adult Education: An Overview." *International Encyclopedia of Education: Research and Studies.* Vol. l.

Kulich, J. (Ed.) (1977) *Training of Adult Educators in East Europe.* Vancouver: The University of British Columbia and the International Council for Adult Education.

Kulich, J. and Kruger, W. (Eds.) (1980) *The Universities and Adult Education in Europe.* Vancouver: The University of British Columbia and the International Council for Adult Education.

Laidlaw, A.(1961) *The Campus and the Community: The Global Impact of the Antigonish Movement.* Montreal: Harvest House.

Laidlaw, A. (Ed.)(1971) *The Man from Margaree.* Toronto: McClelland & Stewart.

Lamoureux, M. (1976) *Marketing continuing education: A study of price strategies.* (Occasional Papers in Continuing Education). Vancouver: Centre for Continuing Education, The University of British Columbia.

Lindeman, E.C. (1961) *The Meaning of Adult Education.* Montreal: Harvest House.

MacKeracher, D. (1979) *Adult Basic Education for Women: A Model of Policy Development.* Toronto: Canadian Congress for Learning Opportunities for Women.

MacLellan, M. (1985) *Coady Remembered.* Antigonish, Nova Scotia: St. Francis Xavier University.

MacPherson, B. (1983) *Aging as a Social Process.* Toronto: Butterworths & Co.

Marshall, V. (1980) *Aging in Canada: Social Perspectives.* Toronto: Fitzhenry & Whiteside.

McIntosh, Clifford M. (1986) *Warriors or Statesmen: The Choice is Yours ....* Atikokan, Ontario: Quetico Press.

McLeish, J.A. (1973) *The Advancement of Professional Education in Canada.* Toronto: Kellogg Foundation.

McLeish, J. (1976) *The Ulyssean Adult: Creativity in the Middle and Later Years.* Toronto: McGraw-Hill Ryerson Press.

Miles, A. and Finn, G. (1989) *Feminism: From Pressure to Politics.* New York: Black Rose Books.

Miller, J.P., Taylor, G. and Walker, K. (1982) *Teachers in transition: Study of an aging teaching force.* (Informal Series No. 44). Toronto: OISE Press.

Ministry of Education, British Columbia (1976) *Report of the committee on continuing and community education in British Columbia.* Victoria: Government of British Columbia.

Ministry of Education and Ministry of Colleges and Universities (1981) *Continuing Education: The Third System.* Toronto.

Ministry of Colleges and Universities (1986) *For Adults Only.* Toronto.

Moore, G., & Waldron, M. (1981) *Helping Adults Learn.* Guelph: University of Guelph, Office for Educational Practice.

Morin, L. (Ed.)(1982) *On Prison Education.* Ottawa: Canadian Government Publishing Centre (Cat. NO. JS82-14/1982E).

Nicol, J., Shea, A.A., Simmons, G.P. and Sim, R.A. (Eds.) (1954) *Canada's Farm Radio Forum.* (Press, film and radio in the world today). Paris:UNESCO.

Ray, D., Bayles, M., and Harley, A. (1983) *Values, Life-Long Education and an Aging Canadian Population.* London: Third Eye Publishing Inc.

Renner, P.F. (1983) *The Instructor's Survival Kit.* Vancouver: Training Associates Ltd.

Renner, P. (1988) *The Quick Instructional Planner.* Vancouver: Training Associates Ltd.

Roberts, H. (1979) *Community Development: Learning and Action.* Toronto: University of Toronto Press.

Roberts, H. (1982) *Culture and Adult Education: A Study of Alberta and Quebec.* Edmonton: University of Alberta Press.

Robinson, J., Saberton, J. and Griffin, V. (1985) *Learning Partnerships: Interdependent Learning in Adult Education.* Toronto: Department of Adult Education, OISE.

Rouillard, H. (Ed.)(n.d.) *Pioneers in Adult Education in Canada.* Toronto: Thomas Nelson & Sons.

Sandiford, P. (Ed.)(1935) *Adult education in Canada: A survey.* Toronto: University of Toronto. (Typescript).

Selman, G.R. (1966) *A History of 50 Years of Extension Service by the University of British Columbia, 1915-1965.* Toronto: Canadian Association for Adult Education.

Selman, G.R.(1976) *Adult educators in British Columbia during the Depression.* (Occasional Papers in Continuing Education No. 12). Vancouver: Centre for Continuing Education, The University of British Columbia.

Selman, G.R. (1981) *The Canadian Association for Adult Education in the Corbett Years.* (Occasional Papers in Continuing Education No. 20). Vancouver: Centre for Continuing Education, University of British Columbia.

Selman, G.R. (1982) *Roby Kidd and the Canadian Association for Adult Education: 1951-1961.* (Occasional Papers in Continuing Education No. 22) Vancouver: Centre for Continuing Education, The University of British Columbia.

Selman, G.R. (1984)" Stages in the development of Canadian adult education." *Canadian Journal of University Continuing Education.* Vol.10, No.1.

Selman, G. (1985) *Alan Thomas and the Canadian Association for Adult Education: 1961-1970.*(Occasional Papers in Continuing Education No. 24) Vancouver: Centre for Continuing Education, The University of British Columbia.

Selman, G. and Dampier, P. (1990) *The Foundations of Adult Education in Canada.* Toronto: Thompson Educational Publishing, Inc.

Selman, G. (1991) *Citizenship and The Adult Movement in Canada.* Vancouver: Centre for Continuing Education, The University of British Columbia.

Sims, R.A. (Ed.) (1954) *Canada's Farm Radio Forum.* Paris: UNESCO.

Smith, R.M., Aker, G.F. and Kidd, J.R. (Eds.) (1970) *Handbook of Adult Education.* New York: The MacMillan Company.

Stabler, M. (1972) *Explorations in a Night Culture, or After Dinner Walks in Night School.* Toronto: Ontario Association for Continuing Education.

Taylor, M.C. and Draper, J.A. (1989,1991) *Adult Learning Perspectives.* Toronto: Culture Concepts Inc.

Taylor, M.C., Lewe, G.R.,and Draper, J.A. (1992) *Basic Skills for the Workplace.* Toronto: Culture Concepts Inc.

Taylor, M. (1981) The social dimensions of adult learning. In L. Salter (Ed.) *Communication Studies in Canada.* Toronto: Butterworths & Co. (Canada)

Thomas, A. M. (1973) *A summary and critique of various reports on post-secondary education in Canada, 1969-1973.* Toronto: Canadian Association for Adult Education.

Thomas, A.M. (1983) *Learning in society: Discussion paper.* Ottawa: Canadian Commission for UNESCO.

Thomas, A.M. and Ploman, E. W. (1986) *Learning and Development: A Global Perspective.* Symposium Series No. 15.Toronto: OISE Press.

Thomas, A.M., Selman, G.R., MacNeil, T. and MacKeracher D. (1982) *Adult Learning About Canada.* Toronto: OISE Press.

Thomas, A.M. (1991) *Beyond Education: A New Perspective on Society's Management of learning.* San Francisco: Jossey-Bass Inc.

Thomas, Audrey M. (1976) *Adult Basic Education and Literacy Activities in Canada, 1973-76.* Toronto: World Literacy of Canada

Thomas, Audrey M. (1983) *Adult illiteracy in Canada: A Challenge.* (Occasional Paper No. 42) Ottawa: Canadian Commission for UNESCO.

Toppin, D. (1969) *This Cybernetic Age.* New York: Human Development Corporation.

Tough, A. (1979) *The Adult's Learning Projects: A Fresh Approach to Theory and Practice in Adult Learning* (2nd edition). Toronto: OISE Press.

Tough, A. (1982) *Intentional Changes: A Fresh Approach to Helping People Change.* Atlanta, GA: Follett Publishing Co.

Tough, A. (1991) *Crucial Questions About the Future.* Maryland: University Press of America.

UNESCO, Canadian Commission for, (1980) *Recommendations on the development of adult education.* Occasional Paper No. 34. Ottawa.

Van Manen, M. (1990) *Researching Live Experience.* London, Ont.: The University of Western Ontario.

Waldron, M., & Moore, G. (1991) *Helping Adults Learn: Course Planning for Adult Learners.* Toronto: Thompson Educational Publishing Inc.

Waniewitz, I. (1976) *Demand for Part-Time Learning in Ontario.* Toronto: OISE Press, for the Ontario Educational Communications Authority.

Welton, M.R. (Ed.)(1987) *Knowledge for the People: The Struggle for Adult Learning in English-Speaking Canada 1828-1973.* Toronto: OISE Press.

Wilson, I. (1980) *Citizen's Forum: Canada's National Platform.* Toronto: Department of Adult Education, OISE .